Synthese Library

Studies in Epistemology, Logic, M
and Philosophy of Science

Volume 442

The aim of *Synthese Library* is to provide a forum for the best current work in the methodology and philosophy of science and in epistemology. A wide variety of different approaches have traditionally been represented in the Library, and every effort is made to maintain this variety, not for its own sake, but because we believe that there are many fruitful and illuminating approaches to the philosophy of science and related disciplines.

Special attention is paid to methodological studies which illustrate the interplay of empirical and philosophical viewpoints and to contributions to the formal (logical, set-theoretical,mathematical, information-theoretical, decision-theoretical, etc.) methodology of empirical sciences. Likewise, the applications of logical methods to epistemology as well as philosophically and methodologically relevant studies in logic are strongly encouraged. The emphasis on logic will be tempered by interest in the psychological, historical, and sociological aspects of science.

Besides monographs *Synthese Library* publishes thematically unified anthologies and edited volumes with a well-defined topical focus inside the aim and scope of the book series. The contributions in the volumes are expected to be focused and structurally organized in accordance with the central theme(s), and should be tied together by an extensive editorial introduction or set of introductions if the volume is divided into parts. An extensive bibliography and index are mandatory.

For further volumes:
http://www.springer.com/series/6607

Brian Garrett

Jeremiah Joven Joaquin
Editor

Time, Identity and the Self: Essays on Metaphysics

Springer

Brian Garrett
School of Philosophy
Australian National University
Canberra, ACT, Australia

Edited by
Jeremiah Joven Joaquin
Department of Philosophy
De La Salle University
Manila, Philippines

ISSN 0166-6991 ISSN 2542-8292 (electronic)
Synthese Library
ISBN 978-3-030-85519-2 ISBN 978-3-030-85517-8 (eBook)
https://doi.org/10.1007/978-3-030-85517-8

This Springer imprint is published by the registered company Springer Nature Switzerland AG
The registered company address is: Gewerbestrasse 11, 6330 Cham, Switzerland

Foreword

Long before I got to know Brian Garrett, I knew about him. Or more to the point, I knew about Garrett's Fork which was named in his honour: *any philosophical view is either false or trivial.* I heard that he was especially adept at deploying this fork at philosophy talks. I also heard that he applied equally exacting standards to his own work. I was told the story of a talk that he gave, at which someone in Q&A raised what Brian recognised as a serious objection. We have all seen philosophers at such a moment prevaricating, blustering, or obfuscating. Instead, the story goes, with admirable forthrightness Brian picked up his paper and threw it in a rubbish bin.

We became colleagues in 2005, and since then he has generously invited me to send him regularly my work in progress. I do my best to dodge the tines of his fork, but Brian invariably gives me trenchant comments that require my serious attention.

To understand how he became the acute philosopher that he is, it helps to know something of the *Life of Brian*. He was an undergraduate at St Andrews (paving the way for Prince William and Kate Middleton). He studied with Crispin Wright and Stephen Read, who inculcated in him the value of clear thinking. He wrote a prize-winning essay for the *Analysis* competition, which appears in this volume (Chap. 14). He went on to do a BPhil at Oxford, winning the John Locke Prize in Mental Philosophy. (It's worth noting that there are many years in which this prize is not awarded at all.) He continued at Oxford for his DPhil, supervised by Sir Peter Strawson, Derek Parfit, Paul Snowdon, and Lord Quinton. After visiting positions at the University of Cincinnati and Indiana University, Bloomington, Brian joined the Australian National University, where he has been ever since. Yet more awards were soon bestowed upon him: he won the 1992 Philosophical Quarterly Essay Prize (see Chap. 23), and an Australian Research Council Queen Elizabeth II Research Fellowship.

Isaiah Berlin distinguished two types of intellectuals: a 'fox' who knows many things, and a 'hedgehog' who knows one big thing. Brian is a fox. While he works squarely in the analytic tradition, he does not cleave to any particular doctrine or school of thought, nor is he a disciple of any particular philosopher. He follows arguments wherever they lead. In his articles, he generally scrutinises classic works by well-known philosophers – respectfully but not reverentially. His critiques are always insightful, and they are often fatal.

Reading the papers in this volume, I think there should be a new entry in the *Philosophical Lexicon.*[1]

> garrett, v.: to strangle the life out of an unsound argument. 'He garretted Max Black's arguments that backwards causation is impossible'.

Brian has also written three books: *What is this thing called Metaphysics?* (now in its third edition, and translated into Spanish and Portuguese), *Personal Identity and Self-Consciousness*, and *Elementary Logic*. He always runs his work through many drafts, and it shows – there is not a wasted word, and it is invariably crystal clear.

I have also enjoyed attending some of his lectures. He is an *Old School* philosopher, in a good sense. Unencumbered by technology, he is serious about his subject matter without taking himself too seriously.

I am especially pleased that my friend J. J. Joaquin has undertaken the task of editing this collection. Brian and JJ have built a bridge between the ANU and De La Salle University, and indeed a bridge between philosophy in Australia and the Philippines. I have benefited personally from that bridge, giving a series of talks in the Philippines a few years ago, and thoroughly enjoying my time there with JJ as my exemplary host. As well as showcasing Brian's fine philosophical work, this volume attests to the strength of this bridge.

Australian National University
ACT, Australia
7 May 2021

Alan Hájek

[1] Edited by Daniel Dennett, available at https://dl.tufts.edu/concern/pdfs/jw827p68f.

Preface

On the occasion of his 60th birthday (16 May 2021), I have put together a volume of essays by my dear mentor and good friend, Brian Garrett. These essays cover topics in Brian's area of philosophical expertise, viz., *Metaphysics*, the beating heart of philosophy. In particular, they delve into topics on the metaphysics of time, the nature of identity, and the importance of the self, persons, and human beings. The essays in this volume represent almost four decades of hard and honest philosophical toil. The volume includes his two award-winning essays published in *Analysis* in 1983 and *The Philosophical Quarterly* in 1992, respectively, and his latest musings about fatalism and the Grandfather Paradox.

'Brian Garrett' might not be a famous name in twentieth or twenty-first century analytic philosophy. But as this volume will show, Brian is one of its best practitioners. His manner of presenting and arguing for (or against) a particular philosophical claim evidence his clarity of thought, sharp and tenacious wit, and ability to follow the argument wherever it leads. Such qualities are deemed by most academic philosophers and philosophy *aficionados* alike as qualities of a truly great philosopher. His dialectical writing style highlights Brian's dialogue with the works of other philosophers. His ripostes of the ideas of these philosophers generate in turn new and original insights, which may be considered as lasting contributions to the discipline of philosophy. In this regard, one might say that Brian is a philosopher's philosopher as his works exhibit the dialogical nature of philosophy.

Brian came into philosophy *via* St. Andrews and Oxford, where he learned to do philosophy from some of the best philosophers of the era. He had Sir Peter Strawson, Derek Parfit, Paul Snowdon, Michael Dummett, and Lord Quinton as supervisors at Oxford. His philosophical training led to academic posts in different parts of the globe, and this includes his long-time post at the Australian National University – which has been his home since 1990. ANU, of course, is one the philosophical centres in the world, with David Chalmers, Alan Hájek, Frank Jackson, Daniel Nolan, Philip Pettit, Jonathan Schaffer, Daniel Stoljar, and a host of other prominent contemporary philosophers being members of its School of Philosophy at one time or other.

Like most of today's practising philosophers, Brian is a well-travelled academic. Not only has he visited the top universities in 'developed' countries, he also visited universities in the 'developing' ones. And this is how we met. During one of his trips in 2009, Brian visited my home university – De La Salle University (Manila, Philippines). I was a starting faculty then, finishing my PhD, and still learning the academic ropes. Being the youngest in the department, I was assigned to be Brian's tour-guide, chauffeur, and overall executive assistant for the duration of his visit. In one of our driving-tours around Manila, Brian and I discussed my dissertation topic on the nature of personal identity. Unbeknownst to me then, Brian was one of the top philosophers on the subject, having published many articles and a book on personal identity and self-consciousness. Despite my ignorance of his prominence within this area of philosophy, I must have impressed him since he offered to supervise my dissertation and invited me to be a visiting PhD fellow at the ANU in 2010. Looking back now, I could say that the discussions we had in 2009 started not only my philosophy education under Brian but also a friendship that has been brewing for more than a decade now.

*****

This volume contains 28 of Brian's essays. I have divided them into four parts. The first part includes eight chapters on time; the second are seven chapters on identity; the third part contains nine chapters on the self; and the fourth and final part contains four discussion chapters of Brian's latest thoughts on time, backwards causation, identity, and personal identity. Most of these essays were originally published from 1983 to 2020. I have edited these essays for uniformity of presentation, and have checked for misprints and other stylistic nuances. In some cases, I have appended an abstract and section headings; in others, I have changed the 'formal' component. I have left out Brian's other published essays which overlap too much with the essays already included in this volume.

What follows will be a short overview of the essays contained in this volume. The first two chapters are rejoinders to Arthur Prior's 'Thank Goodness that's Over' puzzle. Chapters 3 and 4 are discussion notes on the coherence of backward causation as argued by Max Black and Michael Dummett, respectively. Chapter 5 evaluates Michael Dummett's treatment of McTaggart's proof for the unreality of time. Chapters 6 and 7 are evaluations of David Lewis's solution to the Grandfather Paradox. Chapter 8 closes the first part with a dilemma raised against eternalists – philosophers who believe in the existence of the past, present, and the future.

The second part opens with two chapters on best-candidate theories of identity – the view that identity is extrinsically determined. Chapter 9 argues against Penelope Mackie's 'No Extrinsic Determination' principle and Chapter 10 criticises Andrew Brennan's defence of best-candidate theories of identity. The next four chapters are critical rejoinders. Chapter 11 is a critique of Graeme Forbes's views about the metaphysics of identity. Chapter 12 is a critical appraisal of Gareth Evans's view about vague identity and vague objects. Chapter 13 is a riposte to M. J. More's thesis about rigidity and scope. And, Chapter 14 counters Stephen Baker and Phil Dowe's arguments against endurantism – the view that artefacts are three-dimensional entities. The second part closes with Chapter 15, which is Brian's award-winning solution to *Analysis* Problem no. 19, written while he was an undergraduate at St. Andrews.

The third part opens with three chapters concerning three dominant views about the nature of persons. Chapters 16 and 17 evaluate two versions of animalism (the view that we are human animals) – viz., Eric Olson's view and David Wiggins's view, respectively – and contrast them to the Lockean view that we are self-conscious beings. Chapter 18 is a critique of Lynne Rudder Baker's view that each of us is constituted by, but not identical with, a human animal. Chapters 19 and 20 explore the nature of personal identity. The former argues for the extrinsic nature of personal identity; the latter questions Derek Parfit's reductionist view that reference to persons and personal identity is, in principle, eliminable. The next three chapters explore the topic of 'I'-judgements. Chapter 21 argues against José Bermúdez's deflationist theory of self-consciousness. Chapter 22 presents a response to Elizabeth Anscombe's arguments against the referential status of 'I'. Chapter 23 explores Wittgenstein's distinction between the 'as subject' and 'as object' uses of 'I'. The third part closes with Chapter 24, which presents Brian's thoughts on the relationship between the metaphysics of persons and theories of ethics and rationality.

The fourth part contains four chapters where Brian and I discuss his afterthoughts on the topics covered in this volume. Chapter 25 focuses on McTaggart's arguments for the unreality of time. Chapter 26 raises an epistemic puzzle for those who believe in the possibility of backwards causation. Chapter 27 centres on the two puzzles for endurantism and perdurantism – i.e., the two leading theories of identity over time. The chapter that closes the volume, Chapter 28, focuses on four leading personal identity theories: dualism, animalism, constitutionalism, and the Hume/Parfit view, and the problems that befall each theory.

*****

I learned a lot under Brian's tutelage. I learned what is expected of a 'professional academic philosopher' in this day and age. I learned how to write and teach philosophy well. But most of all, I learned that doing philosophy never stops, that it's a life-long process that only true lovers of the discipline will understand. These are the things that I now share with my students and peers through my lectures and published works in metaphysics and logic. May this volume be instructive to you, dear reader, as it not only contains essays at the forefront of research in analytic metaphysics, it also contains the lessons I have learned from my friend, Brian Garrett without whom this whole volume is nought.

*****

This volume is made possible by the constant support and encouragement of colleagues and friends. I want to thank the administrators of De La Salle University, especially Brother Bernard Oca (FSC), Robert Roleda, Rhoderick Nuncio, and Robert James Boyles, for giving me some time off teaching to work on this project. I am also grateful to Ben Blumson, Fides del Castillo, Peter Eldridge-Smith, Soraj Hongladarom, Fernando Santiago, Jr., Daniel Stoljar, and Raymond Tan for their useful comments and suggestions. My thanks also to Otávio Bueno, Alexandra Campbell, Lucy Fleet, Svetlana Kleiner, Palani Murugesan, and the rest of the staff of Springer Nature – Synthese Library Series, for their trust in this volume. Special thanks to Hazel T. Biana, Peter Grundy, Alan Hájek, Thomas Mautner, and Stephen Read for reading through the chapters of this volume and having this journey with Brian and myself.

De La Salle University
Manila, Philippines
5 July 2021

Jeremiah Joven Joaquin

Acknowledgements

The following chapters in this volume appeared in the places listed below. My thanks to the editors and publishers for their permission to reprint them.

- 1988. 'Thank Goodness that's Over' Revisited. *The Philosophical Quarterly* 38(151): 201–205.
- 2018. Experience and Time. *Acta Analytica* 33(4): 427–430.
- 2020. Max Black and Backwards Causation. *Argumenta* (online first): 1–5.
- 2020. Michael Dummett, Reasons to Act, and Bringing About the Past. *Philosophia* 48: 547–556.
- 2018. Dummett on McTaggart's Proof of the Unreality of Time. *Argumenta* 3(2): 347–351.
- 2019. Bulletproof Grandfathers, David Lewis, and 'Can't'-Judgements. *Acta Analytica* 34(2): 177–180.
- 2017. A Dilemma for Eternalists. *Philosophia* 45(4): 1735–1739.
- 1988. Identity and Extrinsicness. *Mind* 97(385): 105–109.
- 1988. Best-candidate Theories and Identity: Reply to Brennan. *Inquiry* 31(1): 79–85.
- 1986. Possible Worlds and Identity. *Philosophical Books* 27(2): 65–72.
- 1991. Vague Identity and Vague Objects. *Noûs* 25(3): 341–351.
- 1984. More on Rigidity and Scope. *Logique et Analyse* 27(5): 97–101.
- 2017. Endurantism Endures: Rejoinder to Barker and Dowe. *Manuscrito* 40(3): 29–32.
- 1983. Identical Truth-conditions. *Analysis* 43 (3): 117–118. (One of two winners of the *Analysis* Problem no. 19.)
- 2003. Some Thoughts on Animalism. In *On Human Persons*, Klaus Petrus (ed.), Frankfurt: Ontos-Verlag.
- 1990. Persons and Human Beings. *Logos: Philosophic Issues in Christian Perspective*, (Proceedings of the Santa Clara Conference on Personal Identity) 11: 47–57.

- 2001. Comments on Rudder Baker's *Persons and Bodies*. In *A Field Guide to the Philosophy of Mind, Book Symposium on Persons and Bodies: A Constitution View*, Marco Nani (ed.) Rome: University of Rome.
- 1990. Personal Identity and Extrinsicness. *Philosophical Studies* 59(2): 177–194.
- 1991. Personal Identity and Reductionism. *Philosophy and Phenomenological Research* 51(2): 361–373.
- 2003. Bermúdez on Self-consciousness. *The Philosophical Quarterly* 53(210): 96–101.
- 1997. Anscombe on 'I'. *The Philosophical Quarterly* 47(189): 507–511.
- 1995. Wittgenstein and the First Person. *Australasian Journal of Philosophy* 73(3): 347–355.
- 1992. Persons and Values. *The Philosophical Quarterly* 42(168): 337–44. (Winner of the 1992 *Philosophical Quarterly* Essay Prize.)

*****

I would like to express my gratitude to J.J. Joaquin for putting in the hard work required to bring this project to completion. JJ is one of the most productive philosophers in the Philippines, and he is doing more than anyone to kick-start analytic philosophy in Southeast Asia. I also have long-standing debts to my teachers, at St Andrews and Oxford, and to colleagues here at the Australian National University, most especially Daniel Stoljar and Alan Hájek.

The Universities, the Humanities, and Philosophy itself are going through hard times at the moment (and not just because of COVID). The Universities have become corporate machines; the Humanities have become infected with identity politics; Philosophy has become, *inter alia*, overly specialised, overly formal, and overly empirical. We can only hope that Philosophy will once again be the leading humane discipline, a paradigm for the culture, as it was last century.

Australian National University Brian Garrett
ACT, Australia
1 July 2021

Contents

Part I
Time

Chapter 1
"Thank Goodness That's Over" Revisited

Abstract Arthur N. Prior's "Thank Goodness that's Over" puzzle is often used as an argument against the tenseless view of the nature of time. In this discussion, I argue that a defender of the tenseless view can resolve Prior's puzzle.

1.1 Prior's Puzzle and the Two Views About the Nature of Time

There are two fundamentally opposed views of the nature of time, two accounts of the truth-conditions of tensed sentences. According to one view – the tensed view – the truth of a tensed sentence-token such as "*e* is past" consists in a particular event, *e*, having a particular property, pastness. According to the opposing view – the tenseless view – this account of the truth-conditions of tensed sentences is illusory. There is no property of pastness (or of presentness or futurity). Tensed sentence-tokens possess tenseless token-reflexive truth-conditions: on this view "*e* is past" is true if and only if *e* is earlier than the utterance "*e* is past". The account is token-reflexive since the sentence itself appears in the statement of its own truth-conditions, and it is tenseless since it is true at all times that a particular event is earlier than some other event. (Of course, defenders of the tensed view of time do not deny that the above biconditional is true; what they deny is that it gives the correct analysis of tensed sentences.)

Arthur Prior has presented the following objection to the tenseless view of time:

> One says, e.g. "Thank goodness that's over", and not only is this, when said, quite clear without any date appended, but it says something which is impossible that any use of a tenseless copula with a date should convey. It certainly doesn't mean the same as "Thank goodness the date of the conclusion of that thing is Friday, June 15, 1954", even if it be said then. (Nor, for that matter, does it mean "Thank goodness the conclusion of that thing is contemporaneous with this utterance". Why should anyone thank goodness for that?) (Prior, 1959, 17).

Thus it appears that the tenseless view of time cannot give utterance of "Thank goodness that's over" their intended content; such utterances can have that content only if the tensed view of time is correct.

B. Garrett, *Time, Identity and the Self: Essays on Metaphysics*, Synthese Library 442, https://doi.org/10.1007/978-3-030-85517-8_1

1.2 Responses to Prior's Puzzle

As stated, however, Prior's puzzle appears to admit of an easy solution. For it is no essential part of the tenseless view of time to claim that any sentence is synonymous with (means the same as) the corresponding sentence which states its truth-condition. The tenseless view of time is simply a view about tensed properties and the nature of the truth-conditions of tensed sentences. Hence the fact that an utterance of "Thank goodness that's over" conveys something which it is impossible that any use of a tenseless copula with a date should convey is quite consistent with the tenseless view of time.

However, Hugh Mellor has pointed out that Prior's puzzle can be restated in order to avoid this reply:

> Suppose you have just had a painful experience, e.g. a headache. Now it is over, you say with relief "Thank goodness that's over". What are you thanking goodness for? On the face it, the fact that the headache is no longer a present experience, i.e. is now past. That is presumably why you make your remark after the pain, and not during or before it. Can this fact still be explained when tensed facts have been traded in ... for tensed tokens with tenseless truth-conditions? (Mellor, 1981, 48)

That is, in order to bestow upon utterances of "Thank goodness that's over" their intended content we must presuppose the reality of tensed facts. But to acknowledge the existence of tensed facts is inconsistent with the tenseless view of time. Hence the tenseless view of time cannot give utterances of "Thank goodness that's over" their intended interpretation.

Mellor's own response to this version of Prior's puzzle is to claim that when I say "Thank goodness that's over" after the ending of a painful headache, I am not thanking goodness for any fact, *a fortiori* I am not thanking goodness for the fact that my headache is past, but merely expressing my relief (not necessarily relief from or about anything, just relief) (Mellor, 1981, 51). However, this account of the matter is unconvincing. Contrary to one of Mellor's assumptions, it is plausible to suppose that relief is a mental state which always has an intentional object – if I am relieved, it is surely always appropriate to ask what I am relieved about. And no other description of this case appears tenable than that I am relieved about the fact that my headache is past. Furthermore, Murray MacBeath has pointed out that not all utterances whose correct interpretation apparently presupposes the existence of tensed facts can plausibly be regarded as expressions of relief (e.g., ..., a father who, looking at his daughter on 1 June 1982 as she studies her finals, says, "Thank goodness I'm never going to sit another examination"' (MacBeath, 1983, 85)).

MacBeath himself attempts to solve Mellor's version of Prior's puzzle by claiming that only tensed beliefs, not tensed facts, are required in order to bestow upon utterances of "Thank goodness that's over" their intended content, and both the truth and content of tensed beliefs can be fixed by purely tenseless facts. Thus: I thank goodness that my headache is past, not because it is past, but because I believe it to be past, and this belief is true in virtue of the tenseless fact that the belief occurs after the headache.

However, I am not convinced by this solution. Certainly, when I thank goodness, after the ending of a painful headache, I thank goodness because I believe that the headache is past (if I didn't have this belief, I wouldn't have thanked goodness). But I do not thank goodness for my belief that the headache is past – I thank goodness for the fact that my headache is past. That I thank goodness because I believe my headache to be past does not serve to undermine the thesis that what I thank goodness for is the fact that my headache is past, and hence the correct account of the content of utterances of "Thank goodness that's over" does require tensed facts. The problem for the tenseless view of time remains – or so it appears.

1.3 A Riposte

I think it is an illusion to suppose that there is any genuine puzzle for the tenseless view of time in the first place. Contrary to the assumption of Mellor, there is a perfectly good sense in which, on the tenseless view of time, there are tensed facts. Mellor claims that "tensed facts are a myth" (Mellor, 1981, 34). But this, I believe, is no essential part of the tenseless view of time. Since the tenseless view of time acknowledges the existence of tensed truths (e.g. a 1988 utterance of 'Hitler's death is past'), there is a harmless sense in which it acknowledges the existence of tensed facts (the fact, expressed by that utterance, that Hitler's death is past). If we allow that an utterance '*P*' expresses a truth, there ought to be no objection to the locution 'it is a fact that *P*'. The tenseless view of time only denies the existence of tensed properties, not of tensed truths or facts, and it is quite consistent to hold that it is a fact that Hitler's death is past and that this fact does not consist in a particular event having a particular tensed property.

Examples from other areas may help to illustrate this point. It appears quite consistent for someone to believe that there are no negative, disjunctive or intensional properties, and yet to hold that there are negative, disjunctive or intensional facts. For example, one could hold that it is a fact that Socrates is believed by Jones to have been a famous Roman philosopher without holding that the predicate "is believed by Jones to have been a famous Roman philosopher" denotes a genuine property of Socrates. In general, then, it seems that we can acknowledge the fact that a is F without thereby incurring any commitment to the existence of a property of F-ness. A defender of the tenseless view of time ought, I suggest, to exploit this result. Consequently, there is no good reason why a defender of the tenseless view of time cannot agree with Prior: when I say "Thank goodness that's over" after the ending of a painful headache, I am thanking goodness for the fact that my headache is past.

At this point, it may be objected that if, on the tenseless view of time, tensed sentences are analysed in terms of tenseless sentences, then when I say "Thank goodness that's over" after the ending of a painful headache, what I am thanking goodness for must, ultimately, be a tenseless fact. But this, as Prior and Mellor rightly stress, is absurd. If I was thanking goodness for the tenseless fact that the utterance "My headache is over" is later than my headache, then, since this tenseless fact was a fact before and during my headache, as well as after it, I could just as well have thanked goodness for it before or during the headache – which is absurd.

This objection is, I think, fallacious. The operator "Thank goodness [...]" appears to generate a non-extensional context: I can thank goodness for the fact that *P*, where the fact that *P* is identical with, or logically equivalent to, the fact that *Q*, yet not thank goodness for the fact *Q*. For example, suppose that, after an accident and suffering from temporary amnesia, I thank goodness for the fact that I am still alive. Then, it might be supposed, I do not thank goodness for the fact that Garrett is still alive, even though – on one plausible view – the former fact just is the latter fact, under a different mode of presentation. Similarly, on the tenseless view of time, I can thank goodness for the fact that my headache is past without thanking goodness for the tenseless fact that my headache is earlier than my utterance "My headache is over".

Hence, once we (i) acknowledge the distinction between tensed facts and tensed properties, (ii) appreciate that the tenseless view of time is quite consistent with the existence of tensed facts, and (iii) recognise the non-extensionality of the operator "Thank goodness for the fact that [...]", Prior's puzzle for the tenseless view of time disappears. The tenseless view of time can, after all, bestow upon utterances of "Thank goodness that's over" their intended content.[1]

However, even if this is so, it might be objected that the defenders of the tenseless view of time must regard utterances of "Thank goodness that's over" (which are expressions of what Parfit has called "the bias towards the future") as symptoms of an irrational preference structure (Parfit, 1984, ch. 8). It seems irrational, on the tenseless view of time, to thank goodness for the fact that a pain is past. Why should the fact that a pain is past justify caring less about it? On the tenseless view, the fact that a particular pain, *e*, is past simply consists in the fact that *e* is earlier than the judgement that *e* is past. But there appears to be no relevant, intrinsic asymmetry between the relations *earlier than* and *later than* which justifies caring less about pains which are earlier than the time of judgement. On the tenseless view of time, it appears that the bias towards the future cannot be justified.

It might be thought that it is justifiable to care more about future experiences since we can control or bring about future states of affairs, whereas we cannot control or bring about past states of affairs, and it is perfectly rational to care more about states of affairs which we can now affect. However, as Parfit points out, if the explanation of why we care more about future pains was simply that we care only about those states of affairs which we can now affect, then inevitable future pains ought to have the same value for us as past pains (Parfit, 1984, 168). Yet, clearly, our attitude to inevitable future pains (states of affairs which, *ex hypothesi*, we cannot

[1] This solution is not the same as MacBeath's. Despite its involvement with intensional notions, MacBeath's solution is one which (like Mellor's) attempts to resolve Prior's puzzle for the tenseless view of time without invoking tensed facts.

affect) is not the same as our attitude to past pains. We are biased towards the future – we care more about future experiences simply because they are future – and this bias would appear to be unjustified if the tenseless view of time is correct.

However, whether this is an objection to the tenseless view of time depends upon whether the tensed view of time can justify the bias towards the future. But, *prima facie*, it is difficult to see how the tensed view of time is any better placed to provide a rationale for the bias towards the future. It is difficult to see how acknowledging the existence of tensed properties is supposed thereby to justify the bias towards the future. For the question still remains: what is it about the property of pastness which justifies caring less about past pains? I am sceptical as to whether this question can be answered, and appeal to time's passage and the metaphor of the moving NOW appears to provide little illumination.

1.4 Concluding Remarks

Clearly, this is not the place to go into the general question of the rationality of the bias towards the future. My point is simply that if the tenseless view of time is unable to provide a justification of the rationality of the attitude expressed in utterances of "Thank goodness that's over", this is not necessarily an objection to that view of time. And, of course, if the correct thing to say about the bias towards the future is that it is an attitude so deep and fundamental that it is rational even though it does not admit of justification, this is a response which can be made on either view of the nature of time.

References

MacBeath, M. (1983). Mellor's Emeritus headache. *Ratio, 25*(1), 81–88.
Mellor, D. H. (1981). *Real time*. Cambridge: Cambridge University Press.
Parfit, D. (1984). *Reasons and persons*. Oxford: Oxford University Press.
Prior, A. N. (1959). Thank goodness that's over. *Philosophy, 34*(128), 12–17.

Chapter 2
Experience and Time

Abstract In this discussion, I claim that the debate over "the bias towards the present" turns on an axiological question: Is the value of a present experience greater than its value when past? I argue not and hold that our bias towards the present, understood as a pure time preference, is irrational.

2.1 Justifying Our Bias Towards the Present

I am presented with two scenarios. On each scenario, my life contains a severe headache lasting one hour. The end of the headache induces total amnesia concerning the events of the previous hour. The two scenarios are

(a) The headache is past.
(b) The headache is present.

If asked which scenario I would prefer to obtain, I answer (a). I take it this would be the most popular answer. We are, in Parfit's phrase, "biased towards the present", that is, we care more about present headaches than we do about past ones simply in virtue of their presentness (Parfit, 1984, 179). But can this attitude be justified?

It is natural to suppose that we are right to care more about present headaches than about past ones only if present headaches have a greater (dis)value than past headaches. On this view, the primary question concerns the value of experiences.[1] A defender of (a) over (b) must reason as follows: a headache which is present (i.e. currently experienced) has a certain value; once that headache becomes past, it has a lesser value, either the same (lesser) value at all past times or else less and less value the further it recedes into the past. Only if something like this picture is correct can it be rational to prefer (a) to (b), as opposed to being indifferent between them.

[1] It matters not whether the value is understood to be impersonal or subject-relative.

B. Garrett, *Time, Identity and the Self: Essays on Metaphysics*, Synthese Library 442, https://doi.org/10.1007/978-3-030-85517-8_2

2.2 Value and the Metaphysics of Time

Perhaps, a defender of (a) over (b) must hold that the mere passage of time can affect the value of a headache. A given headache has a certain value when present and a lesser value when past. Its value decreases simply in virtue of losing the property of presentness and gaining the property of pastness. But how can this be? It is natural to think that the value of an experience supervenes on its underlying hedonic properties. When a headache moves from present to past, its hedonic properties do not change. It has the same hedonic properties in the past as it did when present. How then can its value change? Of course, a defender of the bias towards the present may simply deny supervenience, or at least deny that it holds over time, and so assert that the passage of time itself affects the value of experiences.

However, if we look at the standard theories of the metaphysics of time – with the notable exception of Presentism – it is hard to see how the passage of time can underwrite any difference in value. On the Moving Spotlight and Growing Universe views, past and present are equally real. When my present headache becomes past, therefore, it loses none of its hedonic properties. It exists in the past with those same hedonic properties. How then can the transition from present to past affect its value? A defender of the bias towards the present must ultimately insist that past headaches matter less simply because they are past. (See, e.g., (Heathwood, 2008, 61–62).) No further explanation can be given. But this is unsatisfactory.

For familiar reasons, appeal to the B-theory of time is to no avail. As with defenders of the Moving Spotlight and Growing Universe views, the B-theorist takes past and present headaches to be equally real. So how can the shift from present to past affect value? Moreover, the B-theorist's surrogate for the "passage of time" – one event following another in the B-series – seems incapable of justifying the assignment of lesser value to a past headache. Being earlier than some event in the B-series is not a reason for valuing a headache (or anything else) less.

Matters are different with respect to Presentism, according to which the present is real but the past (and future) are unreal. If headaches only exist when present, then presumably they only have value when present. This view justifies the bias towards the present, but it goes too far. If past headaches do not exist, they have no properties, hence no value properties. In that case, it would be rational for me to prefer any number of past headaches in preference to a present headache. But this is hard to believe. It cannot be right completely to discount the value of past headaches.[2]

---

[2] The Presentist might respond: "Past headaches don't exist, but they did exist." However, even if the Presentist is entitled to say this, it does not help. How can something which does not exist have any value?

Chris Heathwood is sympathetic to the view that one's past pains should be of no concern. In relation to Parfit's amnesia case, he writes that it is quite reasonable to refuse:

> [A]any reduction in past suffering, however large, in exchange for any increase in future suffering, however small (Heathwood, 2008, 56).

Then, of Parfit's past pain, he writes:

> Why should he care about it now? No reason – it's over and done with. When things become past, the reasons they provide can change (Heathwood, 2008, 57).

Then later:

> Look – don't you get it? If you're the patient whose operation was yesterday, then your suffering is over and done with. It's a thing of the past. Stop getting worked up about it. That doesn't make any sense (Heathwood, 2008, 63).

However, as noted above, I find the idea in the first quotation – that no weight be given to past suffering – implausible.[3] One way to see its implausibility is to consider a different case. I wake up in hospital with amnesia. The nurse does not know which of two patients I am, but she tells me that either I had a past life filled with unpleasant headaches or I had a headache-free past. According to Heathwood, I should be indifferent as to which past I had. This is hard to believe. It would, at least, not be irrational to prefer the headache-free past.

In the second quotation, Heathwood says that reasons can change when pains become past. But which reasons? Some reasons change, of course, e.g. reasons to act, to anticipate, to worry, etc. But why should reasons to care or to care less for something change? The third quotation introduces considerations which distract from the key issue. Of course, in cases where we have memories of past pains, it is psychologically unhealthy to obsess about them. But merely expressing concern and endorsing certain preferences is not obsessive behaviour.

2.3 Concluding Remarks

Presentism aside, then, the passage from present to past cannot reduce the value of a headache. But only thus can it be rational to care less about a headache once it has become past. In addition, any (less than total) discounting of past experiences faces the problem of arbitrariness. What value should be assigned to experiences once they become past 50% of its value when present? Is there, instead, a sliding scale and what is the discount rate of say 1% per day? These questions seem unanswerable. The inevitable conclusion is that we have no reason to prefer (a) to (b) (other things being equal). Of course, even given this conclusion, it may sometimes be rational

[3] Parfit would agree. He wrote: "When we are discussing distribution, past pains count. Those who have suffered more have more claim to be spared future pain" (Parfit, 1978, 297).

to care more about an experience when present than when past, but not simply in virtue of its being present.

Similar reasoning to the above shows that the "bias towards the future" – e.g., caring more about future headaches than about past ones simply in virtue of their being future – is also irrational (Parfit, 1984, 160). This bias is hard to justify on all the above theories of time, including Presentism. Again, we need to enter the qualification that it may sometimes be rational to care more about a future headache because one can influence its severity or duration. But this is not a case of pure time preference, i.e. it is not a case of valuing an experience more simply in virtue of its being future.

Arthur Prior famously argued that an utterance of "Thank goodness that's over!" only makes sense on the A-theory of time. Prior wrote:

> One says, e.g. "Thank goodness that's over!", and not only is this, when said, quite clear without any date appended, but it says something which it is impossible that any use of a tenseless copula with a date should convey. It certainly doesn't mean the same as, e.g. "Thank goodness the date of the conclusion of that thing is Friday, June I5, I954", even if it be said then. (Nor, for that matter, does it mean "Thank goodness the conclusion of that thing is contemporaneous with this utterance". Why should anyone thank goodness for that?) (Prior, 1959, 17)

According to Prior, utterances of "Thank goodness that's over!" presuppose an ontology of shifting A-series facts.[4] However, Prior's argument is controversial. For example, could we not use analogous reasoning ("Thank goodness that's happening over there!"; "Thank goodness that's not happening to me!") to establish an 'A-theory' of space and personality? More to the present point, even if the argument worked, it would only show that utterances of "Thank goodness that's over!", understood as expressions of pure time preference, require A-series facts for their correct interpretation. It would not follow that the attitudes expressed by such utterances are rational. Hence, Prior's argument, even if cogent, does not conflict with the conclusion that it is irrational to prefer (a) to (b).

References

Heathwood, C. (2008). Fitting attitudes and welfare. In R. Shafer-Landau (Ed.), *Oxford studies in metaethics*, volume 3. Oxford: Oxford University Press.

Parfit, D. (1978). Innumerate ethics. *Philosophy and Public Affairs, 7*(4), 285–301.

Parfit, D. (1984). *Reasons and persons*. Oxford: Oxford University Press.

Prior, A. N. (1959). Thank goodness that's over. *Philosophy, 34*(128), 12–17.

[4] Here is an alternative take on Prior's example: what you are thanking goodness for is the temporally neutral fact that the headache was not longer than, e.g., one hour.

Chapter 3
Max Black and Backward Causation

Abstract In this discussion, I point out that Max Black offers not one but two arguments against the (logical/metaphysical) possibility of backwards causation. Although both arguments fail in their intended aim, they show something important, viz., that defenders of backwards causation should understand Black's Houdini example (and others like it) in terms of the "multiple causes" model.

3.1 Black's Main Claim

In order to understand and assess Max Black's arguments against the possibility of backwards causation, we should revisit Black's original Houdini thought-experiment (Black, 1956, 52–55). Although the so-called 'bilking argument' against backwards causation has been much discussed over the years, commentators have overlooked the fact that Black offers not one but two arguments against the possibility of backwards causation.[1] Moreover, properly formulated, Black's arguments teach us something important about the strange and complex causal laws which would have to hold in the kind of situations Black envisages.

Black's example involves an alleged case of precognition in which Houdini announces whether a penny coin will land heads or tails. The coin is tossed one minute after his announcement. In repeated trials, Houdini always gives the right answer. Following Black's terminology we can label Houdini's predictions 'A- type events' and the outcomes of the coin tosses 'T-type events'. Let us suppose that the conditions which have obtained to date are maximally conducive to describing the example as a case of backwards causation. That is, suppose – thus far and prior to any intervention – we have good evidence for the following: Houdini's predictions exercise no causal influence on the coin tosses; the predictions and the coin tosses are not joint effects of a common cause; and no prediction was caused by a prior or simultaneous event.

[1] Neither 'bilk' nor 'bilking' (nor any cognate words) appear in Black's article. The term was first introduced into the philosophical lexicon by Antony Flew two years earlier. See Flew (1954, 57).

B. Garrett, *Time, Identity and the Self: Essays on Metaphysics*, Synthese Library 442, https://doi.org/10.1007/978-3-030-85517-8_3

Might this be considered a case of backwards causation? Black writes:

> There is at least one good reason for saying "No". In the circumstances described, we can wait until A has happened and then prevent T. For we assumed that the causes of T (the way the penny was thrown, the air currents in the room, and so on) were causally independent of A. So, A having occurred, it is within our power to prevent T's occurring – by simply not tossing a coin.
>
> This being so, a man who insists upon describing the circumstances as a case of effect preceding cause must qualify his assertion that the character of T causes A by adding that this is so only when T occurs. In other words: T causes A if T occurs, yet A may occur without T occurring at all.[2] So A may sometimes occur without being caused either by an earlier or a later event,[3] and yet on other occasions, a precisely similar A, though again not caused by an earlier event, is now held to be caused by a later one. This would be hard, if not impossible, to reconcile with our present uses of causal terminology.
>
> But there is a still better reason for refusing to call T a cause of A. If T's causal antecedents are independent of A as we found ourselves required to stipulate, we can arrange for T to disagree with A. Thus, it would be theoretically possible to learn to toss the coin so that it came down heads or tails as we pleased; all we need to do is to wait for Houdini's answer, and then arrange for the coin to fall contrary to his prediction. If we can do this, the stipulations for the supposed precognition are logically impossible of fulfilment, because Houdini's answer will not always agree with the subsequent trial. On the other hand, if we find that once Houdini has answered we cannot arrange for the penny to come down as we please, we shall be compelled to say that the causal antecedents of T are not independent of A. We shall have to say that Houdini's answer exerts a causal influence of an esoteric sort upon the subsequent toss of the coin. This would be extraordinary enough, to be sure. Yet it would not be preposterous, as would be the logical absurdity of saying that an effect precedes its cause (Black, 1956, 54–55).

3.2 Black's Two Arguments

Black offers two arguments against the possibility of backwards causation. His first argument (contained in the initial two paragraphs of the quotation) proceeds as follows:

1. Suppose, for *reductio*, that the coin tosses cause the earlier predictions;
2. After a prediction has occurred, it is within our power to prevent a coin toss from occurring one minute later;
3. Occasionally we do so intervene (i.e., bilk); so

[2] Black's discussion in this paragraph and elsewhere is compromised by his failure to distinguish event-tokens from event-types. However, I assume that this can easily be rectified. What Black finds absurd is the idea that A-type events are sometimes caused by T-type events and sometimes not.

[3] Clearly this doesn't follow. If an A-type event is not caused by a later T-type event, it doesn't follow that it wasn't caused by an earlier or later event (i.e., that it was either uncaused or caused by a simultaneous event). It might have been caused by another later event. That is the main point of the present chapter.

4. Houdini's predictions are sometimes caused by coin tosses (when we don't intervene) and sometimes not caused by coin tosses (when we do intervene);
5. This conjunction (i.e., (4)) is impossible; so
6. (1) is false: the coin tosses never cause the predictions; so
7. Backwards causation is impossible.

It might be questioned whether Black does endorse premise (5). He says that (4) would be "hard, if not impossible, to reconcile with our present uses of causal terminology" (Black, 1956, 54). However Black needs (5) if he is to establish (6) and (7). Any weaker claim – e.g., that (4) is merely odd or unusual – would not secure the desired result. I also assume, given his appeal to our 'causal terminology', that Black would regard (4) as analytically impossible. I urge below that it is neither analytically nor metaphysically impossible.

Black's first argument faces the following objection. According to Black, it is absurd to suppose that Houdini's pronouncements are sometimes caused by coin tosses and sometimes not. But why is this absurd? It is not impossible for events of the same type to have different causes on different occasions. For example, suppose that switch S is normally down and, when down, causes a light to be on. But on the occasions when S is up, switch S* kicks in and causes the light to be on. The light's being on has different causes at different times. There is nothing mysterious here, and this or relevantly similar cases have doubtless occurred many times. It is, of course, a paradigm case of what is known as (forwards) causal preemption.

A defender of the possibility of backwards causation is entitled to suppose that backwards causal preemption is also possible. It could then be proposed that, in Black's example, the act of preventing the coin toss causes the earlier prediction (a prediction which otherwise would have been caused by the coin toss). On this view, Houdini's predictions are always backwardly caused, sometimes by the coin toss and sometimes by the act of preventing the coin toss.

This description is not in tension with our "causal terminology", at least if understood on the model of "multiple causes" (i.e., different causes on different occasions). Note that I do not have to motivate the 'multiple causes' interpretation of Black's example. It is enough that the interpretation represents a metaphysically possible scenario. To refute an impossibility claim we need only describe one coherent scenario in which the alleged impossibility obtains. No other justification is needed.

On this (hitherto unexplored) way of understanding Black's example, if we let the coin toss go ahead, it causes Houdini's prediction; if we prevent the coin toss, our act of prevention causes the prediction. Either way, Houdini's prediction is an explicable and backwardly caused event. It is either caused by a coin toss or caused by an act of preventing the coin toss. So premise (5) is false.

It may, by our standards, be a strange world in which the prevention of a coin toss causes an earlier pronouncement, and such a world may have strange causal laws. But strange is not impossible. As Hume observed, it is never an a priori matter whether one event causes, or does not cause, another. Why has this possibility been overlooked? Perhaps because the coin toss was presented as the only salient candidate for causing the earlier pronouncement. Perhaps because it was assumed that the prevention of a coin toss is not the kind of action that could have any backwards causal effects. Whatever the explanation, this possibility represents a natural way for a defender of backwards causation to make sense of Black's example.

There are other possibilities too. For example, what if the tosser simply decides not to toss the coin? Then his failure to toss the coin causes the earlier pronouncement. Indeed, we can suppose it to be nomically guaranteed that any act or omission which results in the non-occurrence of the coin toss causes the pronouncement. Such 'disjunctive' scenarios are not impossible, however weird and gerrymandered they may be. These scenarios are 'disjunctive', not in the sense that the cause is a disjunction, but in the sense that Houdini's predictions are caused in different ways on different occasions.[4]

It may be that Black endorsed premise (5) because he assumed a simple covering law model of causation. Perhaps he reasoned: if Houdini's predictions are caused by coin tosses, they must fall under an exceptionless law according to which the predictions are always caused by coin tosses; in our imagined scenario Houdini's predictions are sometimes caused by coin tosses, sometimes not; this is not possible; so coin tosses never cause the predictions. The reply to this reasoning is that its starting premise is false. The simple covering law model is refuted by cases of causal preemption (backwards or forwards).

Black's second, and supposedly better, argument (contained in the last paragraph of the quotation) runs as follows:

1. Either we can arrange for the coin to fall contrary to Houdini's prediction or we cannot;
2. If we can, "the stipulations for the supposed precognition are logically impossible of fulfilment, because Houdini's answer will not always agree with the subsequent trial";
3. If we can't, A-type events must be among the causal antecedents of T-type events (in which case we have a strange kind of forwards causation, not backwards causation);
4. Either way, T-type events never cause A-type events; so
5. Backwards causation is impossible.

In order for this argument to be cogent, premises (2) and (3) must be true and each must entail (4). But there is a problem. Premise (2), as stated, is false. If we can, but never do, arrange for the coin to fall contrary to Houdini's predictions, Houdini's answers will always agree with the subsequent coin tosses. We could instead replace premise (2) with:

[4] I put to one side the outre possibility that Houdini's pronouncements, when there is no later coin toss, are uncaused and, hence, inexplicable. This may be a metaphysically possibility, but it would require even stranger laws than those envisaged above.

2' If we can and sometimes do arrange for the coin to fall contrary to Houdini's predictions, Houdini's answers will not always agree with the subsequent coin tosses.

(2') may be what Black had in mind. Unfortunately, it is trivially true and fails to imply that the coin tosses never cause Houdini's predictions. (2') is consistent with the tosses causing the predictions in cases where we don't intervene. The second argument fails too.

3.3 Analysing Black's Arguments

It should be clear from the above that Black's arguments are not hopeless confusions from which we can learn nothing. Black has highlighted a perfectly intuitive worry about backwards causation, at least in situations in which agents can and do prevent the typical cause from occurring. It is puzzling what brings about the effect in such situations. But the puzzlement arises only because Black's example has been under-described. Once we think of such scenarios along the lines of the "multiple causes" model, the worry disappears.

I realise that some may find the "multiple causes" model hard to take seriously. It offers an extraordinarily gerrymandered case of causation. On this model, anything which results in the non-occurrence of the coin toss, after Houdini has made his prediction, causes the prediction. But 'anything' here could mean pretty much anything: intervention by a third-party, forgetfulness on the part of the coin tosser, the death of the tosser, some natural intervention (e.g., a lightning strike etc.). This is not a kind of preemptive causation that we are familiar with. It is wildly disjunctive.

Let me say three things in response. First, it does not seem to be impossible. To appeal to Hume again, no causal connexion, however bizarre, can be excluded *a priori*. Second, even in cases of forwards causation, there are no *a priori* limits on what might have brought about a certain effect had the actual cause been preempted. The same is true in cases of backwards causation. Third, if we do not pursue some such line, it's hard to see how Black's worry can be met. If his worry can't be answered, we must concede that there are no possible worlds containing backwards causal chains and agents (or natural happenings) which can bilk those chains.[5] I would rather not concede this.

Some commentators have thought that Black's reasoning relies on an epistemic premise, viz., that the intervenor knows of Houdini's pronouncement and, as a result, prevents the occurrence of the coin toss (or determines its outcome).[6] This is undoubtedly the picture that Black had in mind. But it is not essential to his arguments. The possibility of an unwitting intervenor (ignorant of Houdini and

[5] This would, e.g., rule out as impossible the time travel stories beloved of philosophers.

[6] See, e.g., Price (1996, 171–174).

his pronouncements), or even the possibility of a natural disruptor (such as a falling tree), would serve Black's purpose just as well. Black's arguments are metaphysical not epistemic. Hence, insistence on the intervenor's ignorance of Houdini's announcements, besides being ad hoc, affords no resolution of Black's worry.

In sum, then, we have good grounds to reject Black's arguments. Black's opponents can render explicable Houdini's predictions if they take the acts of prevention, when they occur, to cause the earlier predictions, predictions which would otherwise have been caused by the coin tosses.

References

Black, M. (1956). Why cannot an effect precede its cause? *Analysis, 16*(3), 49–58.

Flew, A. (1954). Can an effect precede its cause? *Proceedings of the Aristotelian Society, 28*, 45–62.

Price, H. (1996). *Time's arrow and Archimedes' point.* Oxford: Oxford University Press.

Chapter 4
Dummett on Reasons to Act and Bringing About the Past

Abstract My intention in this discussion is to outline and criticise some of the main ideas in Michael Dummett's classic article "Bringing about the Past". From Dummett's remarks we can (I think) reconstruct two sceptical arguments designed to show that it can never be rational to attempt to bring about past events. Dummett is critical of both arguments. Though I am happy with Dummett's reply to the first sceptical argument, I disagree with his reply to the second.

4.1 Introduction

Michael Dummett's "Bringing about the Past" has not, I think, received the detailed attention that it deserves (Dummett, 1964). One of my aims in this discussion is to make clear why Dummett's paper deserves more consideration today. Although the topic of backwards causation may seem esoteric, it intersects with central themes in metaphysics (time, causation) and in epistemology (rationality, reasons for acting). Indeed, as we shall we see, Dummett's concerns in his paper are more epistemic than metaphysical. Although Dummett's article is in dire need of editing and sign-posting, it nonetheless contains many interesting ideas. What follows is very much my own reconstruction of Dummett's reasoning, using nomenclature that Dummett himself does not employ. Even so, I take it to be faithful to the spirit of Dummett's thought.

4.2 Dissecting Dummett's Argument

Dummett's paper divides into three parts. The first is introductory, opening with some remarks about causation in general and backwards causation in particular. Dummett assumes that backwards causation is possible. That is, provided that we imagine ourselves to be mere observers, we can conceive of worlds in which some causation runs in the later-to-earlier direction. Indeed, since we are mere observers

B. Garrett, *Time, Identity and the Self: Essays on Metaphysics*, Synthese Library 442, https://doi.org/10.1007/978-3-030-85517-8_4

of the motion of the planets, it could have turned out that such motion involved backwards causation and backwards causal laws (Dummett, 1964, 340).

The central concern of Dummett's paper, however, lies elsewhere. It relates to worlds in which there are backwards causal chains and agents who can initiate such chains. (Max Black, similarly, questioned whether backwards causation is possible in the presence of agents who can interfere in backwards causal chains (Black, 1956).) Dummett's question is: Can agents have a reason to bring about past events, in worlds where there are, or are justifiably believed to be, humanly manipulable backwards causal chains? Dummett's (eventual) answer is in the affirmative.

Dummett is aware that "the conception of doing something in order that something else should have happened appears to be intrinsically absurd" (Dummett, 1964, 340). According to my reconstruction, he identifies two sceptical arguments against such a conception. The first sceptical argument attempts to show that it is pointless to attempt to affect the past since any given past event has already either happened or not. Dummett's reply to this argument is that it cannot be cogent since it is the mirror image of a standard argument for fatalism. (The argument in question is a version of the so-called "Idle Argument"; see (Rice, 2018, sec. 7) for a useful discussion.) Since we reject the latter (fatalist) argument, we should reject the former too.

The second sceptical argument is more complex, and rests on the (natural) assumption that we can have intention-independent knowledge of past events we brought about. Such knowledge might seem to undermine our reasons to bring about past events. For example: what reason can I have to do A tomorrow in order that B occurred last week if I learn today that B occurred? Dummett's reply to this second sceptical argument is a radical one. He denies the assumption that such intention-independent knowledge is possible. This reply is, I think, untenable. Fortunately another reply is available.

One initial argument for thinking it absurd to attempt to affect the past assumes that attempting to affect the past involves attempting to change the past; and since the latter is impossible to achieve, so is the former. But it is generally agreed that this reasoning is confused. In doing *A* to bring about the earlier *B*, I have made it the case that *B* occurred, but I have not changed the past. If *B* occurred at that earlier time, it always was and always will be true that it occurred then. Nothing that occurred at that time was changed, nor could it be.

As Dummett notes, orthodox Jewish theologians thought that retrospective prayer involved a logical impossibility, and that such prayer therefore mocked God. Dummett gives an example of retrospective prayer: a father prays that his son was one of the survivors in a ship that went down a few hours previously. But, as Dummett rightly points out, we don't have to interpret the father as asking God to do the impossible (to make the drowned son not have drowned). Rather, we can interpret the father as asking God to make it the case that his son was among the survivors, and this is not asking for the logically impossible. Dummett interprets this case, not as one in which the father's prayer directly brings about the survival of his son, but as one in which God has foreknowledge that the father will pray and, as a result, ensures that his son is among the survivors.

Having introduced the case of retrospective prayer, Dummett then outlines the first sceptical argument against the rationality of attempts to bring about the past. This argument does not draw on the theological aspect of the prayer example but applies quite generally to any attempt to causally influence the past. The first sceptical argument runs as follows:

> Suppose someone were to say to [the father], "Either your son has drowned or he has not. If he has drowned, then certainly your prayer will not (cannot) be answered. If he has not drowned, your prayer is superfluous. So in either case your prayer is pointless: it cannot make any difference to whether he has drowned or not." (Dummett, 1964, 344–345)

Dummett observes that this argument seems to be the "exact analogue" of one of the standard arguments for fatalism, popular in London during the bombing, viz.,:

> The siren sounds, and I set off for the air-raid shelter in order to avoid being killed by a bomb. The fatalist argues, "Either you are going to be killed by a bomb or you are not going to be. If you are, then any precautions you take will be ineffective. If you are not, all precautions you take are superfluous. Therefore it is pointless to take precautions." This belief was extended even to particular bombs. If a bomb was going to kill me, then it "had my number on it," and there was no point in my attempting to take precautions against being killed by that bomb; if it did not have my number on it, then of course precautions were pointless too. (Dummett, 1964, 345)

Dummett's thought is that since we regard the fatalist's argument as sophistical, so too should we regard the first sceptical argument. Now Dummett concedes that some may not regard the arguments as exact analogues precisely because of the difference in tense. This opens up a way of replying to the fatalist's argument which is not applicable to the sceptical argument, viz., denying the first premise. Thus, on some theories of time which deny the reality of the future (such as C. D. Broad's Growing Universe View) future contingent statements, such as "you will be killed by a bomb", are not true or false. They are indeterminate in truth-value, and hence not true. If we wish to adhere to the classical (non-supervaluationist) principle that a disjunction is true only if at least one of its disjuncts is true, such theories imply that the first premise of the fatalist argument is not true. But, assuming the reality of the past, there is no analogous way of denying the first premise of the sceptical argument.

However, leaving the dispute about the reality of the future to one side, the two arguments are analogous in another respect. The premises of both arguments are assumed to be necessary *a priori* truths. Yet, so understood, the second and third premises of each argument are not true.[1] Consider the second premise of the fatalist's argument: "If you are going to be killed, then any precautions you take will be ineffective". If you are going to be killed, then of course whatever precautions you actually take will be (or would have been) ineffective in preventing your death. But it does not follow that there are no precautions such that, had you taken them,

[1] Dummett's discussion at this point is somewhat opaque (Dummett, 1964, 346–348). J. H. Sobel's discussion clarifies matters (Sobel, 1966). For a different interpretation, see Stalnaker (1975) and Bledin (2019).

you would not have been killed. If there are such life-saving precautions, taking them would have been effective, so not pointless. Hence, it does not follow that all possible precautions are ineffective, which is what the fatalist needs and intends.

Now consider the third premise of the fatalist's argument: "If you are not going to be killed, all precautions you take are superfluous". This is not a necessary truth. It is not necessarily true that if you are not killed, all precautions you took were superfluous. On the contrary, it may be that you were not killed precisely because you took precautions. Superfluity is a counterfactual notion. Precautions were superfluous just if you would (still) not have been killed, had you not taken them. But this counterfactual is obviously not a necessary truth, and presumably was often false during the Second World War and at other times. Sometimes precautions are superfluous, but sometimes they are not.

Consequently, the fatalist's argument is defective, whatever the correct theory of time may be. But the sceptical argument contains analogous premises and is flawed for the same reason. Thus, the son may have been saved precisely because the father prayed. Hence, the first sceptical argument against the rationality of attempting to bring about the past fails.

Since I agree with Dummett's reply to the first sceptical argument, I will spend more time discussing the second sceptical argument. In order to introduce this argument, Dummett proffers the following thought-experiment:

> Every second year the young men of the tribe are sent, as part of their initiation ritual, on a lion hunt: they have to prove their manhood. They travel for 2 days, hunt lions for 2 days, and spend 2 days on the return journey; observers go with them, and report to the chief upon their return whether the young men acquitted themselves with bravery or not. The people of the tribe believe that various ceremonies, carried out by the chief, influence the weather, the crops, and so forth. I do not want these ceremonies to be thought of as religious rites, intended to dispose the gods favourably towards them, but simply as performed on the basis of a wholly mistaken system of causal beliefs. While the young men are away from the village the chief performs ceremonies – dances, let us say – intended to cause the young men to act bravely. We notice that he continues to perform these dances for the whole 6 days that the party is away, that is to say, for 2 days during which the events that the dancing is supposed to influence have already taken place. Now there is generally thought to be a special absurdity in the idea of affecting the past, much greater than the absurdity of believing that the performance of a dance can influence the behaviour of a man 2 days' journey away; so we ought to be able to persuade the chief of the absurdity of his continuing to dance after the first 4 days without questioning his general system of causal beliefs. How are we going to do it? (Dummett, 1964, 348–349)

So: is there a special absurdity in the idea of an agent attempting to affect the past, and how might we establish its absurdity? Dummett approaches these questions by posing a more specific one: viz., "Can we persuade the chief of the irrationality of his post-hunt dancing?" Let us take it that the chief has the best possible grounds to believe that his dancing is causally efficacious.[2] That is, suppose that on every occasion when he danced on the last 2 days, the men were brave, and on every

[2] I assume throughout that the chief only dances in order to influence the men's behaviour (e.g., he is not a "fitness fanatic") and that the chief's desire is to bring it about that the men fought bravely,

occasion when he didn't dance, the men were cowardly. (We don't need to make such a strong assumption – a significant correlation would suffice – but let us make it nonetheless.) Further, the chief tells us that he has never tried to dance and been unable to do so for no explicable reason. Hence, there is no temptation to think that the men's bravery causes his dancing or that their cowardice renders him incapable of dancing.

How then are we to challenge the chief's belief? Dummett takes it as obvious that if the chief somehow knew, prior to dancing on the last 2 days, that the men were brave, he would have no reason to dance. Let us suppose, therefore, that we arrange for the information to reach the chief (e.g., by portable telephone) after the men have fought but prior to his post-hunt dancing. We then invite the chief not to dance when told that the men were brave, and to dance when told that they were not brave. Suppose he does so and, immediately after, we say "Well, you must see that you have no reason to dance. Your dancing is not causally efficacious after all". However, suppose it later turns out that on all the occasions on which the chief was told the men were brave and didn't dance, and on which he was told the men were cowardly and did dance, he was misinformed (the observers lied or were mistaken). Our challenge has failed. The correlations between dancing and bravery, and between non-dancing and cowardice, instead of being undermined, have been reinforced.

Dummett concedes that if this is how things turn out, the chief is quite entitled to believe in the efficacy of his dancing. But the experiment has a further consequence. It has made the chief think that he cannot trust the reports of observers. So the chief concludes that he can know that the young men were brave only through his intention to dance. In this way, his knowledge of the men's bravery is exactly parallel to the knowledge that we have of the intended effects of our own future actions (e.g., I know that I will be home tonight via my current intention to catch my usual train). Dummett regards this symmetry between past and future as a point in favour of his view. Thus, in order to maintain the rationality of his belief in the causal efficacy of his dancing, the chief gives up a belief about the past that we all find natural, viz., the belief "that it is possible for me to find out what has happened (whether the young men have been brave or not) independently of my intentions" (Dummett, 1964, 356–357).

The upshot is that we cannot convict the chief of irrationality, if things turn out as described above. More generally, provided we are willing to give up the principle that we can have intention-independent knowledge of events that we backwardly cause, it can be rational to attempt to bring about the past. Hence, in worlds in which there are humanly manipulable backwards causal chains, it can be rational to use them to bring about past events just as we use future-directed causal chains to bring about future events in this world.

---

as opposed to the egocentric desire to bring it about that he (the chief) caused the men to fight bravely.

4.3 The Second Sceptical Argument

We are now in a position to state the second sceptical argument and Dummett's response to it. The second sceptical argument, addressed to the chief but general in its application, is this:

(i) If you can have intention-independent knowledge, prior to dancing, of the men's bravery, you have no reason to dance.
(ii) You can have intention-independent knowledge, prior to dancing, of the men's bravery; so
(iii) You have no reason to dance.

Dummett's response to this (obviously valid) argument is to endorse premise (i) but to deny premise (ii). Dummett's overall conclusion, therefore, is that there are possible circumstances in which it is rational to attempt to bring about the past, provided we are prepared to give up the principle that we can have intention-independent knowledge of the occurrence of events that we backwardly cause. What should we say about the second sceptical argument and Dummett's response to it? The two key questions are: "Is Dummett right to endorse premise (i)?" and "Is Dummett right to reject premise (ii)?" Let us address these questions in turn.

It's fair to say that Dummett offers no argument for premise (i). In fact, Dummett endorses the slightly different principle (without the modal 'can'):

(i*) If you have intention-independent knowledge, prior to dancing, of the men's bravery, you have no reason to dance.

On the face of it, (i*) does not imply (i). Could one not hold that intention-independent knowledge is reason-undermining, but the mere possibility of such knowledge is not (i.e., cases where you might, but do not, have such knowledge)? After all, it may be said, what you have reason to do, at least in one sense of 'reason', depends on what you know or believe. However, since the falsity of (i*) implies the falsity of (i), I will try to show that (i) is false by demonstrating the falsity of (i*).

Dummett takes it as obvious that once the chief "knows whether the young men have been brave or not ... there is no longer any point in trying to bring it about that they have been" (Dummett, 1964, 349). Similar sentiments were expressed in an earlier symposium with Anthony Flew. There Dummett wrote, using a different example but to the same effect:

> What is true is that if the magician knows that the weather was fine on the date in question, he will not bother to recite the spell; and if he knows that it was not fine, he will not recite it either ... Here it is of no consequence that this argument too can be paralleled for the future. It is of course true that if anyone knew whether or not something was going to happen, he would do nothing now designed to make it happen, for this would be either redundant or fruitless. (Dummett, 1954, 41)

In these quotes, I take it that Dummett has in mind intention-independent knowledge, although this was not clearly formulated in the 1954 article. Flew objects to Dummett's claim that knowledge is reason-undermining. Unfortunately, his counterexample involves intention-dependent knowledge. Imagining a Headmaster about to punish an errant schoolboy, Flew observes that "if the Headmaster knows what he is going to do to Smith, this does not make his efforts redundant and fruitless" (Flew, 1954, 61). This observation seems correct, but since the Headmaster's knowledge is presumably intention-dependent (i.e., acquired via his intention to cane Smith) it is no objection to Dummett's considered view.

It may be possible, however, to reinterpret Flew's example so that it is a counterexample. Suppose that the Headmaster knows that Smith is sitting outside his office at 5 pm on Friday, knows that boys sitting outside his office at 5 pm on Friday are caned, and so infers that Smith will be caned. Intuitively, the Headmaster's intention-independent knowledge that Smith will be caned does not undermine his reason to cane Smith. Here is another example. I travel home every night by train. Suppose that I know, via induction from previous nights, that I will arrive home tonight. Although intention-independent, that knowledge does not undermine my reason to catch tonight's train. In these examples I assume that the Headmaster and I arrive at our knowledge purely by induction, so that our knowledge is (unequivocally) intention-independent. Alternatively, our knowledge might be over-determined. Perhaps the Headmaster knows via his intention that he will cane Smith and knows by induction that he will do so. Even so, the second way of knowing has no tendency to undermine the Headmaster's reason to cane Smith.

These examples show that Dummett was wrong to endorse (i*): intention-independent knowledge is not, or at least not always, reason-undermining. Since (i*), and hence (i), are false, the door is now open to a different response to the second sceptical argument: reject premise (i).

What of premise (ii)? Since premise (i) is false, it is of course not necessary to reject premise (ii) in order to avoid the conclusion (iii). Still, is Dummett's rejection of premise (ii) plausible or even coherent? It is natural to think that agents can, in principle, have knowledge of past events – including knowledge of past events they bring about – independently of their intentions. Yet this is what Dummett denies in order to make room for the idea that an agent can have a reason to bring about a past event. The only scenario, according to Dummett, in which the chief can have a reason to dance is one in which he cannot know, independently of his intention to dance, that the young men were brave. There was, it will be recalled, a reason for this. The chief realised that he could not trust the reports of his observers, so concluded that he could only know that the men were brave via his intention to dance. But does this conclusion follow and is it tenable?

According to Dummett, the chief has a reason to dance provided he cannot have intention-independent knowledge of the men's bravery prior to his dancing. Now it is typical of past events to leave myriad future traces. Suppose that the men fought bravely and that information to that effect was spread in many ways into the future: by testimony, memory, newspaper reports and so on. This information presumably constitutes knowledge for the observers and many others – they can know that the men were brave – but such information cannot constitute knowledge for the chief, according to Dummett. This, however, is hard to believe.

Moreover, even if the chief decides that he cannot trust the reports of others, what if he was to witness the men fighting bravely? (Gorovitz, 1964, 368). Should he discount that information too? Does the chief's own perceptual information not constitute knowledge for him? What of a different case where the chief's dancing caused him to have had a headache the previous Wednesday? Could he not have intention-independent knowledge of his own headache prior to dancing? Another problem: can the chief have intention-independent knowledge that the men were brave after he has danced? It would seem so. Yet this implies the oddity that the same item of information, say a newspaper report, may constitute knowledge for the chief after he dances but not before.

There is another, more extreme, possibility. Perhaps the men's bravery has no causal consequences at all and thus yields no information for anyone. Knowledge of the men's bravery, even via perception or memory, is therefore impossible for anyone. This would underwrite Dummett's epistemic restriction but at the cost of removing backwardly caused events from the causal swim (they are caused but uncausing). This consequence is metaphysically bizarre and makes such events forever unknowable. This is too high a price to pay in order to make sense of bringing about the past. Dummett's project, after all, is to find out whether we can accommodate the idea of agents bringing about the past in ways recognisable to us, involving minimal distortion of our own conceptual scheme. We must be able to draw a moral for our own case from the example of the dancing chief (Dummett, 1954, 351).

The upshot is that the chief was too quick to move to the conclusion that he could only know that the men were brave via his intention to dance, and Dummett was wrong to endorse this conclusion. Moreover, the conclusion is, if not incoherent, completely at odds with our ways of knowing about the world. Dummett was, I submit, wrong to reject premise (ii). We should accept (ii).

4.4 The Third Sceptical Argument

Is that the end of the matter? Is the second sceptical argument flawed because premise (i) is false? The counterexamples to premise (i) involved knowledge acquired by inductive reasoning. But much of our knowledge of past events is direct, where direct knowledge of an event's occurrence can be defined as knowledge that derives causally from that event. Thus, my reading in this morning's newspaper that the Raiders won last night's game is direct knowledge; my knowledge that the sun will rise tomorrow is indirect. Perhaps we can improve on the second sceptical argument by replacing Dummett's intention-independent/intention-dependent distinction with the direct/indirect distinction. This may yield a better argument.

We should therefore consider the following (third) sceptical argument, again addressed to the chief:

(1) If you can have direct knowledge, prior to dancing, of the men's bravery, you have no reason to dance.
(2) You can have direct knowledge, prior to dancing, of the men's bravery; so
(3) You have no reason to dance.

Since denying premise (2) is not an option, for the reasons given in the previous section, the question is whether premise (1) is more plausible than premise (i). Unlike (i), it is hard to think of uncontroversial and everyday cases in which direct knowledge is not reason-undermining. This is unsurprising since in our world we don't have direct knowledge of future events, and events of which we do have direct knowledge, we cannot affect.

Suppose that the chief has direct knowledge that the men were brave. Might he reason to himself: "I know that the men were brave; so the men were brave. That fact is not going to change. So it will still be true that the men were brave if I refrain from dancing. So I have no reason to dance."? He might so reason, but it looks suspiciously similar to the fatalist reasoning mooted earlier. Suppose I have knowledge (in the normal way or by induction) that I will be home tonight. Then I might reason: "I know that I will be home tonight; so I will be home tonight. That fact is not going to change. So it will still be true that I will be home tonight if I refrain from catching my usual train. So I have no reason to catch my train". This reasoning is sophistical, yet it is the analogue of the chief's reasoning. Where does it go wrong?

First, the reasoning assumes that the natural language indicative conditional is material and hence that from any proposition '*p*' we can derive 'if *q* then *p*' ("if the men were brave then if I refrain from dancing it will still be the case that the men were brave"). But it is controversial to hold that the indicative conditional is material. The principle "if *p* then if *q* then *p*" is, after all, often referred to as "the paradox of material implication". Many would gibe at the idea that, e.g., "if Trump wins the next election then, if his opponent wins, Trump wins" is a tautology.

Second, even if we grant that the indicative conditional is material, the fatalist conclusion does not follow. I have no reason to catch my train in order to arrive home just if catching my train is superfluous with respect to achieving this end. But superfluity, as noted earlier, is a counterfactual notion: catching my train is superfluous just if, were I not to catch my train, I would still arrive home tonight. But we may have good reason to think this counterfactual false. Nor does it follow from the tautology (if it is a tautology) that if I arrive home tonight then if I don't catch my train, I arrive home tonight. (Indeed, how could it? Tautologies only imply tautologies.) The same diagnosis applies to the chief's imagined chain of reasoning.

It might be replied that I am not comparing like with like. Consider a world in which the chief dances in order that the young men fight bravely the following week. Suppose that the correlations are strong enough reasonably to take this to be a case of (forwards) causation. Now suppose that the chief has a crystal ball which affords him direct knowledge of the outcomes of future hunts (i.e., those outcomes cause him to have true beliefs about the men's bravery or lack of it). Question: if the chief is in receipt of information that the men will fight bravely next week does this undermine his reason to dance? Arguably not. Again, a fatalist fallacy lurks in the wings: "I know the men will fight bravely; so I know the men will fight bravely if I don't dance; so I have no reason to dance". This is no better than standard (logical) fatalist argument which makes no reference to knowledge: "Either the men will fight bravely or they won't. If they will, they will if I don't dance; if they won't, they won't if I don't dance; so I have no reason to dance". It's ironic that having spent many pages criticising fatalist reasoning, Dummett endorses a premise (premise (i) and, by implication, premise (1)) which can seemingly only be supported by analogous reasoning.

Hence, a natural and tempting argument for premise (1) is fallacious, and it is the mirror-image of fatalist reasoning. Pending some better argument for premise (1), and I cannot think of one, we are free to reject that premise and thus leave room for the idea that we can, in appropriate circumstances, have reason to bring about past events. So I agree with Dummett that we should reject the conclusion of the second and third sceptical arguments. We differ over which premise to reject.

4.5 Conclusion

At the end of this discussion, I am in broad agreement with Dummett. It is no more unreasonable for agents to make use of backwards causal chains in order to achieve their ends than it is for us to make use of forward causal chains to achieve our ends. I think that opposition to this conclusion has to take the form of a blank denial of the possibility of backwards causation. It would be odd, instead, to allow that backwards causation is possible, but not in the presence of agents; or that backwards causation is possible in the presence of agents, but that agents could never initiate backwards causal chains; or that they could initiate such chains (as mere causes), but could never have any reason to do so. It seems essential to the idea that A-type events cause B-type events that if an agent wants to bring about a B-type event, and has it within his power to bring about an A-type event, then he has reason to do so. The upshot is that anyone who wants to disagree with Dummett's overall conclusion, e.g., someone who endorses both premises of the third sceptical argument, had better maintain that backwards causation is impossible.

One might suggest that (1) is an intuitively plausible principle, even if there is a bad argument for it. (True propositions can, after all, be the conclusions of fallacious arguments.) But if we endorse (1), then how do we respond to the third sceptical argument? Since denying (2) is not an option, do we want to be committed to the conclusion (3)? (3) is not intrinsically absurd but accepting it sits ill with the idea that backwards causation is possible, for reasons given in the previous paragraph. Since I want to make room for the possibility of backwards causation, and find the denial of (2) much more implausible than the denial of (1), I accept (2) and deny (1). Whether the reader agrees with this response or not, it is to Dummett's credit that he makes these sceptical arguments visible.

References

Black, M. (1956). Why cannot an effect precede its cause? *Analysis, 16*(3), 49–58.
Bledin, J. (2019). Fatalism and the logic of unconditionals. *Noûs, 54*(1), 126–161.
Dummett, M. A. E. (1954). Can an effect precede its cause? *Proceedings of the Aristotelian Society, 28*, 27–44.
Dummett, M. A. E. (1964). Bringing about the Past. *The Philosophical Review, 73*(3), 338–359.
Flew, A. (1954). Can an effect precede its cause? *Proceedings of the Aristotelian Society, 28*, 45–62.
Gorovitz, S. (1964). Leaving the past alone. *The Philosophical Review, 73*(3), 360–371.
Rice, H. (2018). Fatalism. In E. N. Zalta (Ed.), *The Stanford encyclopedia of philosophy*. Metaphysics Research Lab, Stanford University, Winter 2018 edition.
Sobel, J. H. (1966). Dummett on fatalism. *The Philosophical Review, 75*(1), 78–90.
Stalnaker, R. C. (1975). Indicative conditionals. *Philosophia, 5*(3), 269–286.

Chapter 5
Dummett on McTaggart's Proof of the Unreality of Time

Abstract Michael Dummett's paper "A Defence of McTaggart's Proof of the Unreality of Time" puts forward an ingenious interpretation of McTaggart's famous proof. My aim in this discussion is not to assess the cogency of McTaggart's reasoning, but to criticise Dummett's interpretation of McTaggart.

5.1 Introduction

The reasoning of McTaggart's 1908 article "The Unreality of Time" runs as follows. We distinguish positions in time in two ways: a permanent B-series (in which events and facts are distinguished using the relations of earlier than and later than) and a dynamic A-series (in which events and facts are future, then present, then past). Both series are essential to time, yet the A-series is more fundamental since only it allows for change (McTaggart, 1908, 458). This concludes the first part of McTaggart's reasoning: his argument for the fundamentality of the A-series.

Having established this conclusion, McTaggart then claims that the A-series "involves a contradiction" (McTaggart, 1908, 466). His argument for the contradiction is seemingly straightforward: past, present and future are "incompatible determinations" yet "every event has them all" (McTaggart, 1908, 469). This argument is typically known as McTaggart's Paradox. McTaggart is aware of a natural rejoinder to his argument. No event, it will be urged, is simultaneously past, present and future, only successively, and from this no contradiction follows. But, claims McTaggart, this rejoinder entails either a vicious circle or a vicious infinite regress, and so the contradiction is not removed.

In sum, McTaggart's first argument establishes that the A-series is fundamental to time. His paradox then establishes that the A-series is contradictory. From these conclusions it follows that time is unreal. My aim here is not to assess McTaggart's reasoning, but to call into question Michael Dummett's well-known interpretation of McTaggart's proof of the unreality of time (Dummett, 1960).

In his paper Dummett does not use the terms 'A-series' and 'B-series'. Instead, he talks of "facts of kind (a)" viz., facts into the statement of which tensed expressions enter essentially (Dummett, 1960, 500). Presumably, facts of kind (b) would be facts

B. Garrett, *Time, Identity and the Self: Essays on Metaphysics*, Synthese Library 442, https://doi.org/10.1007/978-3-030-85517-8_5

into the statement of which no tensed expressions enter (or do so inessentially). Clearly, facts of kind (a) – tensed facts – are meant to correspond to A-series facts (e.g., the fact that Hitler's death is past), and facts of kind (b) – tenseless facts – are meant to correspond to B-series facts (e.g., the fact that Hitler's death is later than Caesar's death).

5.2 Dummett on McTaggart's Argument

Having thus set things up, Dummett begins by making the following claim. With regard to McTaggart's arguments, "[p]art two depends upon part one" (Dummett, 1960, 500). That is, the success of McTaggart's Paradox, a plausible rendering of which Dummett sketches in his opening pages, depends upon the success of McTaggart's argument for the fundamentality of the A-series. This might seem a puzzling claim. Could not one hold that the A-series is contradictory even if it is not fundamental?

However, I take it that Dummett's point is that McTaggart's Paradox (part two) is directed against the A-series as understood by the A-theorist. That is, McTaggart's Paradox is intended to show that the A-series is contradictory on the assumption that tensed facts are fundamental and (hence) irreducible. No one thinks that the A-series is contradictory if tensed facts are taken to be reducible to B-theoretic facts (e.g., it's not contradictory for X to be earlier than t2 but later than t1). McTaggart's Paradox is directed against the A-theory of time, i.e., the theory according to which the A-series is fundamental and consistent. So understood, Dummett's claim is correct: McTaggart's proof of the inconsistency of the A-series presupposes the fundamentality of that series. This explains why Dummett continues as follows:

> it is because the analogue of part one does not hold for space or for personality that the analogue of part two for space or for personality has no force (Dummett, 1960, 500).

The analogue of part one does indeed fail for space and personality. Spatially and personally token-reflexive expressions ('here', 'there', 'I', 'you', etc.) need not feature in a full description of reality. A description using only spatial co-ordinates and personal proper names would suffice.

The conclusion of McTaggart's first argument – that the A-series is fundamental to time – implies the tensed thesis (as we can call it) that what is in time cannot be fully described without the use of tensed expressions. Dummett is sympathetic to this A-theoretic thesis and offers his own argument for it. Consider any description of events containing no tensed expressions. We can, he says, always ask the question "And which of these events is happening now?" This question, Dummett thinks, deserves an answer, yet can be given one only if tensed expressions are added to the description. Hence, the tensed thesis is true (Dummett, 1960, 591).

This argument is unconvincing. Unlike the A theorist, the B-theorist rejects the tensed thesis and accepts instead the tenseless thesis that what is in time can be fully described without the use of tensed expressions. According to the B-theorist,

Dummett's question is either illegitimate or else can be answered in tenseless terms. If Dummett's question is asked from "outside time", it makes no sense, just as the question "What is happening here?", asked from "outside space", makes no sense. For the B-theorist, a question containing a temporal indexical can only be asked and answered from a position in time. In that case, the answer to Dummett's question ("And which of these events is happening now?") is straightforward: those events whose occurrence is simultaneous with the posing of that very question.

5.3 Temporal versus Spatial Immersion

Dummett takes the tensed thesis to be equivalent to the temporal immersion thesis that a description of events in time can only be "given by someone who is himself in that time" (Dummett, 1960, 501). Dummett is well-disposed towards this thesis, but unhesitatingly rejects the spatial immersion thesis that a description of objects in space can only be given by someone who is himself in that space. He writes:

> [T]he use of spatially token-reflexive expressions is not essential to the description of objects as being in a space. That is, I can describe an arrangement of objects in space although I do not myself have any position in that space. An example would be the space of my visual field. In that space there is no here or there, no near or far: I am not in that space. We can, I think, conceive, on the strength of this analogy, of a being who could perceive objects in our three-dimensional physical space although he occupied no position in that space. He would have no use for any spatially token-reflexive expressions in giving a description of the physical universe, and yet that description might be a perfectly correct description of the objects of the universe as arranged in space. (Dummett, 1960, 500–501)

Dummett's reasoning in this passage is somewhat convoluted. He cites the space of one's visual field as a counterexample to the spatial immersion thesis. On the basis of the analogy with the space of one's visual field, we can imagine a being who could perceive objects in our three-dimensional physical space without occupying any position in that space. Such a being could give a full description of objects in physical space without occupying any position in that space, thus yielding another counterexample to the spatial immersion thesis.

The spatial immersion thesis may well be implausible, but the analogy with the space of the visual field does not help Dummett's case. If the objects of my visual field are non-physical sense-data, they occupy no space. In that case, the 'space' of my visual field is irrelevant to the spatial immersion thesis. If, instead, the objects of my visual field are those objects in my immediate physical environment, then I am in the same space as them. Again, we have no counterexample to the spatial immersion thesis (Thomson, 2001, 243–247).

5.4 Observer-independence

With regard to part two of McTaggart's argument, Dummett asks, "does not the objection we considered – that McTaggart's attempt to uncover a contradiction rested on a neglect of the obvious properties of token-reflexive expressions – at least invalidate part two of the argument?" (Dummett, 1960, 501). Rightly or wrongly, Dummett uses 'token-reflexive' interchangeably with 'indexical'. The objection Dummett is alluding to holds that, if McTaggart's argument for a contradiction in the A-series were sound, we could equally well argue for the inconsistency of space and personality by showing that every place can be both 'here' and 'there', and every person can be both 'I' and 'you'. Since the latter arguments are confused, so is McTaggart's.

It is odd that Dummett asks this question at this point since he already has the means to answer it, viz., by appeal to the falsity of the analogue of part one for space and personality. However, instead of giving this answer, Dummett takes a new tack and ascribes to McTaggart the assumption that:

> reality must be something of which there exists in principle a complete description. I can make drawings of a rock from various angles, but if I am asked to say what the real shape of the rock is, I can give a description of it as in three-dimensional space which is independent of the angle from which it is looked at. The description of what is really there, as it really is, must be independent of any particular point of view. Now if time were real, then since what is temporal cannot be completely described without the use of token-reflexive expressions, there would be no such thing as the complete description of reality. (Dummett, 1960, 503)

According to Dummett's use of 'complete', a complete description is "independent of any particular point of view", i.e., observer-independent. Dummett thus ascribes to McTaggart the observer-independence thesis that there can be an observer-independent description of temporal reality.

As the above quote makes clear, Dummett takes the tensed thesis to imply the falsity of the observer-independence thesis. If what is temporal cannot be completely described without the use of perspectival terms such as 'past', 'present' and 'future', then what is temporal can only be fully described from the perspective of a being in time. This seems correct. Dummett takes McTaggart to endorse both the tensed and observer-independence theses, and hence to be (knowingly) in the grip of a contradiction which can be avoided only by declaring time to be unreal. Hence, McTaggart is forced to his infamous conclusion that time is unreal.

However, Dummett offers no textual support for this interpretation of McTaggart. No passage is cited in which McTaggart endorses the observer-independence thesis. It is, in addition, a strange and self-stultifying argument. Any supporter of the tensed thesis will automatically reject the observer-independence thesis, and vice-versa. Moreover, the observer-independence thesis has no theory-independent plausibility. Its acceptance could only be motivated by a belief in the tenseless thesis (i.e., the denial of the tensed thesis). For these reasons, then, Dummett has given us no reason to revise the standard and textually-grounded interpretation of McTaggart's argument which emphasises the role played by McTaggart's well-known (if ill-understood) proof of the self-contradictory nature of the A-series, as that series is understood by the A-theorist.

Furthermore, the argument which Dummett himself endorses – (*contra* McTaggart) time is real; the tensed thesis is true; so observer-independence is false – is an argument that any A-theorist should endorse. Evidence that this is Dummett's argument can be seen from the following remark: "If this last piece of reasoning, to the effect that the belief that time is unreal is self-refuting, is correct, then McTaggart's argument shows that we must abandon our prejudice that there must be a complete [observer-independent] description of reality" (Dummett, 1960, 504).

Note that rejection of the 'prejudice' that there must be an observer-independent description of reality sits comfortably with the central idea of Dummett's anti-realist programme in semantics and epistemology (the idea that reality cannot outrun what we can, in principle, know). Finally, we can now see that the title of Dummett's article is something of a misnomer. Dummett is not defending McTaggart's proof of the unreality of time, but arguing that it can be transformed into a (quite different) proof of the falsity of the observer-independence thesis.

References

Dummett, M. A. E. (1960). A defense of McTaggart's proof of the unreality of time. *The Philosophical Review, 69*(4), 497–504.

McTaggart, J. M. E. (1908). The unreality of time. *Mind, 17*(68), 457–474.

Thomson, J. J. (2001). McTaggart on time. *Philosophical Perspectives, 15*, 229–252.

Chapter 6
A Note on the Grandfather Paradox

Abstract In this note, I am critical of some aspects of David Lewis's resolution of the Grandfather Paradox. I argue that Lewis gives the wrong explanation of Tim's inability to kill Grandfather, and that the correct explanation makes essential reference to the self-undermining character of Tim's attempt at grampicide.

6.1 Lewis's Theory

The philosophy of time travel is, in large part, an attempt to answer the exam question: To what extent, if any, do you disagree with the views expressed in David Lewis's eminently readable "The Paradoxes of Time Travel"? (Lewis, 1976). One of the most interesting and influential discussions in Lewis's paper concerns what a traveller to the past can or can't do. In particular, can such a traveller kill his own grandfather? In Lewis's thought-experiment, we are asked to consider Tim, who evidently dislikes his grandfather, and has built a time machine in order to go back to 1920 and kill him, many years before Tim's father was conceived. Tim duly travels back to 1920, buys a rifle, and tracks the route of his grandfather's daily walk (Lewis, 1976, 149).

According to Lewis, Tim can kill his grandfather. He has a high-powered rifle; he's a good shot; weather conditions are perfect, etc. On the other hand, Tim can't kill his grandfather. Grandfather died in his bed in 1957. Consistency demands, despite Tim's best efforts, that he fail in his attempts to kill his grandfather, and fail for some commonplace reason (an errant seagull, a distracting noise, an observant policeman, etc.) (Lewis, 1976, 150).

Since Lewis holds that Tim can and can't kill his grandfather, it might be thought that his position is contradictory. Lewis has a nice reply to this charge. There is no contradiction since 'can' is context-dependent. He writes:

> To say that something can happen means that its happening is compossible with certain facts. Which facts? That is determined, but sometimes not determined well enough, by context. An ape can't speak a human language, say, Finnish, but I can. Facts about the anatomy and operation of the ape's larynx and nervous system are not compossible with his speaking Finnish. The corresponding facts about my larynx and nervous system are

B. Garrett, *Time, Identity and the Self: Essays on Metaphysics*, Synthese Library 442, https://doi.org/10.1007/978-3-030-85517-8_6

> compossible with my speaking Finnish. But don't take me along to Helsinki as your interpreter: I can't speak Finnish. My speaking Finnish is compossible with the facts considered so far, but not with further facts about my lack of training. What I can do, relative to one set of facts, I can't do, relative to another, more inclusive, set (Lewis, 1976, 150).

According to Lewis, then, 'can'-judgements are context-dependent. Relative to one context "A can do F" is true, relative to another it's not. In Lewis's example, given the facts about the structure of my larynx and nervous system, I can speak Finnish. But given a wider set of facts, including the fact that I have never learnt Finnish, I can't. Similarly, given one set of facts, e.g., facts about Tim's rifle, his shooting ability, the weather conditions, etc., Tim can kill his grandfather. But given another, more inclusive, set of facts, including, e.g., the fact that grandfather wasn't killed in 1920, Tim can't kill his grandfather.[1]

6.2 Against Lewis's Theory

But what are the truth-conditions for these 'can'-judgements? Surely, we cannot endorse:

> A can do F if and only if A's doing F is compossible (consistent) with some fact or set of facts.

My jumping 20 feet in the air, for example, is consistent with the fact that 2 is the only even prime number; but I can't jump 20 feet in the air. Presumably, then, this is why Lewis talks of 'context', thus yielding the more plausible analysis:

> A can do F if and only if A's doing F is compossible with all contextually salient facts or set of such facts.

However, we still need to be told something about the nature of the context (is it the conversational context?) and also about how the context selects the salient facts. In addition, with no restriction on admissible contexts, the problem of making it too easy for 'can'-judgements to come out true remains.[2] There is also the problem of what is meant by 'compossible' and 'incompossible'. Lewis doesn't say explicitly, but presumably he meant logical compatibility and incompatibility. However, this reading creates problems for his own example. My speaking Finnish isn't logically incompatible with my never having learnt to speak it; nor is the structure of an ape's larynx and central nervous system logically incompatible with its speaking Finnish.

However these issues are to be resolved, let's concede to Lewis that there is a sense in which Tim can kill Grandfather. That is, let's concede that, relative to facts only about Tim's means, motive and opportunity, Tim can kill Grandfather. I do so with reluctance since I would prefer to say that Tim can't kill Grandfather, full stop.

[1] I disagree with Lewis that this is the right fact to cite here; see (Garrett, 2019), published in this volume as Chapter 7.

[2] Jaster has a more concrete version of this worry, see (Jaster, 2020, 98).

But many think that there is a sense in which Tim can kill Grandfather, and I have no knockdown argument against this thought. Here, I want to focus instead on the sense in which Tim can't kill Grandfather, and on what Lewis has to say about this. Lewis writes: "Tim cannot kill Grandfather. Grandfather lived, so to kill him would be to change the past" (Lewis, 1976, 150). It is, as Lewis rightly notes, impossible – indeed, logically impossible – to change the past. That is, no one can make it the case that some event both happened and didn't happen. Lewis then immediately points out that, in the very same way, it's logically impossible to change the present or the future.

However, the second sentence in Lewis's quote does not support the first. The impossibility of changing the past implies only that since Grandfather wasn't killed in 1920, Tim won't kill him then. It doesn't imply that he can't kill him then.[3] Indeed, if it did, it would follow by analogous reasoning that I can't kill my Grandson tomorrow, given that he lives until 2050. More generally, it would follow that for any act which an agent can do but doesn't, there is a sense in which he can't do it (viz., he can't do it relative to the fact that he didn't do it). This concedes too much to the Fatalist. The Fatalist holds that I can't do what I won't do (or, equivalently, that I can only do what I will do).[4] If, as we may suppose, I have the means, motive and opportunity to kill Grandson tomorrow, I can kill him then (though I won't, since we stipulated that he lives until 2050). Crucially, however, we shouldn't concede any sense of 'can' such that I can't kill him tomorrow. The same is true of Tim. Given that Grandfather wasn't killed in 1920, we are entitled to conclude only that Tim won't kill him then, not that he can't kill him.

Lewis does have something to say about cases like the Grandson one. This is the point of his discussion of Tom (see below). Applying his remarks to my Grandson example, Lewis would say that since Grandson's death (in 2050) is later than my attempted assassination (tomorrow), it's not to be counted as relevant to saying what I can do tomorrow (Lewis, 1976, 151). However, Lewis's context-dependent theory gives him no license to say this. The context fixes which facts are salient to a given 'can'-judgement, and those facts can be about the past, the present or the future. No context is 'better' or 'worse' than any other. The only way we could legitimately discount future facts is if the future were unreal and there were no future facts. But the unreality of the future is no part of Lewis's (eternalist, B-theoretic) conception of time and it's not the view of most philosophers who allow for the possibility of travel to the past.

---

[3] Jaster, in her discussion, also fails to vindicate any sense in which Tim can't kill Grandfather. According to her version of the context-dependent view of 'can'-judgements, Tim can't kill Grandfather because "[he] does not shoot [Grandfather] in a sufficient proportion of the possible situations in which he intends to shoot him *and the fact that he does not shoot him obtains*" (italics in text) (Jaster, 2020, 104). Since this sentence is trivially true it can hardly imply that Tim can't kill Grandfather. Trivialities only imply trivialities.

[4] Later in his article, Lewis rightly criticises a particularly egregious specimen of Fatalist reasoning (Lewis, 1976, 151–152). But there are many varieties of Fatalism, some more subtle than others, and Lewis seems to have succumbed to one of the more subtle variants.

However, we shouldn't conclude that there's no sense in which Tim can't kill Grandfather. There is a fact relative to which Tim can't kill Grandfather. As Lewis acknowledges, but fails to press into service, Tim's attempted grampicide is self-undermining: "No Grandfather, no Father; no Father, no Tim; no Tim, no killing" (Lewis, 1976, 152). A self-undermining action by an agent A is one which undermines a causally necessary condition for A's existence in the first place. (Suicide, of course, is not a self-undermining act in this sense.) No agent can perform a self-undermining act, in any sense of 'can' appropriate to human ability. That is, no agent can make it the case that he never existed.

In terms of Lewis's context-dependent theory, we can put the point as follows: relative to the fact that Tim's action is self-undermining, he can't kill Grandfather. Vihvelin also holds Tim can't kill Grandfather, but on the grounds that no matter how often Tim had tried to kill Grandfather, he would have failed (Vihvelin, 1996, 2020). The account offered here is preferable since it explains why Vihvelin's counterfactual is true (viz., no one can perform a self-undermining action).

6.3 Tim and Tom

Given the preceding discussion, we can see that Lewis is wrong to urge a complete parallel between Tim and Tom. Tom is a normal (non-time travelling) inhabitant of 1920 and wants to kill Grandfather's partner, who lives until 1960. Tom will of course fail in his attempt since we have stipulated that the partner die in 1960. Thus, Tim and Tom are alike to the extent that each will fail in their homicidal attempts. However, Lewis says that Tom can't kill the partner for the very same reason that Tim can't kill Grandfather: viz., neither man was killed in that year (Lewis, 1976, 151). As we have seen, this reasoning is flawed. Furthermore, since Tom's action, unlike Tim's, is not self-undermining, there is no sense in which Tom can't kill Grandfather's partner in 1920 (given that Tom has the means, motive and opportunity).

What is true of Tom's attempt is true of all non-self-undermining attempts to undo the past. Presumably, many actions that Tim can perform in 1920 would not undermine his own existence ("butterfly effects" notwithstanding). In these cases, I would urge, only descriptions of the "can but won't" variety apply. For example, suppose that Tim never shook Grandfather's hand in 1920. Can Tim shake his hand then? Yes, he can, although he won't. Indeed, to think otherwise – to think that Tim can't shake Grandfather's hand because it wasn't shaken then – is to succumb to the Fatalist reasoning outlined above.

6.4 Conclusion

In sum, then, I am critical of Lewis's account on four fronts. First, there are difficulties internal to Lewis's theory of 'can'-judgements. Second, Lewis gives the wrong explanation of the sense in which Tim can't kill Grandfather. Third, Lewis fails to appreciate that it is the self-undermining nature of Tim's attempted grampicide which explains why Tim can't kill Grandfather. Fourth, since Tom's attempt to kill Grandfather's partner is not self-undermining, Lewis is wrong to press for a complete parallel between Tim and Tom. In Tom's case, there is no fact relative to which Tom can't kill Grandfather's partner (assuming, as we have throughout, that Tom has the requisite means, motive and opportunity).

References

Garrett, B. (2019). Bulletproof grandfathers, David Lewis, and 'can't'-judgements. *Acta Analytica, 34*(2), 177–180.

Jaster, K. (2020). What Tim can and cannot do: A paradox of time travel revisited. *Kriterion Journal of Philosophy, 34*(4), 93–110.

Lewis, D. (1976). The paradoxes of time travel. *American Philosophical Quarterly, 13*(1), 145–152.

Vihvelin, K. (1996). What time travelers cannot do. *Philosophical Studies, 81*(2/3), 315–30.

Vihvelin, K. (2020). Killing time again. *The Monist, 103*(3), 312–327.

Chapter 7
Bulletproof Grandfathers, David Lewis, and 'Can't'-Judgements

Abstract In this discussion, I argue that David Lewis fails to support his claim that (relative to one context) time-travelling Tim cannot kill his Grandfather in 1921. This result, in turn, undermines Lewis's contextualist solution to the Grandfather Paradox – i.e., conceding that Tim can and cannot kill Grandfather, but relative to different contexts in each case.

7.1 A General Argument

It is invalid to infer "*X* can't do *F*" from "*X* won't do *F*", as some fatalists are wont to do. Intuitively, there are no end of things we can do but will not. Nor does "*X* won't do *F*" lend any inductive support to "*X* can't do *F*". (I put to one side arguments that appeal to the thesis of causal determinism in order to derive "*X* cannot do *F*" from "*X* won't do *F*".)

Further, the fact that *X* will not do *F* is never an admissible reason why *X* cannot do *F*. We might say that Fred cannot hit the bull's eye tonight because he has had too much beer, but we would not say that Fred cannot hit the bull's eye tonight because he will not. (If anything, that would be a philosophical joke.) The reason why someone cannot do some humanly achievable task must advert to a lack of means or opportunity on their part, not to the fact that they will fail in their attempt. So much seems common sense.

Suppose that Grandson will die in 2060. Can I kill him tomorrow, assuming that I have the wherewithal to do so? The answer seems to be unequivocally yes. The stipulated fact that he will die in 2060 implies, of course, that any attempted homicide tomorrow will fail. But, as noted, 'will not' does not imply 'cannot', so it does not follow that any homicide attempt tomorrow must fail. We should resist the temptation to say that I cannot kill him tomorrow because he will not be killed then. This is no better than saying that Fred cannot hit the bull's eye tonight because he will not. If it really is true that I cannot kill Grandson tomorrow, that can only be for some quotidian reason (e.g., Grandson suddenly goes on holiday, I break my arm etc.), and not because he will not be killed then.

B. Garrett, *Time, Identity and the Self: Essays on Metaphysics*, Synthese Library 442, https://doi.org/10.1007/978-3-030-85517-8_7

7.2 Misapplied Contextualism

These platitudes, however, have been overlooked in discussions of travel to the past. Lewis's Tim travels back from 1975 to 1920 in order to kill his Grandfather, who, we are told, died in his bed in 1957. Tim lies in wait in 1921, rifle at the ready. Can Tim kill Grandfather? Yes, says Lewis: he has the means and opportunity. But also, in a different sense: No, he cannot. Why not? Because Grandfather wasn't killed in 1921 (Lewis, 1976, 151). That is, Grandfather cannot be killed in 1921 because he was not killed then. This is an instance of the invalid inference criticised in the opening paragraph.

Note the contrast with Lewis's Finnish example (Lewis, 1976, 150). It is plausible that, relative to one context (e.g., discussing differences between humans and other primates), I can speak Finnish, but, relative to another context (e.g., choosing a translator), I cannot. However, according to Lewis, the reason why I cannot speak Finnish is because I have never learnt it ("lack of training", as he says). This is a perfectly admissible reason, in contrast to Lewis's reason for Tim's inability to kill Grandfather. Lewis has, I think, misapplied his contextualist theory of 'can'-judgements in the case of Tim. The fact that Grandfather died in 1957 does not belong in any range of facts relative to which Tim cannot kill him in 1921.[1]

7.3 A Time Symmetry Argument

Lewis elaborates as follows: "Tim cannot kill Grandfather. Grandfather lived, so to kill him would be to change the past" (Lewis, 1976, 156). Lewis takes the second sentence to entail the first. But does it? Certainly, it is a necessary truth that no one can change the past. That is, there is no possible world in which someone brings it about that some event which did not happen happened (or vice versa). But how do we get from "It's impossible that (Grandfather lives and Tim kills him)" to "Tim can't kill him"?

If "It's impossible that (Grandfather lives and Tim kills him)" implied "If Grandfather lives, it's impossible that Tim kill him", we could apply *modus ponens* to the resulting conditional, infer "It's impossible that Tim kill him", and so derive "Tim can't kill him". But, of course, "It's impossible that (Grandfather lives and Tim kills him)" does not imply "If Grandfather lives, it's impossible that Tim kill

[1] What distinguishes the admissible facts from the inadmissible ones? Admissible facts will typically be facts about the presence or absence of contextually salient means or opportunities. Inadmissible facts will presumably be all the rest, including facts about the agent's lack of success. One way in which the salient means and opportunities are selected is presumably the conversational context. (Perhaps this observation goes some way towards defusing Van Cleve's crocodile objection and the threat of rampant relativity (Van Cleve, 2019).)

him". That is an instance of a familiar modal fallacy to be found in some fatalist arguments: $\sim \diamond(P \wedge Q) \models (P \rightarrow \sim \diamond Q)$.

It is hard to see any valid route from the impossibility of changing the past to the conclusion that Tim cannot kill Grandfather. Moreover, if there were such a route, there ought to be an analogous route to the unacceptable conclusion that I cannot kill Grandson tomorrow. The future, assuming it is real, can no more be changed than the past can, as Lewis acknowledges (Lewis, 1976, 150). (See also Russell 1913, 21.)

What follows from the above? The important lesson is that Lewis has not supported his conclusion that Tim cannot kill Grandfather in 1921. His case for that conclusion involves an invalid step from 'will not' to 'cannot' and the apparent commission of a familiar modal fallacy.

7.4 Alternative Arguments

However, it does not follow that Tim can kill Grandfather. There may be different and better reasons to hold that Tim cannot kill Grandfather than those offered by Lewis. Kadri Vihvelin would argue: Tim can kill Grandfather only if he might succeed; it's not true that Tim might succeed; so Tim cannot kill Grandfather (Vihvelin, 1996). Or consider the fact, of which Lewis is aware but fails to exploit, that Tim's attempted grampicide is self-undermining. "No Grandfather, no Father; no Father, no Tim; no Tim, no killing" (Lewis, 1976, 152). It does seem to be logically impossible for an agent to do something which would make it the case that he never existed. In which case, Tim cannot kill Grandfather. (I note that these reasons are not reasons for the unwelcome conclusion that I cannot kill Grandson tomorrow.) However, even if these are good reasons for concluding that Tim cannot kill Grandfather, my point is that, contrary to what many have thought, Lewis gave us no good reason to believe this conclusion.

James Van Cleve is also concerned with Lewis's contextualist theory of 'can'-judgements and its application to the case of Tim (Van Cleve, 2019). Van Cleve's main claim is that Lewis's contextualist theory of 'can'-judgements is fatalistic. According to Lewis, "[t]o say that something can happen means that its happening is compossible with certain facts" (Lewis, 1976, 150). Equally, to say that something cannot happen means that its happening is incompossible with certain facts.[2] Thus: it cannot happen that P, relative to fact Q, just if $\sim \diamond(P \wedge Q)$ and Q. But, read right

[2] But what is meant by 'compossible' and 'incompossible'? Lewis does not say explicitly, but commentators have assumed that he meant logical compatibility and incompatibility. However, this reading creates problems for Lewis's own Finnish example. My speaking Finnish is not logically incompatible with my never having learnt to speak Finnish; nor is the structure of an ape's larynx and central nervous system logically incompatible with its speaking Finnish. (I pointed this out in Garrett (2016, 248); Van Cleve also picks up on it, see Van Cleve (2019).) Perhaps Lewis's analysis can be revised to avoid these difficulties.

to left, this is just a version of the modal fallacy (mentioned above): $\sim \diamond(P \wedge Q) \models (P \rightarrow\sim \diamond Q)$. Moreover, as Van Cleve observes, we find this fallacy at work in a well-known fatalist argument due to Richard Taylor (Taylor, 1962).

This is an interesting criticism to make, and it is distinct from the more specific point that I have made, viz., that Lewis's reasons why Tim cannot kill Grandfather are fallacious and fatalist. The fact that Grandfather was not killed in 1921 does not imply that Tim cannot kill him then, only that he will not. Equally, the fact that Grandson will die in 2060 does not imply that I cannot kill him tomorrow, only that I will not. Nor does the impossibility of changing the past imply that Tim cannot kill Grandfather, only that he will not.

7.5 Concluding Remarks

I did not intend these claims to undermine Lewis's contextualist theory of 'can'-judgements, only to restrict its application (to the right kind of facts). If Van Cleve is right and Lewis's theory is itself fatalist, it is perhaps unsurprising that Lewis's case for the conclusion that Tim cannot kill Grandfather contains fatalist elements.[3]

With regard to the Lewis vs. Van Cleve battle, it is worth pointing out that the following line of reasoning seems perfectly intuitive: I never learned to swim; my never having learnt to swim precludes or rules out my swimming; so I cannot swim. In other words: I cannot swim because I have never learnt to swim, and the latter reason is relevant (to whether or not I can swim) because it precludes my swimming. If this is a good piece of reasoning, as it seems, it should be possible to formalise it other than as a modal fallacy.

References

Garrett, B. (2016). Tim, Tom, Time and Fate: Lewis on time travel. *Analytic Philosophy, 57*(3), 247–252.

Lewis, D. (1976). The paradoxes of time travel. *American Philosophical Quarterly, 13*(1), 145–152.

Russell, B. (1913). On the notion of cause. *Proceedings of the Aristotelian Society, 13*(1), 1–26.

Taylor, R. (1962). Fatalism. *The Philosophical Review, 71*(1), 56–66.

Van Cleve, J. (2019). Lewis and Taylor as partners in sin. *Acta Analytica, 34*, 165–175.

Vihvelin, K. (1996). What time travelers cannot do. *Philosophical Studies, 81*(2/3), 315–30.

[3] It is troubling to attribute an obviously fallacious inference to one of the world's greatest modal logicians. Troubling also to suggest that his reasoning has fatalist elements. Lewis, after all, takes pains to advertise his anti-fatalist credentials by criticising a particularly egregious piece of fatalist trickery (Lewis, 1976, 151–152). Nonetheless, I do not think that anything I have said distorts or misinterprets Lewis's line of argument. Fortunately, the point I make in the last paragraph of the text may go some way towards rehabilitating Lewis's reasoning.

Chapter 8
A Dilemma for Eternalists

Abstract In this discussion, I argue that given the possibility of travel to the past, eternalists face a dilemma. They must choose between fatalism and the denial of an intuitive claim about what a traveller to the past cannot do. The eternalist should deny this seemingly intuitive claim which is in fact a version of fatalism about the past.

8.1 Introduction

Eternalism is the metaphysical thesis that past, present and future are equally real. I argue that this thesis leads to an uncomfortable dilemma, of which fatalism is one fork. Naturally we want to avoid that fork, but embracing the other fork is not without consequences.

8.2 The Dilemma

Consider the following case involving travel to the past. Hitler died in 1945. Suppose I build a time machine and travel back to 1930 with the intention of killing him. I arrive in 1930, buy a rifle, and shadow Hitler's movements. Consider:

(i) Given that Hitler died in 1945, I can't kill him in 1930.

Many accept (i). According to David Lewis, relative to the fact that Hitler died in 1945, I can't kill him in 1930. To justify this, the Lewisian would say: I cannot kill Hitler; Hitler lived, so to kill him would be to change the past. Lewis writes of his time traveller Tim: "Tim cannot kill Grandfather. Grandfather lived, so to kill him would be to change the past." (Lewis, 1976, 150). However, the Lewisian would add that relative to a different set of facts, about my means, motive and opportunity, I can kill Hitler in 1930 (Lewis, 1976, 149–152). We thus have an illustration of Lewis's well-known context-dependent theory of 'can'-judgements. Others may accept (i) but deny – *contra* Lewis – that there is a sense in which I can kill Hitler in 1930.

B. Garrett, *Time, Identity and the Self: Essays on Metaphysics*, Synthese Library 442, https://doi.org/10.1007/978-3-030-85517-8_8

According to eternalism, future facts exist as much as past and present ones. Suppose that my Grandson will die in 2060, but that I want to kill him tomorrow. Consider:

(ii) Given that Grandson will die in 2060, I can't kill him tomorrow.

To accept (ii) is to embrace the disturbing idea that given a certain fact concerning 2060, I can't accomplish a relatively straightforward task tomorrow. The idea that the mere existence of a future fact, or the truth of a future contingent statement, constrains what an agent can do is a fatalist one. Since fatalism is best avoided, we should deny (ii). Provided I have the wherewithal to kill Grandson, I can kill him tomorrow, even if he lives until 2060 (i.e., I can kill him tomorrow but I won't). On the other hand, if I can't kill Grandson tomorrow, that can only be for some quotidian reason (e.g., Grandson suddenly goes on holiday, I break my arm tonight, etc.), and not because Grandson will die in 2060.

Accepting (i) and denying (ii) is obviously a tenable option if the past is real and the future unreal (since (ii) presupposes the reality of the future). But this observation is of no use here since we are assuming eternalism. Is an eternalist justified in accepting (i) and rejecting (ii)? No!

8.3 Some Options

Here are three attempts to answer this question affirmatively.

(a) Is it possible to change the future but not the past? Not on standard thinking. Consider the following passages from Lewis:

> Could a time traveller change the past? It seems not: the events of a past moment could no more change than numbers could...
>
> ...Not that past moments are special; no more can anyone change the present or the future. Present and future momentary events no more have temporal parts than past ones do. You cannot change a present or future event from what it was originally to what it is after you change it. (Lewis, 1976, 149–150)

Lewis is right that it is impossible to change the past and, in the same sense, impossible to change the present and the future. So we have been given no reason to accept (i) and deny (ii). Note that we need not invoke temporal parts in order to explain why it is impossible to change the past. No one can change the past since no one can make it the case that some event which happened didn't happen or vice versa.

(b) Are we entitled to discount future facts, but not past ones, in saying what someone can do? (Lewis, 1976, 150–151) This proposal can be understood in two ways but neither successfully explains why (i) is true and (ii) false. The first way takes our current perspective to be what matters. From that perspective, Hitler's death is past and Grandson's death is future; hence, the latter fact should be discounted in saying what I can do. But this will not work. For an eternalist there is nothing privileged about our current perspective. Nor are matters improved if we combine eternalism with the moving NOW, as the Moving Spotlight theory does. On this theory, the events of 1930 are just as real as those of 2060. Indeed, it's hard to see what is special or privileged about the NOW if it is as real as past and future moments.

According to the second way of understanding the proposal, it is the perspective at the time of acting which matters, as Lewis clearly intends when he talks of discounting "facts about the future of the time in question" (Lewis, 1976, 150–151). But this proposal does not work either; indeed it has the opposite effect. From my perspective in 1930, Hitler's death is future. Hence, Hitler's death in 1945, being in the future of the time in question, ought to be discounted in saying what I can do in 1930. But then we lose our reason for thinking (i) is true. Yet the point of the proposal is to show why (i) is true and (ii) false. If we discount future facts, (i) and (ii) come out false; if we count them, both come out true.

Can Lewis's personal time/external time distinction be pressed into service here? In 1930, my personal past is externally future, so that I have knowledge of externally future events. In 1930, I presumably know that Hitler died in 1945. Could this knowledge ground the truth of (i)? No. First, if there is a sense in which I can't kill Hitler in 1930, it should not depend on the contingency that I happen to remember when he died. Second, my 1930 knowledge is partly about an externally future time (1945) and, according to Lewis, should be discounted in saying what I can do in 1930 (Lewis, 1976, 151–152). But then we are back with our original problem: discount future facts and we undermine both (i) and (ii).

(c) Is it helpful to point out that in real life we don't know when our grandchildren will die, but we do know when historical figures such as Hitler died? Does the epistemic asymmetry between past and future validate discounting future facts? Again, the answer must be negative.

First, it is not in general true that what we can or cannot do is dependent on, or relative to, what we know (nor is there any suggestion of this in Lewis). A man in a locked room can't escape, whether he knows the room is locked or not. Second, the present proposal rests on the assumption that we have knowledge only of the past and present, together with the assumption that if I have knowledge of E's occurrence, I can't bring it about that not-E. However, it's plausible to think that we have knowledge of the future via two sources: inductive extrapolation and knowledge of our own intentions. As an example of the latter, I know that I will have porridge for breakfast tomorrow. Yet, intuitively, this knowledge does not imply that I can't have eggs for breakfast, only that I won't. So both assumptions underlying the proposal are false.

There is a final possibility. Perhaps our initial question – what could justify an eternalist in accepting (i) and rejecting (ii)? – is misplaced. It is our practice to discount future facts in saying what ordinary (non-time-travelling) people can do, but not in saying what travellers to the past can do. Normative questions do not come into it: that is simply what we do. However, even if that is what we do, it's hard to believe that such a relatively sophisticated practice is immune from normative assessment. We have hardly reached bedrock. In which case, since our practice of accepting statements of type-(i) and denying those of type-(ii) is arbitrary, it should be revised. That is what I have been urging here.

8.4 An Upshot

Unless some further answer to our original question emerges, accepting (i) and denying (ii) is not a tenable option for the eternalist. Nor is the option of denying (i) and accepting (ii), which would be bizarre and unmotivated (akin to embracing an open past and closed future). Hence, (i) and (ii) stand or fall together. This yields the following dilemma for eternalists: either accept (i) and (ii) but then incur the fatalist consequence of accepting (ii), or reject (i) and (ii) thereby avoiding fatalism but overriding the *prima facie* powerful intuition which tells in favour of (i).

Lewis accepts (i) but would he accept (ii)? In his article, Lewis discusses the non-time-traveller Tom who attempts, but fails, to kill Grandfather's partner. (Tom's case is essentially the same as my Grandson case.) Lewis writes:

> Exactly the same goes for Tom's parallel failure. For Tom to kill Grandfather's partner also is compossible with all facts of the sorts we ordinarily count as relevant, but not compossible with a larger set including, for instance, the fact that the intended victim lived until 1934. In Tom's case we are not puzzled. We say without hesitation that he can do it, because we see at once that the facts that are not compossible with his success are facts about the future of the time in question and therefore not the sort of facts we count as relevant in saying what Tom can do. (Lewis, 1976, 151)

However, the conclusion in Lewis's last sentence is ambiguous. Does he mean "not the sort of facts we *ever* count as relevant in saying what Tom can do" or "not the sort of facts we *ordinarily* count as relevant in saying what Tom can do"? If the former, Lewis would deny (ii); if the latter, he would not deny it. I take it that the latter interpretation is more in the spirit of Lewis's theory of 'can'-judgements. We can, at least, safely say that Lewis would either endorse (i) but not (ii), or endorse (i) and (ii). Neither option is acceptable – the first because it's arbitrary; the second because it validates the fatalistic (ii).

My own view is that the eternalist should deny (i) and (ii) since fatalism is worse than the denial of (i). Thus, I do not take the dilemma to refute eternalism, but to show that eternalists should deny (i) and (ii) if they are to avoid fatalism. With regard to the Lewisian rationale for (i), it is not true that to kill Hitler in 1930 is to change the past. It is logically impossible to change the past, but it's not logically impossible for me to kill Hitler in 1930. We can make good sense of the counterfactual "Had I killed Hitler in 1930. . .", but only, as with any counterfactual, by supposing various actual truths not to hold (e.g., in this imaginary world Hitler dies in 1930). Lewis makes the same point about the analogous counterfactual in his example of Tim and Grandfather (Lewis, 1976, 152).

To see that the denial of (i) is not just tenable but plausible, consider the following simple analogy. Suppose that no one will hit the bull's eye at tonight's darts tournament. It doesn't follow from this that I can't hit the bull's eye tonight, only that I won't. No one, except the fatalist, thinks that I can't hit the bull's eye because it won't be hit. Similarly, given that Hitler died in 1945, it doesn't follow that I can't kill him in 1930, only that I won't. What this shows is that we should extend the meaning of 'fatalism' so that it can apply to the past. To hold that I can't kill Hitler in 1930 because he didn't die then is to embrace a version of fatalism about the past.

We can make the same point in terms of admissible and inadmissible reasons why someone can't do something. Just as "because it will not be hit" is not an admissible reason why I can't hit the bull's eye, so "because Hitler wasn't killed in 1930" is not an admissible reason why I can't kill Hitler in 1930. The fatalist's mistake is to count such pseudo-reasons as admissible.

Reference

Lewis, D. (1976). The paradoxes of time travel. *American Philosophical Quarterly, 13*(1), 145–152.

Part II
Identity

Chapter 9
Identity and Extrinsicness

Abstract In this discussion, I criticise Penelope Mackie's rejection of the so-called "No Extrinsic Determination" principle and suggest that this principle may not be as unattractive as Mackie makes it out to be.

9.1 Introduction

In "Essence, Origin and Bare Identity", Penelope Mackie analyses possible responses to a problematic set of possible worlds and argues that our reaction to this set must be either: (1) to abandon talk of transworld identity in favour of some counterpart relation; (2) to embrace some non-trivial form of essentialism, such as the necessity of origin; (3) to reject the principle that there can be no 'bare' transworld identities or non-identities; or (4) to reject the principle that transworld identities and non-identities cannot be "extrinsically determined". Mackie argues for the third solution to the problem. In this discussion, I want to discuss one of her arguments in connection with the fourth response, a response which I have endorsed elsewhere,[1] and to suggest that it may not be as unattractive as she makes out.

9.2 Setting Up the Problem

The problem, in rough outline, is this. Suppose that in the actual world, w_1, an oaktree, O_1, developed from acorn A_1 at place p_1. Suppose, further, that there are two other possible worlds, w_2 and w_3, such that in w_2, O_1 develops from a different acorn A_2 at p_1, and, in w_3, O_1 develops from A_1, as in the actual world, but at a different place, p_2. There appears to be no objection to the existence of a fourth

[1] See my critical notice of Graeme Forbes's *The Metaphysics of Modality* (reprinted here as Chap. 11). Note that my aim in this discussion is not to criticise Mackie's own preferred solution to the problem, but merely to counter her arguments for thinking that rejection of the No Extrinsic Determination principle is not a possible response.

B. Garrett, *Time, Identity and the Self: Essays on Metaphysics*, Synthese Library 442, https://doi.org/10.1007/978-3-030-85517-8_9

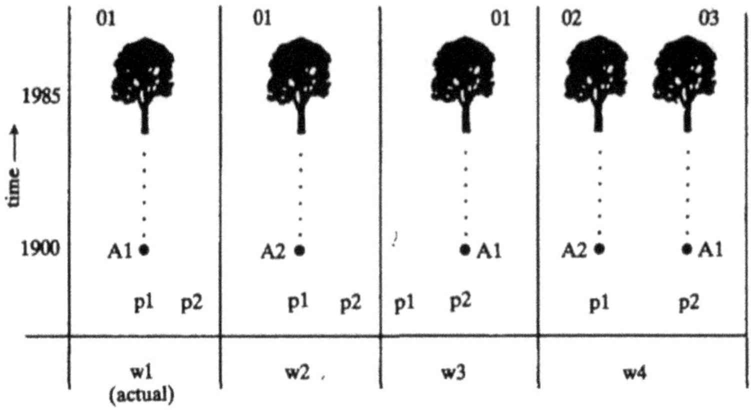

Fig. 9.1 Four possibilities for an oak tree

world, w_4, in which an oak-tree, O_2, develops from acorn A_2 at p_1 and another oak-tree, O_3, develops from A_1 at p_2. (See Fig. 9.1) Since O_2 and O_3 are clearly distinct trees, it must be the case that either O_1 in $w_2 \neq O_2$ in w_4, or O_1 in $w_3 \neq O_3$ in w_4 (or both). If we want to avoid commitment to non-trivial essential properties such as the necessity of origin (which would imply, in effect, that w_2 is not a possible world relative to w_1) and retain talk of transworld identity then, whichever we choose, we are forced to reject either the No Bare Identities principle or the No Extrinsic Determination principle.

Either O_1 in $w_2 \neq O_2$ in w_4 or O_1 in $w_3 \neq O_3$ in w_4 (or both). Suppose that O_1 in $w_2 \neq O_2$ in w_4. This non-identity is either bare (i.e., it does not supervene upon facts of any sort) or else it holds in virtue of the existence of another, equally good candidate for identity with O_1 in w_4 (namely, O_3). The latter explanation of the non-identity implies "that although the oak tree O_1 could have grown from the acorn A_2 at p_1 and have had the material composition, and so on exemplified in w_2, and although there could have been an oak tree that had all those characteristics and also had a companion growing some distance away at p_2, nonetheless O_1 could not have been like that and also have had such a companion" (Mackie, 1987, 190–191). Mackie finds this consequence 'extraordinary', and advocates rejection of the No Bare Identities principle.

9.3 Mackie on Best-Candidate Theories of Identity

Mackie notes that best-candidate theories have attained some degree of popularity as accounts of the identity over time of entities of various sorts (e.g., persons and artefacts), and such theories imply that transworld identities and non-identities can depend upon the absence of competing candidates (see, e.g., Parfit 1984, ch. 12,

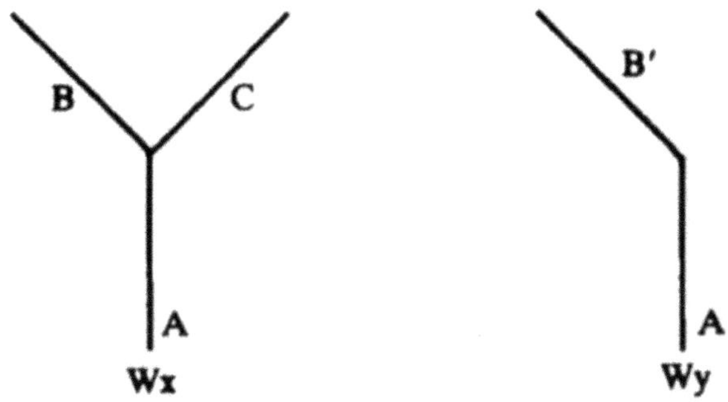

Fig. 9.2 Branching and Non-branching cases

sec. 9; Shoemaker and Swinburne 1984, chs. 12 & 13; and Wiggins 1980, ch. 3). Mackie does not want to say that a transworld identity or non-identity can never depend upon the absence of competing candidates. But she argues that rejection of the No Extrinsic Determination principle is extraordinary as a response to the present problem because the competitor trees in w_4 are causally isolated from one another (they are spatially distinct from each other, and have no causal antecedents in common) (Mackie, 1987, 190–191).

In the sorts of cases which have been of interest to best-candidate theorists of identity over time, however, the causal isolation requirement has been violated. Thus, consider a theorist who proposes to analyse the identity of a person over time in terms of the obtaining of the relation of non-branching psychological continuity. Imagine that, in W_x, the brain of person A is divided and each (equipollent) hemisphere is placed in a separate body, resulting in the creation of two persons, B and C, both of whom are fully psychologically continuous with A. Since branching of the relevant sort has occurred, our best-candidate theorist will claim that $A \neq B$ and $A \neq C$. But had C not existed (as in W_y), A would have continued to exist and would have been identical with the person then occupying B's body (B'), who, by the necessity and transitivity of identity, is not B. (See Fig. 9.2) (Hence, the non-identity of B in W_x and B' in W_y parallels the non-identity of O_1 in w_2 and O_2 in w_4. In both cases, the non-identity holds in virtue of the existence of a rival candidate.)

Mackie suggests that the commitment to the extrinsicness of identity in this case may not be absurd on the grounds that B and C are not "causally isolated" (Mackie, 1987, 191–192). Although B and C may live their lives in complete ignorance of the existence of each other, and may exert no causal influence upon each other, they are causally connected with each other, indirectly, in virtue of their individual causal connections with A. It is this lack of causal isolation which renders the commitment of best-candidate theories of identity over time to extrinsicness, non-absurd.[2]

[2] Note that the best-candidate theorist of transworld identity is not committed to the claim that in a world (w_5) just like w_4 except that O_3 does not exist, O_2 in w_5 is identical to O_1 in w_1 (Mackie 1987, 185–186). Such a result appears to violate the necessity of identity since it implies that, in

9.4 Assessing Mackie

How convincing is Mackie's explanation here? The commitment of (certain) best-candidate theories of personal identity over time to the consequence that B in $W_x \neq B'$ in W_y, in virtue of the existence of C in W_x, is supposed to be non-absurd on the grounds that B and C are causally connected to each other, via their connections with A. But what is opaque is why that indirect causal connection between B and C should be credited with so much significance. Philosophers who think that extrinsic identity is absurd are not going to be pacified by the reflection that B and C are causally connected with A. The existence of that causal connection is irrelevant, they will claim; it is the lack of causal influence of B upon C, and vice versa, which makes the judgement that B in $W_x \neq B'$ in W_y, in virtue of the existence of C in W_x, absurd. Is it not absurd to suppose that, after the destruction of A's body, the identity of the person occupying the B-body (the B-body person)[3] can depend upon what happens elsewhere, perhaps in a distant region of space, at a time after the transplant operation has been carried out? The absurdity (if absurdity there be) consequent upon the fact that B can truly say, on hearing that the other transplant operation was successful: "Thank goodness C 'took', otherwise I wouldn't have existed", is not alleviated by the fact that B and C stand in certain causal relations to the now dead A.

Moreover, consideration of the respective commitments of the following two theories of personal identity appears to undermine Mackie's proposal. The first theory analyses personal identity over time in terms of non-branching psychological continuity. The second theory analyses personal identity over time in terms of non-branching psychological similarity. Both theories are committed to the extrinsicness of identity. Now, consider the following two scenarios.

In the first scenario, a blueprint is made of A's physical and psychological states, by a process which leaves A otherwise unaffected, and then an exact physical and psychological replica of A is created, from the blueprint, by a scientist on Mars (call the replica C). According to both theories of personal identity, A ceases to exist upon the creation of the replica (since psychological branching has occurred) and a distinct person, B, comes to occupy A's body. According to either theory it is

w_4, O_2 is not O_1, and that, in w_5, O_2 is O_1. Fortunately, however, the best-candidate theorist is committed only to the claim that in w_5, O_1 is identical to the oak tree which develops from A_2, call it 'O_2'', which he will not identify with O_2. This account parallels the best-candidate theorist's treatment of identity over time: in the example of the division of persons, there is no possible world in which $A = B$, though there is a possible world (W_y) in which A is the person (B') there occupying B's body. Thus, it is important to note, B and C are not candidates for identity with A in the sense that there is a possible world in which one of the candidates is identical to A. Similarly, O_2 and O_3 are not candidates for identity with O_1 in the sense that there is a possible world in which one of the candidates is identical to O_1. Rather, it is the hunk of matter which composes, e.g., O_2, which is a candidate for being the hunk of matter which, in tome possible world, e.g. w_5, constitutes O_1.

[3] The designator "the B-body person" is to be taken as non-rigid.

true that, had C not existed, B would not have existed – a distinct person, $B'(= A)$, would then have continued to occupy A's body.

In the second scenario, the occurrence of a set of entirely random events results in the spontaneous creation of an exact physical and psychological replica of A on Mars (again call the replica C). According to the second theory, A ceases to exist when the replica comes into existence (since there are now two persons exactly psychologically similar to A), and a distinct person, B, comes to occupy A's body. But on this theory it is true that, had C not existed, B would not have existed – $B'(= A)$ would then have continued to occupy A's body.

Given that psychological continuity is a causal concept, whereas psychological similarity is not, Mackie is forced to say that the commitment to extrinsicness (i.e. commitment to the thesis that $B \neq B'$ in virtue of the existence of the replica C, and hence to the truth of the conditional that, had C not existed, B would not have existed) is absurd in the second scenario, but not in the first. This is surely very implausible – the commitment to extrinsicness of the continuity theory is as absurd (or not) as that of the similarity theory. (Of course, the psychological similarity theory of personal identity over time is logically inadequate – the relation of non-branching (psychological) similarity is neither transitive nor congruent – but the point is that its commitment to extrinsicness does not appear, in itself, to be any more absurd than the parallel commitment of the psychological continuity theory.)

One response which Mackie could make here would be to restrict the "causal isolation" requirement so that two candidates are regarded as causally isolated from an earlier individual if they have no matter in common with the original (or, at least, if they are not in any way physically continuous with the original). In each scenario, one of the candidates is causally isolated from the original individual, and hence in both cases the commitment to the extrinsicness of transworld identity (i.e. to the non-identity of B and B' in virtue of the existence of the replica C) is absurd.

Apart from its *ad hoc* character, however, this response risks squeezing out theories of personal identity over time (e.g. the theory that personal identity over time is analysed in terms of non-branching psychological continuity, whether or not the relation of non-branching psychological continuity has its normal cause, i.e., the continued existence of the brain and central nervous system) which many philosophers find plausible. (Think of the beam-transporter device in the TV series *Star Trek*: is the transporter, when functioning normally, really a form of self-destruction, or rather, as we are inclined to regard it, simply a very fast way of travelling around the universe?)

9.5 Conclusion

The upshot therefore, unless more is said, is that there is no significant asymmetry between best-candidate theories of identity over time and identity across worlds in respect of the absurdity or otherwise of their respective commitments to the extrinsicness of transworld identity. The implications of this conclusion can, of course, cut in two opposing directions. Either it implies, given the absurdity of rejecting the No Extrinsic Determination principle as a solution to the problems created by worlds 1–4, that all best-candidate theories are flawed, or it implies, given that the commitment to the extrinsicness of transworld identity on the part of best-candidate theories of identity over time is not absurd, that the commitment to extrinsicness of any best-candidate theory is unexceptionable.

I believe that we ought to accept the latter implication. The commitment to the extrinsicness (or relationality) of identity shows that a predicate such as "constituting the person identical with *B*" does not denote a genuine property of the hunk of matter which constitutes *B*, and that "constituting the oak-tree identical to O_2" does not denote a genuine property of the hunk of matter of which O_2 is constituted in w_4. It would not, I think, be an unreasonable extension of the sense of Geach's concept of a "mere Cambridge" property to describe such properties as mere Cambridge (Geach, 1972, 321–322).

I can see no reason to regard such a consequence as absurd (Garrett, 1987). Indeed, if the "causal powers" account of (genuine) propertyhood is correct, one would not expect such predicates to denote genuine properties. (Reference to such a property would surely not feature in an account of the causal potentialities of the hunk of matter which constitutes O_2.) If so, we have no reason to regard the commitment to the extrinsicness of identity on the part of best-candidate theories of identity as absurd, and rejection of the No Extrinsic Determination principle constitutes a legitimate response to Mackie's puzzle.

References

Garrett, B. (1987). A further reply to Noonan. *Analysis, 47*(4), 204–207.
Geach, P. T. (1972). *Logic matters*. Oxford: Blackwell.
Mackie, P. (1987). Essence, origin, and bare identity. *Mind, 96*(382), 173–201.
Parfit, D. (1984). *Reasons and persons*. Oxford: Oxford University Press.
Shoemaker, S., & Swinburne, R. (1984). Personal identity: A materialist's account. In *Personal identity*. Oxford: Blackwell.
Wiggins, D. (1980). *Sameness and substance*. Cambridge: Harvard University Press.

Chapter 10
Best Candidate Theories and Identity

Abstract In this discussion, I criticise Andrew Brennan's attempt to defend best-candidate theories of the identity of artefacts over time against certain now familiar objections. Adoption of a mereological conception of individuals does not, in itself, provide the means for a satisfactory response to objections of Wiggins and Noonan (some of which are anyway ill-focused). The way forward consists in recognising that the consequences of best-candidate theories which have been thought objectionable (in particular, commitment to the extrinsicness of identity) do not violate the necessity of identity and imply – what anyway ought to seem unexceptionable – that a predicate such as "constituting the ship which is the Ship of Theseus" does not denote a genuine property of the hunk of matter of which the predicate is true. Once these consequences have been clearly mapped out, the best-candidate theorist's commitment to the extrinsicness of identity does not appear absurd.

10.1 Introduction

In "Best Candidates and Theories of Identity", Andrew Brennan attempts to defend best-candidate theories of identity against objections posed by Wiggins and Noonan. In this reply, I argue that Brennan's characterisation of best-candidate theories is ill-motivated, and that he does not give an adequate response to the objections of Wiggins and Noonan. I then outline what I take to be the most promising strategy of reply which the best-candidate theorist ought to make to these objections.

10.2 Best-Candidate Theories of Identity

A best-candidate theory of the identity over time of entities of a certain sort, say Fs, asserts that an F at t_1 is identical with an F at t_2 iff (or, at least, only if) the F at t_1 stands to the F at t_2 in certain empirical relations appropriate to the sort F and there is no other F at t_2 which is a better or equally good candidate for identity with the

B. Garrett, *Time, Identity and the Self: Essays on Metaphysics*, Synthese Library 442, https://doi.org/10.1007/978-3-030-85517-8_10

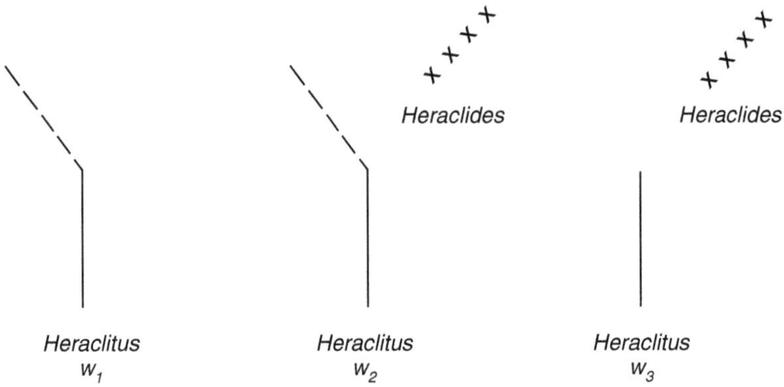

Fig. 10.1 Three possible histories of the Ship of Theseus

F at t_1. Best-candidate theories of personal identity over time have been advocated by Parfit (1984) and Shoemaker and Swinburne (1984).

The logical structure of the common-sense theory of the identity of artefacts over time, revealed most perspicuously in our descriptions of various possible histories of the Ship of Theseus, appears to be that of a best-candidate theory. It is thus a matter of some importance if our best theory of personal identity or artefact-identity is incoherent. Brennan's discussion is confined entirely to artefact-identity, but his points generalise to best-candidate theories of the identity of entities of any sort.

10.3 Brennan's Interpretation

Brennan represents three possible histories of the Ship of Theseus as seen in Fig. 10.1. In all three worlds, 'Heraclitus' denotes Theseus's original ship. In worlds 2 and 3, 'Heraclides' denotes the plank-hoarder's ship, reconstituted from the Heraclitus's original planks. Worlds 2 and 3 differ only in that there are two candidates for identity with the Heraclitus in world 2 – the Heraclides, and the continuously repaired ship, represented by the left-hand branch, which is spatio-temporally continuous (under the sortal *ship*) with the Heraclitus.

Given that we regard spatio-temporal continuity (under a sortal) as the dominant criterion of artefact identity, outweighing the identity-of-original-parts criterion, but acknowledge the fact that an artefact can survive dismantlement and reassembly, we must, it seems, claim that, in world 2, the Heraclitus is not the same ship as the Heraclides but that, in world 3, the Heraclitus is the same ship as the Heraclides. This common-sense theory is clearly a best-candidate theory: the continuously repaired ship and the Heraclides are both candidates for identity with Theseus's ship, though the former ship has the stronger claim.

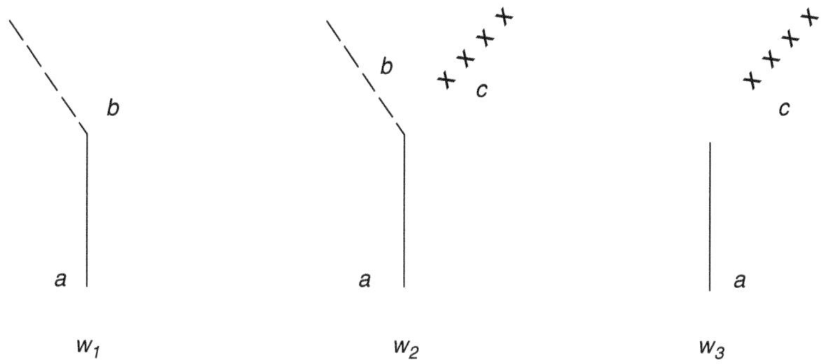

Fig. 10.2 Brennan's three scenarios

However, this description of worlds 2 and 3 seems to violate a principle – variously known as the "only *a* and *b*" rule (Wiggins) and the "only *x* and *y*" principle (Noonan) – which has been taken to represent a constitutive constraint on any relation which purports to be that of strict numerical identity. According to this constraint whether *x* is identical to *y* can never depend upon what happens to objects distinct from *x* and *y*. The common-sense description of worlds 2 and 3 appears to violate this principle – according to that description, whether the Heraclides is identical to the Heraclitus depends upon whether or not there exists a better candidate for identity with the Heraclitus.

Moreover, if proper names are rigid designators, the above description of worlds 1 and 2 is also objectionable since it violates the necessity of identity. (Indeed, contrary to one of Wiggins's claims (Wiggins 1980, 208), the absurdity involved in violating the "only *a* and *b* rule arguably just is the absurdity involved in denying the necessity of identity – why should counterexamples to the "only *a* and *b*" rule be thought exceptionable if identity were contingent?) The above description of worlds 2 and 3 is thus intensely problematic; as Wiggins notes, it licences the thought that:

> we could walk up to the antiquarian's relic [the Heraclides in world 2], seen as a candidate to be Theseus's ship, and say that but for the existence of its rival . . . it would have veritably coincided as a ship with Theseus's original ship. But the idea that in that case it would have been Theseus's very ship seems to be absurd. (Wiggins, 1980, 95)

Brennan's response to this objection is to recommend adoption of a four-dimensional conception of ordinary material objects, and to relabel worlds 1, 2, and 3 as follows (where the constants *a*, *b*, and *c* rigidly designate ship-stages). (See Fig. 10.2.)

If we further employ the concept of a mereological individual, where '+' represents the mereological fusion of individuals, the best-candidate theorist will claim that the mereological individual $a + b$ constitutes Theseus's ship in worlds 1 and 2, and that the distinct mereological individual $a + c$ constitutes Theseus's ship in world 3. This account respects the necessity of identity (it is not true that $a \neq c$ in world 2 and $a = c$ in world 3; '*a*' and '*c*' in both worlds refer to distinct ship-stages) and respects the "only a and b' rule (whether the mereological individual $a + c$ exists does not depend upon facts about the existence of some distinct object).

Prima facie, the adoption of the mereological conception of individuals has considerable point. Of course, this description has the consequence that a (mereological) individual can be a single ship in one possible world, but not in another, and that two individuals may share a common collection of stages; but as Brennan emphasises, there is (within the framework of a four-dimensional ontology) nothing *inherently* absurd about such consequences (Brennan, 1986, 431).

However, any best-candidate account of worlds 2 and 3, including Brennan's, appears to be committed to the following pair of claims, the commitment to which Noonan regards as a *reductio* of the best-candidate theory:

(a*) events which constitute the origin of some object of a certain sort in one situation may not constitute the origin of that, or any object of the kind, in a second situation, even though all the events constituting the history of that object in the first situation remain present in the second;

(b*) two events may be parts of the history of a single object in some situation, but may fail to be parts of the history of that, or any single object of the kind, in a second situation in which both they, and all the events which were parts of the history of the object in the first situation, remain present. (Brennan 1986, 432; Noonan 1985a, 81)[1]

(Following Brennan, I take 'objects' to include mereological individuals.)

Claims (a*) and (b*) are clearly true on Brennan's description of worlds 2 and 3 – events which constitute the origin of an object of the sort *ship* in world 2 do not constitute the origin of a ship in world 3,[2] and events which are parts of the history of a single ship in world 3 are not parts of the history of a single ship in world 2. Brennan regards (a*) and (b*) as important truths. But nothing has been done to alleviate the apparent absurdity of these claims. Discussing the fact that, on his description of worlds 2 and 3, the mereological individual $a + c$ is a ship in world 3 but not in world 2 (i.e., that different collections of temporal parts are allocated to different ships in different possible worlds), Brennan writes:

> This need be no more puzzling, though, than the fact that different spatial components can be allocated to different items in different worlds. In the world where the sides of my desk and the top of my neighbour's desk constitute one desk, there will be a puzzle about where

[1] Analogues of (a*) and (b*) will still be consequences of a best-candidate theory of artefact-identity even if the transworld identity relation is jettisoned in favour of some counterpart relation. Even if, from the point of view of world 2, Theseus's ship does not exist in world 3, it will still be true that the counterpart of the stream of events which constitutes the history of a single ship in world 3, does not constitute the history of a single ship in world 2.

[2] Brennan writes: "Events which constitute the origin of an object of the sort *ship* in w_3, although still constituting the origin of an object in w_2, do not there constitute the origin of an object of the sort ship" (Brennan, 1986, 432–433). This is surely a slip. The events which constitute the origin of a ship in world 3 do constitute the origin of the very same ship in world 2 (i.e., the Heraclitus).

> my desk and my neighbour's desk have gone. The mereologist, however, can reassure us. The spatial parts of things in this world are still present "over there" in the alternative world. So the objects in this world are still present over there (Brennan, 1986, 433).

However, this is patently no explanation. The problem is to make sense of how it can be that $a + c$ is a ship in world 3 but not in world 2 given that, with respect to what happens in the location of $a + c$ in both worlds, the difference between the two situations is (analogous to) a *mere Cambridge one* (only "analogous to" since Geach's Cambridge criterion relates to changes over time, not to differences across possible worlds). How can identity depend upon mere Cambridge differences? The relevant differences between Brennan's two worlds, outlined in the previous quotation, are manifestly real differences, involving different movements and positioning of matter in the appropriate location and not mere Cambridge differences. Brennan has therefore produced no satisfactory response to Noonan. If the best-candidate theorist's commitment to (a*) and (b*) is not to reduce his position to absurdity, we must re-examine Brennan's initial assumptions and provide a better response to the objections of Wiggins and Noonan.

10.4 Assessing Brennan's Response

Consider again Brennan's original – three-dimensional – labelling of the three possible histories of the Ship of Theseus. In worlds 2 and 3, the Heraclides exists but is identical with the Heraclitus only in world 3. This description of the two worlds clearly constitutes a best-candidate theory. But it does not violate the "only *a* and *b*" rule. That rule states that if a relation *R* is to be constitutive of the identity of *a* and *b*, *a*'s having *R* to *b* must be such that objects distinct from *a* and *b* are irrelevant as to whether *a* has *R* to *b* (Wiggins, 1980, 96). Brennan's description of worlds 2 and 3 does not violate this rule – whether the Heraclides is identical with the Heraclitus does not depend upon what happens to an entity distinct from the Heraclides or the Heraclitus (the Heraclitus is the continuously repaired ship in world 2).[3] Nonetheless, Brennan's description does violate the necessity of identity and implies (absurdly) that had Theseus's original ship not been continuously repaired, the Heraclides would have been Theseus's ship. To avoid this consequence, Brennan advocates relabelling the histories depicted in worlds 1–3 in four-dimensional terms.

However, an alternative manoeuvre is available to a best-candidate theorist, one which does not presuppose a four-dimensional conception of ordinary material objects. One of the valuable points made by Noonan (1985b), is that a best-candidate

[3] Best-candidate theories will violate the "only *a* and *b*" rule only if both candidates are equally good. Then three distinct individuals will be involved, and whether the original individual continues to exist in some other possible world will depend upon whether or not both candidates exist.

theorist is not committed to identifying the plank-hoarder's ships in worlds 2 and 3. Given the necessity of identity, it is perfectly reasonable for a best-candidate theorist to complain that Brennan has misdescribed the entities which exist in world 3. Since the Heraclides is not identical with the Heraclitus in world 2, the ship with which the Heraclitus is identical in world 3 cannot be the Heraclides.

Brennan appears to believe that it is a consequence of regarding proper names as rigid designators that the name 'Heraclides', as introduced in world 2, must refer to the plank-hoarder's ship in world 3. I cannot see why this should be so. It is true that the plank-hoarder's ship in world 3 may be called 'Heraclides', but it does not follow that it is the Heraclides. When describing non-actual possible worlds, our words bear the intended interpretation they have in the actual world and not the interpretation they have in some other possible world. (A possible world in which Plato is called 'Socrates' is not a world in which Plato is Socrates.)

Hence, the most natural response for a best-candidate theorist to make is to refuse to identify the plank-hoarder's ships in worlds 2 and 3, thus respecting the necessity of identity and the "only *a* and *b*" rule. Furthermore, as Noonan pointed out, if the best-candidate theorist refuses to identify the plank-hoarder's ships in worlds 2 and 3, he is not even committed to the (supposedly objectionable) counterfactual conditional that were it not for the existence of its rival, the Heraclides would not have existed at all, since world 3 is not a world in which the Heraclides's rival (the ship which is continuously repaired in world 2, i.e., the Heraclitus) does not exist (Noonan, 1986, 208).

Of course, in cases where the candidates are equally good (e.g., cases of the division of persons familiar from the literature on personal identity), best-candidate theories will imply the truth of such a counterfactual since the two candidates are both distinct from the original person. Such cases reveal most clearly that the description "best-candidate theory" can easily be misunderstood. Equally good candidates for identity with an earlier individual are not candidates in the sense that there is a possible world in which one of the candidates is the original individual; nor, in that sense, is the Heraclides a candidate for identity with Theseus's ship. Rather, in the case of Theseus's ship, it is the hunk of matter constituting the Heraclides which is a candidate for being the hunk of matter which constitutes the Ship of Theseus.

10.5 Final Words

What then is objectionable about the best-candidate theorist's proposed description of worlds 2 and 3? The best-candidate theorist, under the present proposal, is committed to the *extrinsicness* of identity. The identity of the plank-hoarder's ship (where this designator is taken to be non-rigid) is determined by what happens elsewhere – if, in some possible world, I am looking at the ship reconstituted from the Heraclitus's original planks, I am entitled to identify that ship with the Heraclides only if I know that, *elsewhere*, the Heraclitus has been continuously repaired. On this view, identity is a relational property: an account of what it is for a ship to be the Heraclides will involve reference to facts pertaining to regions of space outwith the location of the Heraclides.

Given that, with respect to what happens in the location of the plank-hoarder's ships, worlds 2 and 3 differ in a mere Cambridge way, it is a consequence of the best-candidate theorist's account that a predicate such as "constituting the ship which is identical with the Heraclides" does not denote any genuine property of the hunk of matter of which the Heraclides is constituted in world 2. (That is, a predicate such as "constituting the ship which is identical with the Heraclides" is in the same category as other relational predicates such as "being 50 miles south of a burning barn" in that it does not denote any genuine property of an object of which the predicate is true. I do not regard such a consequence as absurd. On the contrary, if it is the conceptual connection between the notions of (genuine) propertyhood and causality which explains why a relational predicate such as "being 50 miles south of a burning barn" does not denote a genuine property then, by that criterion, constituting the ship which is identical with the Heraclides ought not to count as a genuine property. In the first place, would reference to such a property feature in an explanation of the causal potentialities of the hunk of matter which constitutes the Heraclides? (Shoemaker 1985 and Geach 1972).

If the foregoing is correct, then we have no reason to regard (a*) and (b*) as absurd – they are merely consequences of the non-absurd fact that artefact-identity is extrinsic. But unlike Brennan's account, we now have a legitimate explanation of why we should not regard these consequences of our theory of artefact-identity as absurd, an explanation which respects the common-sense view that ordinary material objects have spatial parts but not temporal parts.

References

Brennan, A. (1986). Best candidates and theories of identity. *Inquiry, 29*, 423–38.

Geach, P. T. (1972). *Logic matters*. Oxford: Blackwell.

Noonan, H. (1985a). The "Only *x* and *y*" principle. *Analysis, 46*(4), 202–211.

Noonan, H. (1985b). Wiggins, artefact identity, and best candidate theories. *Analysis, 45*(1), 4–8.

Noonan, H. (1986). Reply to Garrett. *Analysis, 46*(4), 79–85.

Parfit, D. (1984). *Reasons and persons*. Oxford: Oxford University Press.

Shoemaker, S. (1985). Causality and properties. In *Identity, cause and mind*. Cambridge: Cambridge University Press.

Shoemaker, S., & Swinburne, R. (1984). Personal identity: A materialist's account. In *Personal identity*. Oxford: Blackwell.

Wiggins, D. (1980). *Sameness and substance*. Cambridge: Harvard University Press.

Chapter 11
Possible Worlds and Identity

Abstract Graeme Forbes's *The Metaphysics of Modality* presents a *tour de force* of the philosophy of modal concepts. In this chapter, I discuss certain issues relating to Forbes's treatment of the nature of identity and the thesis of the necessity of origin.

11.1 Introduction

Graeme Forbes's *The Metaphysics of Modality* is a thorough examination of the central issues in the metaphysics of modality. There are chapters on modal logic, the *de re/de dicto* distinction and the problem of transworld identity, possible worlds, essences and sets, the necessity of origin, substances, and the epistemology of modal concepts. In this discussion, however, I will concentrate upon issues relating to the nature of identity and the thesis of the necessity of origin.

A small point to start with. In his discussion of the notions of essence and essential property, Forbes does not sufficiently distinguish, with respect to some object x, the property of being identical with x and the property of being self-identical. These properties are distinct – the former is possessed only by x, the latter by everything (Forbes, 1985, 96–100). The point is not unimportant since, if the properties are distinct, it is not obvious that the fact that x possesses the property of necessary self- identity implies that x possesses the property of being necessarily identical with x, thus disrupting the familiar Barcan-Kripke proof of the necessity of identity.

Later in the same chapter, Forbes spends a number of pages defending the thesis that sets have their members essentially. But the thesis that the transtemporal and transworld identity conditions for sets are given in terms of sameness of members is surely just a trivial consequence of our definition of the concept of a set, a definition which serves to distinguish this concept from non-extensional concepts such as group or club. And, certainly, embracing such *a priori* essentialism about sets does not thereby commit one to the non-trivial *a posteriori* essentialist claims generated by the thesis of the necessity of origin.

In the final section of chap. 5, Forbes introduces the grounded/ungrounded distinction and argues that all (transworld and transtemporal) identities and non-

B. Garrett, *Time, Identity and the Self: Essays on Metaphysics*, Synthese Library 442, https://doi.org/10.1007/978-3-030-85517-8_11

identities must be grounded. By this Forbes means that if $a = b$ (or $a \neq b$), then there must be something in virtue of which '$a = b$' (or '$a \neq b$') is true. There cannot be 'bare' or ungrounded transtemporal or transworld identities and non-identities. Forbes argues that the requirement that (transtemporal and transworld) identities and non-identities be grounded is a consequence of the content of our concept of identity. However, I wish to argue that Forbes does not establish this constitutive thesis, and that the appropriateness of the grounding requirement, where it is appropriate, follows not from the content of the concept of identity itself, but from the (transtemporal and/or transworld) identity conditions of the object or objects concerned. Thus, for example, if set X is not identical with set Y, then this non-identity (whether transtemporal or transworld) must indeed be grounded in difference in members. But this requirement is a consequence not of the character of identity itself, but of facts about the identity conditions for sets. In particular, the fact that there is nothing more to the identity of sets than the identity of their members.

11.2 Forbes's Cases

Forbes gives four examples in support of his constitutive thesis that all identities and non-identities must be grounded. I do not believe that these examples support this thesis. I will discuss the examples in turn.

Case 1: "Consider the supposition that things could have been exactly as they are except that the steel tower in Paris opposite the Palais du Chaillot is different from the one actually there ... The only respect in which the imagined situation is different from the actual world is in the identity of the tower" (Forbes, 1985, 128).

Forbes finds this supposition unintelligible and claims that it supports the thesis that transworld non-identities must be grounded. However, I do not find the supposition unintelligible. It is not absurd to suppose that the transworld identity conditions for towers are sufficiently weak as to be compatible with such a supposition.

Case 2: This case concerns transworld identity. Consider the supposition that an actual untwinned human might have been one of a pair of identical twins. Thus imagine the untwinned A in the actual world and consider the world in which A is one of a pair of identical twins, B and C. According to Forbes, "it is evident that there is nothing in such a situation to determine which of B and C is identical to A: nothing grounds one of the identities rather than the other" (Forbes, 1985, 129).

However, again, I do not find this supposition unintelligible. The supposition is unintelligible, I think, only if one implicitly presupposes the "distant planets" conception of possible worlds according to which one has to discover the identities of the individuals in some possible world. If we reject this conception of possible worlds (justly criticised by Kripke (1980) in the preface to *Naming and Necessity*) then the supposition that, e.g., $A = B$ ceases to be absurd.

Case 3: This case concerns the splitting of an amoeba. When an amoeba divides it is plausible to say that the original has ceased to exist and that two new amoebae have come into existence composed of the matter of the original. "It would be very strange to hold that, in fact, the parent amoeba survives the splitting and only one new amoeba comes into existence" (Forbes, 1985, 130).

Case 4: This case concerns the division of persons, familiar from the literature on personal identity. Oldman's brain is divided and each (functionally equivalent) hemisphere is housed in two new bodies resulting in the creation of Newman 1 and Newman 2. If persons are not immaterial substances, the supposition that Oldman is identical with only one of Newman 1 and Newman 2 cannot credibly be maintained: and any (Cartesian) conception of personal identity which would sustain such a supposition is "extremely puzzling" (Forbes, 1985, 130).

In both these cases, Forbes assumes that the absurdity in the suppositions, that the parent amoeba is identical with only one of the resulting amoebae and that Oldman is identical with only one of the 'new' men, results from violation of the constitutive thesis that all identities must be grounded. However, as I have indicated above, an alternative explanation is available. The fact that these transtemporal identities require grounds follows not from the content of our concept of identity, but from facts about what it is for persons and amoebae to persist over time, facts grounded in the nature of persons and amoebae. It is because the identities of persons and amoebae over time do not consist in anything over and above the obtaining of certain non-branching continuities (physical continuity in the case of amoebae, physical and/or psychological continuity in the case of persons) that the above suppositions are unintelligible, and not because it is a consequence of the nature of identity that all identities must be grounded.

The fact that such ungrounded identities are unintelligible in the temporal case does not imply that analogous identities are unintelligible in the modal case. For, unlike the temporal case, there is nothing in the nature of persons and amoebae which excludes the possibility of ungrounded transworld identities and non-identities. From the fact that transtemporal identities and non-identities must be grounded, it does not follow that the same requirement holds for their transworld analogues. It is quite plausible to suppose that the restrictions on transtemporal identities are tighter than those on transworld identities.

Thus, I do not believe that Forbes's examples establish the constitutive thesis. Certainly, transworld and transtemporal identities and non-identities concerning sets, persons and amoebae must be grounded. But this fact does not follow from the nature of identity itself, but from the nature of sets, persons and amoebae. And, most importantly, for many objects, such as persons, towers and amoebae, the thesis that all transworld identities and non-identities concerning such objects must be grounded has simply not been made out.

11.3 On Forbes's Grounded Transworld Identities

The thesis that all transworld identities and non-identities must be grounded is essential to Forbes's defence of the thesis of the necessity of origin. Forbes's strategy is to point out that someone who rejects the necessity of origin and holds that a material object could have originated from completely different matter is committed to the possibility of bare or ungrounded transworld identities and non-identities. For example, suppose that an oak tree T in world w developed from acorn c. If origin is contingent, we may suppose that, in another world w^*, T developed from a different acorn c', and that, in w^*, c also exists and develops into an oak tree T', indistinguishable from T in w. Thus, T in $w \neq T'$ in w^*. But this transworld non-identity is ungrounded. Since ungrounded transworld identities and non-identities are unintelligible, T and T' cannot be distinct. Hence, T could not have developed from c'. And since this argument can be applied to any material object, it follows that the thesis of the necessity of origin is true.

Forbes anticipates a possible reply to this argument (Forbes, 1985, 140–145). Someone might reply that the truth of "T in $w \neq T'$ in w^*" is grounded, that there is something in virtue of which T and T' are distinct: for T' in w^* shares a world with a c'-tree, while T in w does not. As Forbes notes, the question of whether such relational differences are relevant to questions of identity and non-identity is the question of whether identity is only intrinsically, or also extrinsically, determinable. The answer to this question will impose constraints upon the conditions which may be regarded as grounding identities and non-identities. If identity is extrinsic, someone who rejected the thesis of the necessity of origin but accepted that all transworld identities and non-identities must be grounded could justifiably claim that the truth of "T in $w \neq T'$ in w^*" is grounded in virtue of the external, relational differences between T and T' in their respective worlds.

Our initial reaction is to claim that identity must be intrinsic for "How can what goes on concerning another acorn affect the identity of this tree?" (Forbes, 1985, 141). This is Forbes's reaction: identity is intrinsic and, hence, the above reply fails. However, I think that the thesis that identity is intrinsic cannot plausibly be sustained.[1]

Forbes appeals again to the example of division of persons and argues that it exposes the absurdity implicit in the thesis that identity is extrinsic. We may suppose that Oldman is identical with neither Newman 1 nor Newman 2. Someone who believes that identity is extrinsic may hold that, although Oldman $\neq$ Newman 1, had Newman 2 not existed, Oldman would have been identical with the person then occupying Newman 1's body (who, by the necessity of identity, is not Newman 1).

[1] The thesis that identity is intrinsic should not be confused with the (true) thesis that identity conforms to the *Only a and b* condition (Wiggins 1980, 90). Since only rigid designators feature in the statement of that condition (otherwise it would be false), the *Only a and b* condition is simply a consequence of the necessity of identity. And the extrinsicness defended below is quite consistent with the necessity of identity.

But then, as Forbes points out, Newman 1 is entitled to think "Thank goodness the other half-brain wasn't thrown away, otherwise I wouldn't have existed". This is absurd, and the source of the absurdity is the assumption that identity is extrinsic.

However, a defender of the extrinsicness of identity can make a number of replies to this argument. First, someone who accepts that Oldman is identical with neither Newman 1 nor Newman 2 and rejects the extrinsicness thesis must deny that, in the world in which Newman 2 does not exist, there exists a single individual throughout (Oldman). But, in that case, there must be more to the identity of persons over time than non-branching physical and/or psychological continuity, and such a (Cartesian) conception of personal identity is implausible (if not incoherent). If such a conception of personal identity is rejected (and assuming, *contra* Wiggins, that division is a genuine conceptual possibility for persons), it follows that identity cannot be intrinsic. (In a later chapter, Forbes argues that the correct description of the case of division is that Oldman is identical with both Newman 1 and Newman 2, who are themselves distinct (Forbes, 1985, 188–189). Accepting this description blocks the conclusion that (personal) identity is extrinsic, compatibly with a non-Cartesian conception of persons, but does so at the cost of violating the transitivity of identity. Hence, if identity is transitive and Cartesianism is false, identity is extrinsic. In general: any account of the division of persons which attempts to preserve the intrinsicness of identity either distorts our concept of a person or violates the logic of identity.)

Secondly, the story of the Ship of Theseus (not discussed by Forbes) reinforces the conclusion that identity is extrinsic. In the story we are inclined to identify the Ship of Theseus a with the continuously repaired ship b and not with the plank-hoarder's ship c. But, since we allow that artefacts can survive dismantlement and reassembly, we acknowledge the fact that, had ship b not existed, a would have been identical with the plank-hoarder's ship c', numerically distinct from, but qualitatively identical with, c. Hence, identity is extrinsic. And here the intrinsicness thesis cannot be salvaged by a retreat into 'ship-dualism' – it is uncontentious that the identity of artefacts over time consists in the obtaining of certain sorts of continuity (spatio-temporal continuity or identity of original parts). Our common-sense description of these possible histories of the Ship of Theseus presupposes the extrinsicness of identity.

Thirdly, if that were all there was to be said, Forbes could reply that, even if the Ship of Theseus story shows that identity is extrinsic, we have done nothing to remove the air of paradox which surrounds the possibility that identity might fail to be intrinsic. However, the air of paradox can, I think, be dispelled. For the thesis that identity is extrinsic is paradoxical only if we suppose that identity, and hence existence, is "what matters" in identity over time. If, like Parfit and Shoemaker, we deny this, then Newman 1's thought that, but for the existence of Newman 2, he would not have existed, ceases to be absurd. The example of the division of persons and the story of the Ship of Theseus supports the thesis that identity is extrinsic and the thesis that identity is not "what matters" (that what matters in the survival of persons over time, for example, is not identity but psychological continuity and/or connectedness, relations which may obtain in a branching form).

For these reasons, I think that the thesis that identity is extrinsic can be defended. Consequently, even if my belief in the intelligibility of bare transworld identities and non-identities were rejected, the fact that identity is extrinsic suffices to obstruct Forbes's argument for the necessity of origin. Indeed, the combination of views – the grounding requirement, the contingency of origin and the extrinsicness of identity – may seem to many to be an attractive position. Forbes's argument for the necessity of origin is thus doubly unsuccessful – firstly, because he has not succeeded in demonstrating the unintelligibility of ungrounded transworld identities and non-identities and, secondly, because the extrinsicness of identity is anyway sufficient to undermine his argument.

Not only has the thesis of the necessity of origin not been established, but there appears to be an argument against the thesis. This anti-essentialist argument is the subject of Forbes's Chap. 7, where he points out that the following principle (essential to the argument) is intuitively very plausible:

(T) Necessarily, any artefact could have originated from a slightly different collection of parts from any one collection from which it could have originated.

Imagine that a ship has just been built and that one plank has been left over. It is surely very plausible to suppose that, had that plank been used in place of one of the original planks, the identity of the ship would not have been affected. However, principle (T) appears to undermine the thesis of the necessity of origin. For consider a ship S_1 in world w_1, constructed out of 100 planks. Suppose that any ship could have been constructed out of a collection of planks which differs by just one plank from any one collection out of which it could have been constructed. Then there will be a series of worlds $\langle w_1, [\ldots], w_{100}\rangle$, and a series of ships $\langle S_1, [\ldots], S_{100}\rangle$ in those worlds, which are such that adjacent ships differ in their original construction by just one plank, and S_1 and S_{100} have no (original) planks in common. Now, by (T), or rather its ship-version, we may suppose that adjacent ships in the sequence are identical. But then, by the transitivity of identity, $S_1 = S_{100}$. But S_1 and S_{100} were constructed out of completely different collections of planks. Hence, the thesis of the necessity of origin is false.

There have been a number of reactions to this argument. Harold Noonan regards the argument as valid but the conclusion as absurd (since, like Forbes, he finds the idea of bare transworld identities and non-identities unintelligible) and, hence, denies principle (T) (Noonan, 1983). This, however, is very implausible. It is highly counter-intuitive to suppose that an artefact could not have been constructed out of even slightly different matter (differing by just a few molecules, for example). Hence, I do not think that this response is tenable.

A different response has been made by Nathan Salmon (Salmon, 1981, Appendix 1). Salmon claims that the anti-essentialist argument is to be blocked, not by jettisoning principle (T), but by denying the argument's validity on the grounds that the accessibility relation between worlds (the relation "is possible relative to") is non-transitive, and that w_1 and w_{100} are mutually inaccessible. However, as Forbes points out, such a response is blatantly *ad hoc* (Forbes, 1985, 165). The only reason for denying the transitivity of accessibility and regarding w_1 and w_{100} as mutually inaccessible is a belief in the necessity of origin. But it is precisely the truth of this belief which is in question – it cannot simply be assumed. Moreover, even if w_1 and w_{100} could (non-question-beggingly) be regarded as mutually inaccessible, it is not obvious that the anti-essentialist argument is thereby invalidated. For it is still true that adjacent worlds in the sequence are mutually accessible and (presumably) still true that $S_1 = S_2$, $S_2 = S_3$, [...], $S_{99} = S_{100}$. Consequently, by the transitivity of identity, we still get the conclusion that $S_1 = S_{100}$. Hence, unless denying the transitivity of accessibility involves denying the transitivity of identity, thus risking incoherence, I cannot see how it helps defuse the anti-essentialist argument.

Forbes's response is different from either of the above. He believes that the anti-essentialist argument is simply a modal version of the Sorites Paradox, in virtue of the obvious formal similarities between (T) and the tolerance principles which give rise to familiar versions of the Sorites Paradox. Consequently, the modal version of the paradox is to be solved in the same way as other versions of the paradox, which, for Forbes, is by utilising the machinery of degree-theoretic semantics.

However, it is not clear that degree-theoretic semantics can intelligibly be applied to the anti-essentialist argument. For such an application would require that an identity predicate such as '$\sigma = S_1$' be treated as a predicate of degree. But the notion of degrees of identity is scarcely coherent. Forbes's response here is to jettison the transworld identity relation in favour of a transworld relation which it does make sense to regard as holding to varying degrees – the counterpart relation. For this relation is fixed by relations of crossworld similarity and the notion of degrees of similarity is obviously unproblematic. (Although Forbes advocates a degree-theoretic solution, it is worth noting that in order to refute the anti-essentialist argument counterpart-theoretically, it would be sufficient simply to point to the fact that the counterpart relation is non-transitive. Since the relation is non-transitive, the conclusion that S_{100} is a counterpart of S_1 cannot validly be inferred.)

However, in adopting a counterpart-theoretic framework, Forbes appears to be undermining his original argument for the necessity of origin. His argument relied upon the premise that all transworld identities and non-identities must be (intrinsically) grounded. But such a restriction does not hold for the counterpart relation. This relation is extrinsic in character: whether A in w_x is a counterpart of B in w_y depends upon there being no other object in w_x which is more similar to B in the relevant respects than A. The extrinsicness of the counterpart relation undermines Forbes's argument for the necessity of origin.

Moreover, on general grounds, it is clear that the necessity of origin is a thesis which it would be difficult to justify within a counterpart-theoretic framework. For, given that counterpart relation is a relation of crossworld similarity, why should origin have a special status within the similarity metric? If A and B can be counterparts whilst being dissimilar in many respects, why can't origin be one of them? Suppose that A and B are as similar as possible compatibly with the assumption that they had different origins. Would it not be mere prejudice to deny that they may be counterparts?

An alternative response to the anti-essentialist argument would be to claim that since the requirement of groundedness of transworld identities and non-identities has not been made out, we ought to accept the conclusion that $S_1 = S_{100}$ and, hence, regard the argument as refuting the thesis of the necessity of origin. However, despite the non-absurdity of its conclusion, if Forbes is right to think that the anti-essentialist argument is, in virtue of its form, a modal version of the Sorites Paradox (and I can see no reason to suppose that he is not) then, clearly, we cannot legitimately appeal to this argument in order to establish the falsity of the thesis of the necessity of origin. However, since Forbes's argument for the necessity of origin is unsuccessful, we have been given no reason to accept this thesis.[2]

11.4 Conclusion

In conclusion, I am in fairly radical disagreement with Forbes over some of the major issues in his book – the grounding requirement, the intrinsic/extrinsic debate, and the necessity of origin. Nevertheless, it is refreshing to find someone discussing in such a perspicuous and engaging way problems which are central to the philosophy of identity and modality.

References

Forbes, G. (1985). *The metaphysics of modality*. Oxford: Clarendon Press.
Kripke, S. (1980). *Naming and necessity*. Cambridge: Harvard University Press.
Noonan, H. (1983). The necessity of origin. *Mind, 92*(365), 1–20.
Salmon, N. (1981). *Reference and essence*. New Jersey: Princeton University Press.
Wiggins, D. (1980). *Sameness and substance*. Cambridge: Harvard University Press.

[2] Needless to say, one can reject the thesis of the necessity of origin consistently with accepting other (plausible) essentialist theses such as natural kind essentialism and "substance sortal" essentialism.

Chapter 12
Vague Identity and Vague Objects

Abstract In this discussion I want to argue – with certain qualifications – that there cannot be any vague identities, and to outline reasons for scepticism about the view that the world contains vague objects. I also argue that even if there were vague identities, this would lend no support to the vague objects view.

12.1 Getting Clear About the Vague Identity Thesis

What would constitute a defence of the vague-identity thesis? It would be an example in which a sentence of numerical identity is indeterminate in truth-value (i.e., neither true nor false), where the indeterminacy is due to vagueness. (Thus we are not concerned with identity sentences whose indeterminacy is due to reference-failure or to cross-category identification.)

It seems clear that there are such examples: where the vagueness of an identity is a consequence of the vagueness of one or both of its singular terms. For example, the singular term "the world's greatest ruler" is vague because of the vagueness of the predicate "[…] great ruler". This predicate is vague not because it lacks sharp boundaries, but because of its multi-criterial application conditions. Many different factors contribute to the greatness of a ruler – wisdom, fortitude, diplomacy, prudence, etc. – and the rules of our language do not fix in advance what weight to assign to each factor.

Because of this vagueness, the singular term "the world's greatest ruler" has no determinate reference: it is vague which person it singles out. (Though, as Wiggins has emphasised, from the fact that it is vague which object a term singles out, it does not follow that it singles out something vague (Wiggins, 1980, 140).) Consequently, an utterance of, e.g., "the world's greatest ruler was the world's wisest ruler" is a plausible example of a vague identity.[1]

It seems, therefore, that there can be vague identities. But, in the example just given, the vagueness of the identity was due to the vagueness of (at least) one of its

[1] This example is taken from (Wiggins, 1986, 174).

B. Garrett, *Time, Identity and the Self: Essays on Metaphysics*, Synthese Library 442, https://doi.org/10.1007/978-3-030-85517-8_12

component singular terms. Is this the only way in which an identity sentence might be vague? Could $A = B$ be vague even if 'A' and 'B' were both precise designators? We can define 'precision' as follows: a designator 'Z' is precise just in case the reference of 'Z' is not fixed by any vague description or vague ostension, and it is not vague what 'Z' singles out.[2] Ordinary proper names are typically precise designators.

Ordinary proper names are also rigid designators. But it is worth pointing out that precision and rigidity are not the same phenomenon. Although rigid designators (terms whose reference does not shift across possible worlds) will typically be precise, not all precise designators are rigid. For example, it may be perfectly determinate who is singled out by the definite description "the tallest man in the room", even if the description is used non-rigidly.

Let us reformulate the vague-identity thesis as follows: there can be vague identities whose singular terms are both precise. Is this true? Consider a diachronic identity: X (at t_1) is identical with Y (at t_2). It is assumed – *contra* Wiggins – that "singling out" can be successfully accomplished synchronically (Wiggins 1986, 171–172). Can this identity be indeterminate in truth-value due to vagueness, even if 'X' and 'Y' are both precise designators?

12.2 Considering the Ship of Theseus

Consider the ship of Theseus, which we will call 'A', is composed of 100 planks.

Case 1 At time t_1, one plank is removed from A, and quickly replaced with another plank. Call the ship at t_2, thus altered, 'B'. It seems uncontentious – in the absence of any other changes – that it's true that A is identical with B.

Case 2

...

Case 99

Case 100 At t_1, all A's planks are (quickly) removed and then replaced with a new set. As before, call the ship at t_2, 'B'. Since there is complete material discontinuity between A and B in *Case 100*, it seems uncontentious that it's *false* that A is B.

Consider *Case 50*. In this case, half of A's planks are removed and replaced. It is plausible to suppose that it is indeterminate whether A is the same ship as B. There are not sufficiently many continuities to say that, definitely, A is the same ship as B; but nor are there sufficiently few continuities to say that, definitely, A is not the same ship as B. There is simply no "fact of the matter" as to whether A and B are one and the same ship.

This description of *Case 50* rests on more than just an appeal to intuition. If you refuse to accept this description, but accept the above descriptions of *Cases 1*

[2] The term "precise designator" is due to Thomason (1982, 331).

and *100*, you are committed to the existence of a sharp cut-off point in the spectrum from 1 to 100 (i.e., adjacent cases such that in one case, but not the other, the relevant changes are identity-preserving). This commitment is very implausible. How could the replacement of just one plank make such a difference? (If you think one plank could make a difference, change the example and choose a smaller unit of matter.) Further, whatever unit is chosen, how could we ever know where the cut-off point lay?

Since, we may assume, the references of '*A*' and '*B*' have not been fixed by any vague means, and there is no vagueness concerning what is being singled out at either t_1 or t_2, the sentence $A = B$ in *Case 50* appears to be an example of a vague identity, the singular terms of which are both precise.

12.3 Evans's Proof

Despite such examples, Gareth Evans, Nathan Salmon, and David Wiggins have put forward arguments designed to show that no identity statement can be vague and contain only precise designators (Evans 1978; Salmon 1981; Wiggins 1986). I will focus on Evans's *reductio proof*, which is an integral part of his argument against vague objects.[3] This proof, as I present it, is not watertight, but I shall indicate how repairs can easily be carried out.

My interpretation of Evans's argument is, I think, perfectly straightforward. However, having seen an exchange of letters between Evans and David Lewis, I can no longer claim that my presentation corresponds to Evans's understanding of his own argument.[4] This is puzzling, not least because the interpretation offered by Lewis, and endorsed by Evans, seems obviously flawed. In contrast, Evans's argument, as I shall present it, points clearly towards a powerful result.

Evans's proof is in two stages: (1)-(5) and (1')-(5'). Consider first the (1)-(5) argument, which runs as follows:

Where '∇' is a sentential operator expressing indeterminacy, suppose, for *reductio*:

(1) $\nabla(a = b)$

(1) reports a fact about b which we may express as follows:

(2) $\hat{x}[\nabla(x = a)]b$

(That is, b has the property being such that it is indeterminate whether it belongs to the class of objects identical with a.)

But: (3) $\sim \nabla(a = a)$

[3] Elsewhere, I have criticised Wiggins's argument; see Garrett (1988).

[4] Lewis allowed me to see these letters. In his letter, Lewis essentially puts forward the interpretation, see Lewis (1988).

Hence: (4) $\sim \hat{x}[\nabla(x = a)]a$

Since the predicate '$\hat{x}[\nabla(x = a)]$' is true of b but not of a, it follows, by the contrapositive of Leibniz's Law (i. e., $\sim (\phi)(\phi a \equiv \phi b) \rightarrow (a = b)$), that:

(5) $\sim (a = b)$

"contradicting" (1) which states that it is indeterminate whether $a = b$.

12.4 Responses to Evans's Proof

There are five possible responses to Evans's argument. We could endorse one or more of the following:

(i) (3) is not true;
(ii) the move from (1) to (2) is fallacious;
(iii) the move from (3) to (4) is fallacious;
(iv) the move from (2) and (4) to (5) is fallacious;
(v) (1) and (5) do not contradict each other.

Let us take response (i). Clearly, Evans took premise (3) to be a truism, analogous perhaps to the truism that $\Box(a = a)$. It might be thought that if a is a vague object (whatever exactly this claim involves), it would then be vague whether $a = a$. However, I think Wiggins is right to claim that:

> even if ... *a* were a vague object, we still ought to be able to obtain a (so to speak) perfect case of identity, provided we were careful to mate a with exactly the right object. And surely a is exactly the right object to mate with a. There is a complete correspondence. All their vagueness matches exactly. (Wiggins, 1986, 175)

Response (ii) is something that Lewis considered (Lewis, 1988, 128–129). Lewis has objected to the step from (1) to (2), comparing it to the familiar modal fallacy of reasoning from:

(A) It is contingent whether the number of planets is 9 (True)

to:

(B) The number of planets is such that it is contingent whether it is 9 (False).

Lewis's interpretation of Evans's argument against vague objects runs as follows. The *reductio* proof cannot be correct since its conclusion is manifestly false: there are vague identities (Lewis's example: "Princeton = Princeton Borough"). The fallacy in the proof lies in the step from (1) to (2). Believers in vague objects cannot account for this fallacy. Hence, the vague-objects view "is in bad trouble" (Lewis, 1988, 129).

However, if the inference from (1) to (2) is invalid, in virtue of the presence of imprecise designators, this ought to be a fact which any theorist can and should acknowledge. Believers in the existence of vague objects do not hold absurdly that all designators are precise; they can acknowledge the existence of imprecise designators and the fallacious patterns of inference in which they participate. Hence, Lewis's interpretation yields no good argument against the vague-objects view.

Richmond Thomason has supported response (iii). Thomason has criticised the step from (3) to (4). Like Lewis, Thomason draws on the modal analogy, and charges Evans with begging the question. He writes:

> The fallacy is analogous to the modal one that would have been committed had ∇ been interpreted as "neither necessarily true nor necessarily false". In the modal case $\nabla[a = b]$ is equivalent to $\hat{x}\nabla[x = a]$ (a) only if 'a' is a "rigid designator"; so to assume the equivalence in arguing for $a = b \rightarrow \Box[a = b]$ is to beg the question. In the case of vague singular terms, $\sim \nabla[a = b]$ is equivalent to $\sim \hat{x}\nabla[x = a]$ (a) only if a is a "precise designator", and when Evans infers the second from the first he is assuming what he is trying to prove. (Thomason, 1982, 331)

However, the possibility of an invalid inference from (1) to (2), or from (3) to (4), seems to depend essentially upon the imprecision of at least one of 'a' or 'b', just as the invalidity of the inference from (A) to (B) depends essentially upon the non-rigidity of the definite description "the number of planets".

In order to avoid this fallacy we should assume, at the outset, that 'a' and 'b' in Evans's proof are both precise designators. The aim of the proof is to show, by *reductio*, that if 'a' and 'b' are both precise, $a = b$ cannot be indeterminate in truth-value due to vagueness. Hence, the moves from (1) to (2), and from (3) to (4) – thus restricted – are valid, as are analogous modal inferences in which all singular terms are rigid. Or, at least, once restricted, it is no longer clear what grounds there could be for scepticism about the validity of the moves from (1) to (2), or from (3) to (4).

12.5 The Correct Response to Evans's Proof

The correct reaction to Evans's proof, I suggest, is to endorse the disjunction of responses (iv) and (v). On one interpretation of (5), (2) and (4) entail (5), but (1) and (5) are consistent. On another interpretation of (5), (1) and (5) are contradictories, but we have been given no reason to suppose that (5), thus understood, follows from (2) and (4). Either way, there is no *reductio*.

Why is (5) open to different interpretations? The reason is that in three-valued logics we can choose between two types of negation, weak and strong. On the weak interpretation, $\sim P$ is true iff P is either false or indeterminate; hence, $\sim P$ is true if P is indeterminate. Consequently, the truth of (5) is consistent with the truth of (1) – indeed, (1) trivially entails (5) – and there is no *reductio*. (There is a rationale for this interpretation. If P is indeterminate, it's neither true nor false; so it's not true. If P is not true, $\sim P$ is true. Hence $\sim P$ is true if P is indeterminate.)

There may be some resistance to weak negation. On such a view, if Ramon is a borderline bald man, it's not true that Ramon is bald. So Ramon is not bald. Isn't this the wrong result? One response would be to deny that $\sim (a \text{ is } F)$ implies a is not-F, if F is a vague predicate. But this seems *ad hoc*. The best response, I think, is to accept this inference, but deny that it is objectionable. Ramon is not bald. But this does not imply that it is false that Ramon is bald; it simply highlights the fact that Ramon does not fall within the extension of 'bald'.

On the strong interpretation of negation, $\sim P$ is true iff P is false, and $\sim P$ is indeterminate if P is indeterminate. Now (5) and (1) do contradict each other: if (5) is true, $a = b$ must be false; but if (1) is true, $a = b$ cannot be false. However, Evans must earn his entitlement to suppose that (5), thus understood, follows from (2) and (4). Simply to assume that it does, would be to beg the question against a defender of vague identities, who will insist upon the weak reading of negation throughout. Thus, unless there is a compelling reason why the truth of (5) must be taken to imply the falsity of $a = b$, the (1)-(5) argument will be ineffectual against its intended target.

Evans may have been aware of these difficulties facing the (1)-(5) argument, and may have seen that his *reductio* required supplementation. Hence the reason for his final paragraph, and the (1')-(5') argument:

> If 'Indefinitely' [i.e., '∇'] and its dual 'Definitely' ('Δ') generate a modal logic as strong as S5, (1)-(4) and, presumably Leibniz's Law, may each be strengthened with a 'Definitely' prefix, enabling us to derive
>
> (5') $\Delta \sim (a = b)$
>
> which is straightforwardly inconsistent with (1). (Evans, 1978, 208)

This passage has a number of problematic features. First, it is clear that $\{\nabla, \Delta\}$, unlike $\{\diamond, \Box\}$, are not duals: e.g., ∇P is not equivalent to $\Delta \sim P$. Second, '∇' and 'Δ' will not generate a modal logic as strong as S5. The characteristic S5 axiom $(\diamond P \rightarrow \Box \diamond P)$ is not an axiom in vague logic: $(\nabla P \rightarrow \Delta \nabla P)$ fails of truth if '∇P' itself is vague. Hence, Evans cannot always prefix (1) with 'Definitely' as his supplementary argument requires: higher-order vague identities (whose definitisation results in falsity) will fall outwith the scope of Evans's argument.

Third, $\{\nabla, \Delta\}$ will not even generate a logic as strong as S4.[5] The characteristic S4 axiom $(\Box\Box P \rightarrow \Box P)$ is not an axiom of vague logic: $(\Delta\Delta P \rightarrow \Delta P)$ fails of truth if 'ΔP' itself is vague. Further, the analogue of the S4 theorem $(\diamond \diamond P \rightarrow \diamond P)$ is not a theorem in vague logic: $(\nabla\nabla P \rightarrow \nabla P)$ is clearly unacceptable given that there are distinct higher-orders of vagueness. (Even the analogue of the System T theorem $(P \rightarrow \Diamond P)$ fails: $(P \rightarrow \nabla P)$ is false if 'P' is true.)

The preceding paragraphs made four assumptions. First, it was assumed that there are higher-orders of vagueness; in particular, it was assumed that there is second-order vagueness: 'ΔP' and '∇P' may themselves be vague. (This plausible assumption is given a brief defence below.) Second, it was assumed that if A takes the value Indeterminate (vague), and B is the definitisation of A ('$\Delta A'$), then the value of B is False. Third, it was assumed that, under such an assignment, '$A \rightarrow B$' is Indeterminate. (A conditional cannot be true if it has a non-false antecedent and a false consequent.) Fourth, it was assumed that if A is true, '∇A' is false. All these assumptions are plausible.

[5] This result is endorsed by Michael Dummett, see (Dummett, 1980, 257).

However, the central problem with Evans's (1')-(5') argument is that the transition to (5') is either ineffective or unnecessary. If negation is weak negation, there is no contradiction between (1) and (5'): on this view, the indeterminacy of $a = b$ is quite consistent with the definite truth of $\sim (a = b)$. (If P is (definitely) in- determinate, then $\sim P$ is definitely true.) Hence, on the weak reading, the shift to (5') fails to complete the *reductio*.

Alternatively, if negation is strong negation, then (5) already contradicts (1); in which case, there is no need for the final paragraph. Either way, therefore, Evans's argument is not strengthened by the move to (5').

Fortunately, however, these difficulties can easily be side-stepped. It seems clear that:

(2) $\hat{x}[\nabla(x = a)]b$

is true. And that:

(4*) $\hat{x}[\nabla(x = a)]a$

is not just not true but false. Now, for any extensional context G all that follows from $G(x)$ and $\sim G(y)$ is $\sim (x = y)$ (i.e., it is not true that $x = y$). It does not follow that it is false that $x = y$, given the availability of the weak reading of negation.

But the following principle is very plausible:

$$T(G(x))\&F(G(y)) \rightarrow F(x = y).$$

That is, if it is true that x is G and false that y is G, it is false that $x = y$. (What better grounds could there be for judging x and y distinct, than that something true of x is false of y?) Applying this principle to Evans's argument, the falsity of $a = b$ follows from the truth of (2) and the falsity of (4*), and the intended *reductio* is successful.

It was noted above that higher-order vague identities escape Evans's *reductio*, since (1) cannot be prefixed with 'Definitely' if $a = b$ suffers from higher-order vagueness. But what is higher-order vagueness? A proposition P exhibits higher-order vagueness when, e.g., it is vague whether it is vague that P. The grounds for believing in first-order predicate-vagueness – uncertainty over the application of a predicate due to no factual or conceptual ignorance – equally motivate belief in higher orders of vagueness. Thus, just as it may be vague whether some particular (reddish-orange) patch is red, so it may be vague whether it is vague that a particular (red/reddish-orange) patch is red.

Identity certainly appears to be subject to higher orders of vagueness as much as to first-order vagueness. Plausible examples of second-order vague identities are those in *Cases 20–30* of the Ship example. Do such identities escape the strengthened argument of the preceding section? If it is vague whether it is vague that $a = b$, premise (2) will be indeterminate, and hence – so the objection might run – the strengthened argument, since it contains a premise which is not definitely true, cannot serve to undermine the possibility of second-order vague identities (containing only precise designators).

However, it should be apparent that this objection has no force whatsoever. Second-order vague identities do not escape the strengthened argument. We can simply re-state the argument as follows. Assume: $\nabla\nabla(a = b)$. Then:

(2**) $\hat{x}[\nabla\nabla(x = a)]b$

is true. But:

(4**) $\hat{x}[\nabla\nabla(x = a)]a$

is false. Therefore, it is false that $a = b$, contradicting the assumption that $a = b$ suffers from second-order vagueness. (Analogous reasoning can, of course, be applied to an identity of any purported order of vagueness.)

12.6 A General Result

It is important to realise that the dispute over vague identity is far from being a merely technical debate. The most plausible descriptions of many puzzle cases, such as *Case 50* of the Ship Example, commit us to the existence of vague identities containing only precise designators. What are we to say about such examples if the strengthened argument is cogent?

The problem is entirely general. The existence of vague identities is a consequence of accepting Continuity Theories of the persistence conditions of entities of many different sorts (artefacts, persons, social objects, natural objects, etc.). If it is correct to analyse the persistence of Fs in terms of (*inter alia*) the relation of spatio-temporal continuity holding between Fs at different times, then given that the latter relation admits of indeterminacy, the identity of Fs will also admit of indeterminacy.

If we accept the Continuity Theory, the identity of virtually any composite, material entity will admit of indeterminacy. Consequently, the conclusion of the strengthened argument conflicts with an immediate implication of the standard account of persistence.

Nor are matters advanced if we retain the analysis of persistence in terms of continuity, but jettison the relation of strict identity over time in favour of the mereological relations of the four dimensional theory of ordinary continuants. It's true that there is no direct analogue of Evans's argument to the effect that statements of the form "X-at-t_1 is part of the same four dimensional object as Y-at-t_2" cannot be vague (where 'X-at-t_1' and 'Y-at-t_2' are precise designators). But if it is vague whether X-at-t_1 is part of the same four dimensional object as Y-at-t_2, then it is vague whether the four dimensional object of which X-at-t_1 is a part is identical with the four dimensional object of which Y-at-t_2 is a part. This may not be a statement of identity over time, but it is a statement of identity nonetheless; and how can it be vague given the argument above?

What of the vague-objects view? Dummett once wrote that "the notion that things might actually be vague, as well as being vaguely described, is not properly intelligible" (Dummett, 1980, 260).[6] Evans, presumably, would have agreed: the point of his article was to unearth the source of this unintelligibility. But Evans clearly had some idea of what it would be for there to be vague objects, i.e., some criterion of vague objecthood.

On the most natural reading, which links Evans's proof with his critique of vague objects, Evans presupposed the Identity Criterion. We can state this criterion as follows: provided that there are precise singular terms in a language of sufficient expressive power, there are vague objects iff there are identity statements – containing only precise singular terms – which are indeterminate in truth-value due to vagueness. (The criterion is conditionalised in order to avoid the unwelcome consequence that the existence of vague objects depends upon the existence of a language containing precise designators.) Evans's proof is intended to establish that there can be no such identities; from which it follows, *via* the Identity Criterion, that there can be no vague objects.

Prima facie, the Identity Criterion has a good deal to recommend it. If $A = B$ is vague, and 'A' and 'B' are both precise, the sentential indeterminacy must, it seems, simply reflect vagueness in reality (other possible sources of vagueness having been excluded). Further, if it is vague whether, e.g., ship A (at t_1) is identical with ship B (at t_2), then it is vague whether a particular tract of space-time contains one ship or two. This seems to be a perfect illustration of what it is for the world to be vague.

However, I do not think the Identity Criterion is, ultimately, satisfactory. The problem is that alternative sources of vagueness have not been excluded. In particular, the Identity Criterion overlooks the sortal-dependent nature of identity. It is plausible to suppose, as Wiggins has argued, that identity is sortal-dependent: if $A = B$, then, for some sortal F, A is the same F as B (Wiggins, 1980, ch. 2). (It is important to note that the thesis that identity is sortal-dependent does not entail the much more controversial thesis that identity is sortal-relative.) Hence, any sentence $A = B$ is in principle expandable into a lengthier sentence containing explicit reference to a covering sortal concept (*piano*, *kangaroo*, *rainbow*, etc.).

Given the Sortal Dependency thesis, if it is vague whether A is B, even where 'A' and 'B' are precise, we have no reason to regard the indeterminacy as due to the world, rather than to the vagueness of the sortal concept(s) which cover $A = B$.

The apparently ineliminable role of sortal concepts in our practice of individuating and re-identifying particulars also subverts other, initially plausible, criteria of vagueness in reality, such as: (a) an object is vague if it lacks precise spatial boundaries (e.g., clouds, mountains, oceans, etc.); and (b) an object is vague if it is vague whether it has such-and-such a part.[7] Everest may have fuzzy spatial boundaries; but it does not follow that Everest is a vague object. It is open to us

[6] However, Dummett has subsequently withdrawn this claim in (Dummett, 1981, 440).

[7] Michael Tye (1990) proposed (a) (the Fuzzy Boundaries Criterion). Criterion (b) (a version of the Fuzzy Parts Criterion) was proposed by R. M. Sainsbury (1989). Criteria (a) and (b), though related, are not equivalent: an object with precise spatial boundaries will count as vague by (b), but not by (a), if its vague part(s) lies within its spatial boundaries.

to identify the ultimate source of Everest's fuzzy boundaries as our vague sortal, mountain. The vagueness of this concept implies that, in general, it is vague where a mountain ends and a valley begins.

12.7 Conclusion

In this discussion, I have argued that Evans's proof fails to undermine the vague-identity thesis. In contrast, the strengthened argument presented above seems decisive against this thesis. This ought to be a problematic result on either the three or four dimensional conceptions of persistence.

In addition, I argued that even if the vague-identity thesis were true, it would not support the vague-objects thesis in the way that Evans envisaged; and that the latter thesis, if not unintelligible, should receive the verdict: not proven.

References

Dummett, M. A. E. (1980). Wang's paradox. In *Truth and other enigmas*. Cambridge: Harvard University Press.

Dummett, M. A. E. (1981). *The interpretation of Frege's philosophy*. London: Duckworth.

Evans, G. (1978). Can there be vague objects? *Analysis, 38*(4), 208.

Garrett, B. (1988). Vagueness and identity. *Analysis, 48*(3), 130–134.

Lewis, D. (1988). Vague identity: Evans misunderstood. *Analysis, 48*(3), 128–130.

Sainsbury, R. M. (1989). What is a vague object? *Analysis, 49*(3), 99–103.

Salmon, N. (1981). *Reference and essence*. New Jersey: Princeton University Press.

Thomason, R. (1982). Identity and vagueness. *Philosophical Studies, 42*(3), 329–332.

Tye, M. (1990). Vague objects. *Mind, 99*(396), 535–557.

Wiggins, D. (1980). *Sameness and substance*. Cambridge: Harvard University Press.

Wiggins, D. (1986). On singling out an object determinately. In P. Pettit & J. H. McDowell (Eds.), *Subject, thought and context*. Oxford: Oxford University Press.

Chapter 13
More on Rigidity and Scope

Abstract In "Rigidity and Scope" M. J. More attempts to defend the thesis that primacy of scope does not confer rigidity; i.e., the thesis that in *de re* statements of the form "a is necessarily the F" the designator in place of 'a' may take wide scope with respect to the modal operator and yet function non-rigidly. As More points out, the issue is of considerable importance – for if primacy of scope did confer rigidity, then proper names could be both rigid designators and disguised definite descriptions. More's defence of his thesis rests crucially upon the alleged contingency of certain *de re* truths. However, it is my contention that (i) More's arguments establish neither the contingency nor the truth of such statements; and (ii) even if there were compelling arguments for the existence of such contingent *de re* truths, this would entail the thesis that primacy of scope does not confer rigidity only at the cost of rendering the modal operator embedded in such statements totally impotent.

13.1 More's Thesis

More's basic argument for his thesis takes the form of a *Modus Tollens* inference. Consider the following *de re* statement:

(α) The number of planets is necessarily the positive square root of 81.

If primacy of scope did confer rigidity then (α) would be necessarily true. But, argues More, (α) is a contingent truth and therefore primacy of scope does not confer rigidity.

It is worth noting that although More's *Modus Tollens* holds for (α), it does not hold generally – there is no logical connection between rigidity and necessity. For there are many necessary truths which contain no rigid designators (e.g., "Nothing is both round and square at the same time"). And more importantly, there are numerous true statements (including identity statements) containing only rigid designators (e.g., "Tully = Cicero", "Socrates is a person"). The latter statements are contingent since there are possible worlds (precisely those in which Tully and Socrates, respectively, do not exist) in which they are not true and necessary truths

B. Garrett, *Time, Identity and the Self: Essays on Metaphysics*, Synthese Library 442, https://doi.org/10.1007/978-3-030-85517-8_13

are only those which are true in all possible worlds.[1] (What is true, though, is that all statements containing only rigid designators which designate objects that exist in all possible worlds (e.g. numbers) will be, if true, necessarily true.)

However, the major part of More's paper consists of a defence of the second premise of his *Modus Tollens* – the contingency of (α). He gives four arguments for (α)'s contingency, none of which, I claim, is compelling. I will examine each argument in turn.

13.2 More's Arguments

"First, a conjunction (α) and the possible truth

(β) There are 7 planets

entails

(γ) 7 is necessarily the positive square root of 81 which is false. Thus the conjunction of (α) and (β) is false. And, if, as is possible (β) were true, (α) would be false. So there are possible circumstances in which (α) is false" (More, 1980, 328).

Now (γ) is not just false but necessarily false and (β) is contingently false. This is quite consistent with the possible falsity of (α). However, it is equally consistent with the necessary falsity of (α). Consequently, this argument does not establish the contingency of (α) since it will go through if (α) is necessarily false.

"Second, (α) entails (δ) There are 9 planets

But (δ) is contingent; no necessary truth can entail a contingent one, and so (α) is not necessary."

Indeed a necessary truth cannot entail a contingent one, but a necessary falsehood can (e.g., P and $\sim P$ entails P, where P is a contingent truth). This second argument in no way therefore entails the contingency of (α).

"Third, (β) does not entail (α), since if they were conjointly true, then (γ) would be true, which is absurd.

Therefore, (β) does not entail (α), and since a necessary truth is entailed by any proposition, (α) is not necessary."

I think we can agree with More that (β) does not entail (α). But all this shows is that (α) is not a necessary truth and this is far from establishing the contingency of (α)

[1] There is a weaker definition of necessary truth according to which a necessary truth is one which is either true in all possible worlds or true in some worlds but false in none. According to this definition, the above statements about Tully and Socrates (given certain essentialist principles) would count as necessary truths.

"Fourth, (γ) is impossible; thus if the conjunction of (α) and (β) entails (γ), as I contend it does, a conjunction of (α) and (β) is impossible. A conjunction of a necessary truth and a possible truth is itself possible; (β) is possible; therefore (α) is not necessary."

But again this final argument does not establish that (α) is not necessary – it merely establishes that (α) is not a necessary truth. The impossibility of conjoining (α) and (β) counts just as much for the necessary falsity of (α) as for its contingency.

Of course, More may not be much perturbed by these counter-arguments. For he assumes to begin with that (α) is true then argues that it is not a necessary truth and concludes that it is a contingent truth. But my point is simply that one could very well share Quine's view of (α)-type statements (namely, that they are false) (Quine, 1976, 20) and More's actual arguments are quite consistent with the assumption that (α) is necessarily false (and, indeed, with the assumption that (α) is contingently false). More then has not proved his case. At best, his four arguments show that (α) is not a necessary truth, but this is far from establishing either its contingency or its truth.

13.3 Why More's Arguments Fail

I now want to argue that even if persuasive arguments can be given for both the contingency and the truth of (α), then far from supporting the thesis that primacy of scope does not confer rigidity, it renders that thesis totally empty. Let us therefore assume that (α) is indeed a contingent *de re* truth. Consider now the contingently true non-modal counterpart of (α):

(ϵ) The number of planets is the positive square root of 81.

Now if by hypothesis (α) and (ϵ) have the same modal value (i.e., both are contingent) and the same truth value (i.e., both are true), then what is the effect of the modal operator embedded within (α)? It would seem that the only available explanation can be that the operator effects a non-identity between the set of possible worlds in which (α) is true and the set of possible worlds in which (ϵ) is true. However, it can easily be shown that the modal operator induces no such divergence in truth-conditions – (α) is true in any world if and only if (ϵ) is true.

Firstly, then, does (α) entail (ϵ)? Could there be a possible world or counterfactual situation in which (α) was true and (ϵ) false? Well, (ϵ) would be false if there were 10 planets. But if there were 10 planets then (α) would entail the necessary falsehood that 10 is necessarily the positive square root of 81. So (α) would be false. Given that this argument can be generalised for any counterfactual situation concerning the number of planets it follows that it is impossible for (α) to be true and (ϵ) false. (Such an entailment is surely uncontroversial – if "*a* is necessarily the *F*" did not entail "*a* is the *F*" then the notion of *de re* necessity would become totally mysterious.)

Secondly, that (ϵ) entails (α) can be seen clearly from the following argument:

(ϵ) The number of planets is the positive square root of 81

(ζ) The positive square root of 81 is necessarily the positive square root of 81

Therefore

(α) The number of planets is necessarily the positive square root of 81.

Since the argument is valid (by virtue of the referential transparency of *de re* modal contexts) with true premises and (ζ) expresses a necessary truth, it follows that it is impossible for (ϵ) to be true and (α) false.[2]

What the identity of truth-conditions of (α) and (ϵ) reveals is that the contingency of (α) ensures that primacy of scope does not confer rigidity at the cost of effectively eliminating all the relevant scope ambiguities from (α) – the logical equivalence of (α) and (ϵ) renders the modal operator embedded within (α) devoid of logical force and therefore scopeless.

It is evident then that the victory for the contingency theorist is utterly Pyrrhic. For the thesis that primacy of scope does not confer rigidity is achieved only by rendering (α) and (ϵ) logically equivalent. But such an equivalence immediately prompts the question: What is supposed to be (modally) *de re* about contingent *de re* truths such as (α)? And unless the *de re* 'must' can be shown to play some effective role in (a) (a role which differentiates (α) from statements such as (ϵ) in which no such modal operator figures) then the answer, I suggest, is quite simply: nothing.[3]

13.4 Conclusion

My conclusions are therefore twofold: (a) More's arguments fail to establish the contingency of (α); and (b) To base the thesis that primacy of scope does not confer rigidity upon the alleged contingency of (α)-type statements is radically ill-motivated and threatens the coherence of the very position which More is trying to defend.

[2] Note that More cannot object to this substitution move since his arguments for the contingency of (α) rely upon the legitimacy of precisely such a substitution.

[3] Exactly the same question can be posed to those, e.g., Smullyan (1976), who argue for the contingency of certain *de re* truths as a way out of Quine's "paradox of modal logic" (i.e., as a way of establishing that (*de re*) modal contexts are referentially transparent and thus providing a rationale for the project of quantified modal logic).

References

More, M. J. (1980). Rigidity and scope. *Logique et Analyse, 23*(90/91), 327–330.
Quine, W. V. (1976). Reference and modality. In L. Linsky (Ed.), *Reference and modality*. Oxford: Oxford University Press.
Smullyan, A. F. (1976). Modality and description,. In L. Linsky (Ed.), *Reference and modality*. Oxford: Oxford University Press.

Chapter 14
Enduring Endurantism

Abstract In “Paradoxes of Multi-Location”, Stephen Barker and Phil Dowe present three arguments which they take to demonstrate the paradoxical nature of endurantism. I claim that the endurantist has convincing replies to each argument.

14.1 Barker and Dowe’s First Argument

Since some stage-setting is required, I quote the first argument in full (Barker and Dowe cite Beebee and Rush (2003) for this description):

> Eric is a (short-lived) cat. He persists for $100n$, for some small temporal unit n, and thus, assuming Endurantism, is multi-located throughout a 4-D space-time region R of $100n$ temporal size. Consider the 100 temporal slices $r1$, $r2$, [. . .], $r100$ of the region R, where each r has temporal length n. At each region r, there is an object, a cat: Eric at r. We refer collectively to these objects as the Ericrs. Take the fusion, or mereological sum, of the Ericrs and call this fusion F(Eric$r$). Our first paradox of multilocation (version 2) goes as follows:
>
> (a) F(Eric$r$) is the fusion of the Ericrs, which are all identical to Eric since Eric at any r is just Eric. So F(Eric$r$)) is identical to each Eric$r$. As each Eric$r$ has temporal extent n, F(Eric$r$) has temporal extent n. But (b) F(Eric$r$) has a part at each r of $R4$. So F(Eric$r$) is an object with temporal extent $100n$. Thus F(Eric$r$)’s temporal extent both is and is not greater than n. Paradox. (Barker and Dowe, 2005, 69-70)

How should an endurantist respond? The endurantist has to deny the second sentence in (a), viz., that F(Eric$r$) is identical with each Eric$r$ (i.e., with Eric). For F(Eric$r$) is a four-dimensional object and Eric is not.[1] Hence, the endurantist must either reject the first sentence in (a) or deny that it implies the second. The first sentence is true only if the occurrence there of ‘all’ is understood as ‘each’. F(Eric$r$ is the fusion of the Ericrs, each of which is Eric. But it does not follow from this that the fusion is Eric. A fusion of trees is not a tree; and a fusion of ‘Erics’ is not a cat (hence not Eric). Instead, F(Eric$r$) is a fusion of 100 distinct states of affairs involving Eric since Eric will have different properties at each of

[1] Beebee and Rush (2003) and McDaniel (2003) have a similar response.

B. Garrett, *Time, Identity and the Self: Essays on Metaphysics*, Synthese Library 442, https://doi.org/10.1007/978-3-030-85517-8_14

these 100 times. Hence, the endurantist will regard $F(\text{Eric}r)$ as a four-dimensional entity corresponding to Eric's life-history, but not identical with Eric.

Moreover, and this I take to be a new point, it can be demonstrated that $F(\text{Eric}r) \neq \text{Eric}$. Consider some sub-region of R, $R*$, of $50n$ temporal size. Call the fusion of $\text{Eric}r * s$, $F(\text{Eric}r*)$. By Barker and Dowe's (a)-style reasoning, Eric = $F(\text{Eric}r)$. If Eric = $F(\text{Eric}r)$ and Eric = $F(\text{Eric}r*)$, $F(\text{Eric}r = F(\text{Eric}r*)$. But this must be wrong since these fusions occupy different spatio-temporal regions. Hence, Eric cannot be identical to any fusion.

14.2 Barker and Dowe's Second Argument

Barker and Dowe then present an argument using plural reference rather than mereology:

- The Ericrs occupy R (they fill up R).
- Eric does not occupy R (by Endurantism – he is multi-located throughout R).
- The Ericrs are one and the same; they are Eric (by Endurantism).
- Therefore, the Ericrs occupy and don't occupy R. (Barker and Dowe, 2005, 70)

This argument has not been addressed in the literature, but it fares no better than the previous one. The endurantist will insist that the first premise is true only if understood as the claim that Eric persists through R, i.e., that he exists at each region $r1$ through $r100$ and so is multi-located throughout R. Understood thus, all three premises are consistent with each other and so the argument collapses.

14.3 Barker and Dowe's Third Argument

Barker and Dowe next offer the following argument:

> We accept that there are lives, which are 4-D entities, with beginnings, middles and ends. Call the life of Eric, L(Eric). There is a necessary connection between lives and the things that have them. So by the Humean principle that there are no necessary connections between distinct existences it must be that Eric and L(Eric) overlap. We think this means that one must accept that Eric is part of L(Eric). Now the paradox goes as follows:
>
> Divide L(Eric) into two non-overlapping temporal stage: L(Eric)1 and L(Eric)2. L(Eric)1 is located at $R1$, and nowhere else, and L(Eric)2 is located at $R2$, and nowhere else. By hypothesis, Eric is part of L(Eric). So Eric is part of L(Eric)1. But Eric is located at rs that are not in $R1$, so L(Eric)1 cannot, contrary to hypothesis, be confined to $R1$, since Eric is part of L(Eric)1. Similarly for L(Eric)2. Paradox. (Barker and Dowe, 2005, 73)

How should the endurantist respond? Barker and Dowe claim that there is a "necessary connection between lives and the things that have them" (Barker and Dowe, 2005, 73). But this claim is vague. Presumably they are not denying that Eric's life could have gone differently than it actually did. Do they just mean, what everyone accepts, that the life of Eric is necessarily the life of Eric? In addition, the Humean principle they cite is now regarded as far from obvious, in light of plausible Kripkean theses such as the necessity of origin.

However, even if we waive these worries, why should the endurantist accept that Eric is part of L(Eric)? 'L(Eric)' presumably means "the events that comprise Eric's life". The parts of L(Eric) are therefore events. Since the endurantist denies that Eric is an event, he will deny that Eric is part of L(Eric). The totality of things that happen to Eric constitute his life; hence the things that happen to Eric are parts of his life. But, the endurantist insists, Eric is not part of his life.

14.4 Conclusion

Given the foregoing, I argue that Barker and Dowe's arguments against endurantism can be resisted.

References

Barker, S., & Dowe, P. (2005). Endurance is paradoxical. *Analysis, 65*(1), 69–74.
Beebee, H., & Rush, M. (2003). Non-paradoxical multi-location. *Analysis, 63*(4), 311–17.
McDaniel, K. (2003). No paradox of multi-location. *Analysis, 63*(4), 309–311.

Chapter 15
Identity of Truth-Conditions

Abstract What follows is my solution to *Analysis* Problem no. 19, which Professor Colin Radford of the University of Kent (at Canterbury) set on June 1982.

15.1 *Analysis* Problem No. 19

On June 1982, Professor Colin Radford of the University of Kent (at Canterbury) set the *Analysis* Problem no. 19, which goes as follows. If I am looking at myself in a mirror I am directly facing, do I see myself looking at myself? If so, do I also see myself looking at myself looking at myself – and so on? (Radford, 1982)

15.2 The Solution

A natural first thought concerning the two questions is they are both to be answered in the negative since when in a mirror I am directly facing I do not, strictly speaking, see myself, rather I see a reflection of myself. And since reflections do not have intentional properties (in this case, the property of looking) no infinite regress threatens – it is blocked at the first stage.

However, this response overlooks an ambiguity in sentences of the form "I see a reflection of myself looking at *X*". If we take "looking at *X*" to be predicated of my reflection, i.e., effectively to treat such sentences as equivalent to sentences of the form "I see my reflection looking at *X*", then they do indeed make a category mistake (reflections cannot look). But if, more naturally, we take "looking at *X*" to be predicated of myself then such sentences are in perfectly good order – I see a reflection of myself and it is a reflection of myself-looking-at-*X*. And since the above questions can be reformulated in accordance with the latter interpretation (i.e. "If I am looking at a reflection of myself, do I see a reflection of myself-looking-at-a-reflection-of-myself? If so [...] ?"), nothing is here gained by appeal to reflections.

An affirmative answer to the first question requires considerable qualification. To start with, it is quite possible for a person to look at *X* and yet not see *X* ('look'

B. Garrett, *Time, Identity and the Self: Essays on Metaphysics*, Synthese Library 442, https://doi.org/10.1007/978-3-030-85517-8_15

unlike 'see' is not an achievement word, in Ryle's sense). Moreover, even if we are guaranteed such a transition in this case it is still possible for a person to see X whilst X is ϕ-ing and yet not see X ϕ-ing, e.g. I might see John whilst John is looking at me, but not see John looking at me. However, despite the invalidity of the inferences from "I look at X" to "I see X" and from "I see X" and "X is ϕ-ing" to "I see X ϕ-ing", it is nonetheless invariably the case that when I look at myself directly in a mirror, I do see myself and I see myself looking at myself, just as it is invariably the case that when I look at myself eating an apple, I see myself and I see myself eating an apple. In both cases the conclusions are equally legitimate and unambiguous (in the sense in which sentences such as "I saw a man born in Jericho" are not unambiguous) though in the latter case there is no parallel to the second question, no threat of a regress.

Given this, is it true that if I see myself looking at myself then I also see myself looking at myself looking at myself and so on? And if it is true, is the regress which ensues virtuous or vicious? I think it is clear that there is a regress here but that it is entirely virtuous. For the truth-value of every statement in the regress is determined simultaneously and the truth-conditions of each statement in the regressive series are identical. In order to determine the truth of any statement in the series, one does not have first to determine the truth of the following statement in the series and thus the regress is not vicious.

To admit the existence of such a harmless regress is not (as perhaps the occurrence of 'also' in the second question might suggest) to admit the possibility of an infinity of distinct perceptions when I look at myself in mirror. No such absurdities follow. The construction of such a regress, though syntactically and semantically legitimate, is of no philosophical importance.

Reference

Radford, C. (1982). Analysis problem no. 19. *Analysis, 42*(3), 115.

Part III
The Self

Chapter 16
Some Notes on Animalism

Abstract In this discussion I outline Eric Olson's arguments for Animalism – the view that we are human animals. I provide reasons why these arguments might be flawed.

16.1 Animalism

Animalism is the doctrine in the theory of persons according to which each of us is (numerically identical with) an animal, viz., the animal we share our matter with. So if the animal I share my matter with is labelled '*A*', then Animalism implies that I am *A* (and so, *mutatis mutandi*, for everyone else).

Animalism has the initial attraction of being, or seeming to be, a piece of common-sense. Is not man simply flesh and blood? Are we not obviously biological creatures, part of the animal kingdom? Nonetheless, Animalism flies in the face of much traditional philosophical doctrine. Clearly, it is at odds with Cartesian Dualism and with religions which emphasise the survival of the soul after bodily death. But there is also a more recent philosophical tradition, inspired by Locke, which eschews Cartesian Dualism, ye still refuses to identify persons with animals. Clearly, I and the human animal *A* stand to each other in a very intimate relation (sharing the same space as, sharing the same matter as, constitution, or whatever), but, according to the Lockean tradition, this relation falls short of strict numerical identity.

In this discussion, I shall outline the powerful theoretical motivation in support of Animalism, recently outlined convincingly by Eric Olson (1997) in his book, *The Human Animal*. However, I shall give reasons why Animalism cannot be true, drawing on considerations advanced by the Lockean tradition. I shall then describe a model from elsewhere in metaphysics (the theory of artefacts and artworks) in terms of which we can understand how Animalism might be false and its motivation flawed.

Since I am in no position to refute Olson's main point (his theoretical case for Animalism), my conclusion is that, until more is said, we have a paradox on our hands: powerful theoretical considerations support the view that we are identical to animals, yet equally powerful intuitive considerations support the opposite view.

B. Garrett, *Time, Identity and the Self: Essays on Metaphysics*, Synthese Library 442, https://doi.org/10.1007/978-3-030-85517-8_16

16.2 Why Animalism Is True

The central case for Animalism (outlined clearly by Olson in Chapter Five of his book) proceeds by *reductio*: if we suppose Animalism to be false, we end up with an absurdity; so Animalism is true.

Thus suppose Animalism is false: suppose, in particular, that I and *A* are numerically distinct. I am a person. But is *A*, the animal composed of my biological matter, body organs, brain, etc., also a person? Most philosophers in the Lockean tradition have assumed the answer to this question is 'no'. Such philosophers assumed that, strictly speaking, the person is the bearer of mental states (sensations, emotions, beliefs, desires, etc.), but that, strictly speaking, the animal is the bearer of no mental states, and hence is not a person.[1]

However, Olson makes vivid how uncomfortable and just plain wrong that answer is. The animal *A* has my brain, body, abilities, etc. Why deny the full panoply of mental life to *A*? Certainly, such a denial will seem irrational to anyone who believes in the supervenience of the mental on the physical (since I and *A* would be physically identical, yet mentally utterly dissimilar). But, even without relying on supervenience, the denial of mentality to *A* flies in the face of the well-confirmed scientific belief that mentality results from, and depends on, brain structure.

In other words, it seems entirely *ad hoc* to deny mentality to *A*. So we should concede that *A* has just the mental life that I have, and so is a self-conscious subject of experience. But this discussion proceeded on the assumption that I and *A* are distinct. In which case, if both I and *A* are subjects, there are two subjects in my shoes, not one! More generally, the population of the world is twice what we thought it was. But this is absurd.[2] What led to this absurdity? The assumption that I and *A* are numerically distinct. So this assumption must be rejected. But this is just another way of saying that Animalism is true.

It might be thought that there is a way of living with the consequence that I and *A* both have mental states. Could it not be that I and *A* share the same mental states, just as a 1 kilogram bronze statue and the bronze lump which constitutes it share the same matter? In the latter case (see below), the statue and the lump are

[1] Why have Lockeans thought this? Maybe they thought that since a human animal is not essentially a mental being (e.g., it can remain alive even when all mentality has been irretrievably extirpated), so it is not a bearer of mental states at all. But is this not a fallacy? No. Or, rather, not if mental beings are essentially mental. For then it's true that if an animal is not essentially mental, it is not mental at all. *A* is not a mental being since *A* lacks a property (an essential property) had by any mental being. In which case, we are not forced to the conclusion that *A* is identical with a person. This Lockean position has the consequence that, *contra* the point made in the following two paragraphs in the text, *A* has all my physical properties, yet none of my mental properties. To say the least, this commits the Lockean to a view uncongenial to most contemporary philosophers of mind.

[2] In correspondence, Olson has suggested that there is an additional epistemological absurdity: if I'm not *A*, how can I know that I'm not *A*? However, even if there is an epistemological worry here, the metaphysical consequence is absurd enough.

numerically distinct; but we avoid the conclusion that the statue and lump together weigh 2 kilograms by appealing to the fact that they share the same matter.

Similarly, can we not avoid the double-counting consequence by claiming that I and *A* share the same mental states? When I think "Canberra is in Australia" so does *A*: but there are not two thoughts here, just one shared thought. The problem, however, comes with indexical and demonstrative thoughts. Suppose I think "this thinker lives in Canberra". Does *A* think this (token) thought too? No. Thoughts are individuated by truth-conditions, and thoughts about different subjects have different truth-conditions. If I and *A* are distinct subjects/thinkers, we cannot share such a thought. In which case, two demonstrative thoughts are expressed, and this seems one too many. So the double-counting worry remains.

16.3 Why Animalism Can't be True

Nonetheless, Animalism cannot be true. There is a host of thought-experiments, the most plausible description of which imply the falsity of Animalism. I will outline these thought-experiments now.

First, we have brain-transplant cases. Suppose that my brain, or cerebrum, is transplanted into the (brainless) skull of my now dead twin brother. My old (and cancerous) body is allowed to die. The resulting person is fully psychologically continuous with me, and has the kind of body that can allow for the exercise of all my abilities and dispositions. The most plausible description of this case is that I am the resulting person; I survive with my brain and my brother's body. But no human animal has survived, only part of an animal. The human animal (*A*) is allowed to die. But if I can survive a scenario which *A* cannot, then I cannot be identical with *A*. (Of course, Olson wants to resist this description of the case, but that is implausible. That is, it's implausible to think that I die with *A*, and that a new person comes to occupy my twin brother's body.)

Second, we can imagine a slightly different scenario. Suppose that my cerebrum is removed from my skull and the rest of my body is destroyed. My cerebrum is kept alive by a machine, and I am conscious and self-conscious throughout. If a self-conscious being has survived, then a person has survived. I have survived, albeit in a vastly denuded condition. But no animal has survived; the animal was destroyed. Again we seem to have a scenario in which I survive, yet *A* does not. So I cannot be *A*.

Third, we can imagine that technology has reached such an advanced stage that all animal organs, including the brain, can be replaced with bionic organs which serve the very same functions as the animal originals, including psychological functioning.[3] (This at least seems metaphysically or logically possible, which is all that matters here.) So we could imagine that I go through a process of total bionic replacement. Every part of me is (gradually) replaced with a bionic part. At the end of the process, no animal part, hence, no animal, remains. Provided the replacement process in no way interferes with my psychology, abilities and appearance, it is very plausible to say that I survive. Yet, given the plausible essentialist thesis that if x is an animal, then x is essentially and (hence) at all times an animal, no animal has survived; so, again, I cannot be identical with A.

Fourth, we can imagine an even more compelling thought-experiment along similar lines: *Mutation*. I am a space man on the first mission to Mars. The mission is successful; we spend six months on Mars then return. There are no (unaccountable) changes in my abilities, appearance, or psychology. I go to a routine check up, and the doctors find something quite extraordinary. Apart from my appearance, there is nothing human, or animal, about me at all. My biological matter has mutated into that of a non-animal, silicon-based life-form. Given the essentialist thesis of the previous paragraph, it follows that the animal that left for Mars (A) no longer exists. But I still exist. Hence, Animalism is false. (And notice that, unlike the previous example, this transformation is entirely natural and law-governed: mutating from a carbon-based life-form to a silicon-based one in that way is what happens to people like us who go to Mars.)

What our reactions to these thought-experiments suggest is that, at least in these and similar cases, a continuing line of (non-branching) psychological continuity is sufficient for personal identity; and this sufficient condition, together with other plausible assumptions, implies the falsity of Animalism. (And note that one can endorse this sufficient condition while agreeing with Olson that psychological continuity is not everywhere necessary for personal identity, since, e.g., "I once existed as a fetus".)

16.4 A Familiar Analogy

There is a familiar example which, by analogy, tells against Animalism. This is the example of the statue and the lump. Consider a bronze statue. Call the statue 'Statue' and the bronze lump of which it is composed 'Bronze'. It seems uncontroversial that Statue and Bronze are distinct, even though made of the very same matter. They are distinct because they have different properties. For example, Bronze presumably existed prior to Statue; and nothing can exist prior to itself. So, in general, coinciding does not imply identity.[4]

---

[3] This is not to assume that mental processes are computational. John Searle (1980), who famously denied this assumption, took pains to point out that he wasn't thereby denying the possibility of a thinking machine.

[4] The case of the Ship of Theseus provides another motivation for the thesis that an artefact and its constituting matter are numerically distinct, see my discussion in (Garrett, 1998, 65–67).

Of course, conceding that Statue and Bronze are distinct does not force us to conclude that I and *A* are distinct, for there may be relevant differences between the examples. But there is the following complication. It seems that, just as in the case for Animalism, we can pose the following question in the statue/lump case: when I'm admiring Statue, am I not admiring two beautiful objects? The statue is beautiful; the lump is arranged in the very same way as the statue, so surely the lump is beautiful too; the statue is not the lump; so there are two beautiful things before me.

I'm not sure how to respond to this line of reasoning. But note that we do not respond by saying: "The consequence is absurd – I'm obviously not looking at two beautiful things; so the statue and the lump must be identical after all." We don't respond like that because we know, for the reason described above, that the statue and the lump are distinct. That belief we will not give up. So, if the "over-crowding problem" is not a decisive reason for identifying State and Bronze, why do Animalists think that it is a decisive reason for identifying myself with *A*?[5]

16.5 Conclusion

My conclusion is hardly satisfactory. There are powerful considerations in favour of Animalism, yet powerful considerations against. The analogy with the statue example may tip the scales against Animalism. But more needs to be said.

References

Garrett, B. (1998). *Personal identity and self-consciousness*. London: Routledge.
Olson, E. T. (1997). *The human animal*. Oxford: Oxford University Press.
Searle, J. R. (1980). Minds, brains, and programs. *Brain and Behavorial Sciences, 3*(3), 417–457.

[5] The expedient – suggested in correspondence with Olson – of denying the existence of artefacts such as statues seems to me a desperate response to the just mooted argument from analogy. There is another strategy worth considering here. It's not obviously absurd to think that the statue is not a real entity in its own right: it is rather the form or shape of the lump. Could one resolve the paradox about persons by claiming that persons are similarly not substances? However, the non-substantiality claim about the statue is plausible only because the statue could not exist without the lump existing: it depends on the lump. But the analogous claim in the case of persons would, of course, be disputed by the Lockean who thinks that I can exist even if *A* does not.

Chapter 17
Persons and Human Beings

Abstract What is it to be a person? What is the relation between a person and the animal (human being) he shares his matter with? Throughout I shall assume a non-Cartesian conception of persons: persons are not immaterial, non-spatial substances, and have no immaterial parts. Hence, I take it as axiomatic that each person shares his matter with a human being. But are we entitled to assert, in addition, that the relation between a person and the animal he shares his matter with is that of strict numerical identity? In order to answer this question, it is important to be clear about what it is to be a person. I shall therefore begin by attempting to clarify some fundamental aspects of our concept of a person.

17.1 The Lockean Conception of Person

It was Locke who proposed the following, purely functional, definition of personhood: "a person is . . . a thinking intelligent being, that has reason and reflection, and can consider itself as itself, the same thinking thing, in different times and places" (Locke, 1975, II, xxvii, 2).[1]

This definition is purely functional in that it imposes no *a priori* constraints on the sort of thing (animal, spirit, machine) that can qualify as a person. As such, Locke does appear to capture one significant aspect of our ordinary concept of a person. On this view, persons are distinguished from other sorts of beings in virtue of their possession of a powerful and sophisticated psychology. A person is rational (that is, her behaviour admits of rationalisation in terms of the belief/desire schema) and self-conscious (in particular, a person has a conception of herself as a being in time, with a past and a future, and is able to engage in first-person

[1] It is important to note that we are not forced to answer this question affirmatively: matter-sharing does not imply identity. Many philosophers are willing to accept, e.g., that a gold statue is numerically distinct from the lump of gold that spatially coincides with it (e.g., because the statue and the lump have different modal and temporal properties). Yet the statue and the lump of gold are made of the very same matter.

B. Garrett, *Time, Identity and the Self: Essays on Metaphysics*, Synthese Library 442, https://doi.org/10.1007/978-3-030-85517-8_17

counterfactual speculations). It may be that possession of this latter characteristic implies possession of language, but that is a further issue.

Locke's definition is not absolute or all-or-nothing. It can be vague whether a creature is a person, since it can be vague whether a creature instantiates a rational, self-conscious psychology (think of a two-year-old infant). Further, and more radically, given that there are degrees of self-consciousness, a creature can be a person to some degree or other (thus, for example, a neonate gradually becomes a person). But these are not consequences that anyone who finds value in Locke's proposal ought to find disturbing.

One problem with Locke's definition is that, as it stands, it is too exclusive. Consider people who are asleep, temporarily unconscious, or in (reversible) comas. In any of these states, an unconscious person exists. But this ought to be an impossibility on Locke's definition; in which case, Locke's definition cannot be correct. However, it is clear what the Lockean response to this objection should be: what is necessary for personhood is not self-consciousness, but the capacity for self-consciousness.

But under what conditions does a being have this capacity? In particular, what is the connection between the possession of such a capacity and the state of available medical technology? Suppose we say: "There is no connection. A being's capacity for self-consciousness is not a function of the state of medical technology; whether a creature is a person cannot depend upon such contingency". If this is our response, the following modified definition suggests itself: an individual has the capacity for self-consciousness if and only if, irrespective of the state of medical technology, his brain and central nervous system (CNS) could support self-conscious thought.

But what are the truth-conditions of this modal claim? Is it true just in case it is nomologically possible for an individual's brain and CNS to support a self-conscious mental life? But now there are too many persons. The existence of a fresh corpse would imply the existence of a person, since it is presumably nomologically possible (compatible with the laws of nature) that the matter constituting the brain and CNS of the corpse be appropriately rearranged so as to sustain the distinctive psychology of the recently deceased. But surely that person no longer exists. I shall leave it an open question whether the Lockean can elaborate a sense of 'could' in the biconditional of the previous paragraph which falls short of the 'could' of nomological or physical possibility, yet does not make the existence of a person a function merely of the state of available medical technology.

17.2 The Animal Attribute Conception of Persons

David Wiggins proposed the following definition of personhood:

> x is a person if and only if x is an animal falling under the extension of a kind whose typical members perceive, feel, remember, imagine, desire, make projects ... have, and conceive of themselves as having, a past accessible in experience-memory and a future accessible in intention..., etc. (Wiggins, 1980, 171)

This definition differs from Locke's in three significant ways. First, Wiggins's definition is not purely functional. Wiggins is an Animal Attribute Theorist (AAT): he believes that all persons must be animals (of some kind or other, not necessarily human). Hence, the concept of a person is more 'akin to' natural kind concepts such as *tiger*, than to an artefact concept such as *house* (Wiggins, 1980, ch. 6, 7, and 8). Further, although Wiggins's definition does not entail the Animal Identity Thesis (AIT) that, for any person X, there is an animal Y, such that $X = Y$, this thesis is a natural corollary of AAT, and is endorsed by Wiggins (1980, 161; 176–8).

Second, and following from the above, whereas Locke can legitimately claim to have defined personhood *a priori*, Wiggins cannot. The claim that all persons must be animals, if true, is an *a posteriori* truth. Nothing in our concept of a person yields the constraint that all persons must be animals (for example, it does not seem to be an *a priori* truth that I am a human being.)

Third, Wiggins's definition is relational or extrinsic in character: whether a particular animal is a person depends upon the psychology of typical members of its kind (that is, upon the psychology of other individuals). In one way, this feature makes Wiggins's definition less exclusive than Locke's: it allows fetuses and the irreversible comatose to fall under the extension of *person*, in virtue of the fact that typical (adult) human beings are rational and self-conscious. But in another way it makes Wiggins's definition more exclusive, since it would exclude an intelligent, self-conscious creature from the extension of person, if typical members of its kind happen not to be rational and self-conscious.

Both modifications of Locke's definitions are, I think, unwarranted. With respect to the first, many people actually believe in the existence of non-animal persons (God, Satan, the angels, ghosts), and most people have little difficulty in acknowledging the possibility of robot persons. Indeed, can I not coherently imagine, as the result of a consciousness-preserving, bionic replacement process, that I might gradually cease to be an animal, yet continue to exist as a robot? Such beliefs and imaginings do not appear to involve any conceptual mistakes.

Clearly, therefore, Wiggins must rest the argument for AAT upon the premise that animality is a necessary *a posteriori* constraint upon self-consciousness (a constraint which cannot simply 'read-off' the concept of a person). But in that case, Wiggins's AAT rests upon a controversial thesis in the philosophy of mind, for which he gives no argument. In sum, we have been given no reason to believe that there is any constraint, *a priori* or *a posteriori*, to the effect that all persons must be animals.

The second modification of Locke's criterion, the inclusion of a relationality component, is also open to objection. Its effect is to make Wiggins's definition too inclusive and too exclusive. It is too exclusive since, as Paul Snowdon has observed, the resulting definition would – unfairly, it seems – deny the status of personhood to an intelligent and self-conscious orangutan (the unfortunate result, perhaps, of an experiment in genetic engineering), solely on the grounds that typical orangutans are not rational and self-conscious[2] (Snowdon, 1990). Wiggins's definition thus

[2] This objection to Wiggins goes through only if we assume that the resulting creature in Snowdon's example is an orangutan. If, instead, we judge that the effect of the experiment is to

explicitly violates the plausible constraint that whether a creature qualifies as a person is a non-relational and intrinsic matter.

Conversely, the relationality component is too liberal since it would count fetuses as persons on the grounds that typical humans perceive, feel, remember, and so on. (We are to assume that fetuses are human beings.) But to start with, many people would not agree that fetuses ought to be classified as persons. Further, if fetuses are to be counted as persons, it surely cannot be because typical (adult) humans enjoy a rational, self-conscious mental life.[3] To repeat, our intuition is that if a creature is a person, this is because and only because of the character of the mental life of that very creature.

I conclude that Wiggins has given us no good reason to modify Locke's definition of personhood. Even so, it is still worth examining the consequences of these opposing definitions.

17.3 Evaluating the Two Conceptions of Persons

Consider the following thought-experiment (which I trust no one will regard as, in any deep sense, impossible or incoherent). Imagine that person, *A*, exists at time t_1, and later suffers a 'brain-zap' at time t_2; that is, at t_2, *A*'s psychological states are wiped out, completely and irretrievably (much as one might erase a movie from a videocassette). The animal (human being) – call it '*B*' – still exists at t_2, however, and is kept alive by artificial means. *B* is subsequently retrained and, a number of years later, at t_3, a person *C* (psychologically quite unlike *A*) comes to occupy the *A*-body. (It is assumed that *B* exists throughout, since it is plausible to suppose that the continued existence of a human being is tied to the continued existence of its living body, and does not require any psychological continuity.)

How should this case be described? Given his adherence to AAT and AIT, Wiggins would say that *A*, *B* and *C* are identical. The same person (= same animal) persists throughout, albeit with radically different psychological profiles at different times. (The relationality component allows Wiggins to count *B* as a person throughout.) In contrast, a Lockean would say that *A* ceases to exist on being zapped; that no person occupies the *A*-body immediately after zapping; and that at t_3, a person (*C*) exists, and *C* is not identical with *A*.[4]

---

create a new one-member species or kind, the claim that this creature is a person will be consistent with Wiggins's definition.

[3] It is often thought that a fetus is to be counted as a person because it has the potential to be a person (i.e., in the normal course of development, it will become a person). I think this is a bad reason; but even if it were a good reason, the status of the fetus would still not depend on how things are with other people.

[4] It is assumed that, at t_2, *B* does not have the capacity for self-consciousness (otherwise *B* would then count as a person, by Locke's definition). This assumption may seem false in light of *B*'s subsequent retraining. However, this difficulty can easily be side-stepped. Imagine instead that *B*

Which account is correct? Wiggins has offered the following argument against the Lockean description of this case (Wiggins, 1980, 176–177). The Lockean must say that *A* is the same animal as *C*, but not the same person. But then the Lockean, and anyone else who believes that psychological continuity is necessary for personal identity over time, is committed to the relativity of identity.

This is a false charge. Relative identity arises if it is claimed that *X* and *Y* are numerically identical qua *F*s, but numerically distinct qua *G*s. Such a claim verges on incoherence. Can we have any consistent conception of what *X* is if it fails under sortal concepts that yield mutually incompatible criteria of identity over time?

The Lockean, however, should not be interpreted as making a claim of relative identity. The Lockean will deny that "*A* is the same animal as *C*" is an expression of numerical identity. Rather, it is analogous to "Alice's car is the same colour as Whoopi's car", where this sentence is not one of numerical identity, since neither Alice's nor Whoopi's car is identical with a colour. ("*A* is the same *F* as *B*" is a true statement of identity only if *A* is identical to an *F* and *B* is identical to an *F*.)

The Lockean must claim that "*A* is the same animal *C*" does not mean that *A* and *C* are numerically identical, but rather that *A* and *C* share their matter with the very same animal (namely, *B*). Similarly, someone who asserts "the boat (at t_1) is the same as the cabin (at t_2)" should not be interpreted as making a (false) statement of numerical identity, but as claiming (truly) that the boat and the cabin are, at different times, composed of the very same planks. An analogous move is available to the Lockeans; hence, the Lockean is not committed to the relativity of identity.

Hidden dangers, however, lurk for the Lockean (dangers recently exposed by Snowdon (1990) and Carter (1989)). If we say that person *A* ceases to exist at t_2, but the animal with whom *A* shared his matter (*B*) continues to exist, then *A* and *B* must be numerically distinct entities. If two entities are distinct, they must be distinct at all times (by necessity of distinctness). Consequently, two entities (*A* and *B*) occupy the *A*-body at t_1. But, at that time, person *A* and animal *B* both appear to qualify as self-conscious subjects of experience, by Locke's definition; in which case, two persons (with a unified mental life) occupy the same body at the same time. And what is true of *A* and *B*, prior to zapping, is true of all of us now. Is this consequence not plain absurd? (Call this the Two-Person Objection.)

Further, it follows on the Lockean view that *B* is a person at t_1, but not at t_2; consequently, *person* is not a substance sortal, in Wiggins's terminology.[5] Person *B* can cease to be a person (at t_2), yet not cease to be. But this is surely unacceptable: *person* is a substance sortal, not a phase sortal.

---

is rendered irreversibly comatose by the brain-zap, loses all capacity for self-consciousness, and dies soon after. Immediately after this brain-zap, the animal (*B*) continues to exist, even though no potentially self-conscious being (i.e., person) then occupies *B*'s body.

[5] For an account of the distinction between phase and substance sortals, see (Wiggins, 1980, 24–27; 63–66).

Before returning to the Two-Person Objection, let me first try to defend the Lockean against the charge of the previous paragraph. First the phase/substance sortal distinction is not unproblematic, and Wiggins's two characterisations of substance sortalhood are inadequate as they stand.[6] For example, Wiggins's criteria ("*F* is a substance sortal if *F* present-tensedly applies to an individual *x* at every moment throughout *x*'s existence" and "*F* is a substance sortal if *x is no longer F* implies *x is no longer*") imply that, for example, the concept *person born in Edinburgh* counts as a substance sortal, thus severing the connection between the notion of a substance sortal and the notion of a fundamental sort of thing. If it is insisted that only those sortal concepts that do not 'restrict' other sortals count as substance concepts, we run the risk of misclassifying certain concepts (such as *poodle*), which should be regarded as substance sortals.

Second, inasmuch as the phase/substance distinction does correspond to an intuitive division within our concepts, some of the first-person judgements we make suggest that *person* is not a substance sortal. For example, contemplating the possibility of zapping, I might say "I hope *I* never end up like that"; similarly, if asked when I was born, I will respond in the familiar way by giving my date of birth. But, if rationality and self-consciousness are necessary for personhood, neither a zapped individual nor a neonate qualifies as a person. Such first-person judgements, if their surface grammar is not misleading, imply that *person* is a phase sortal. Consequently, it need be no objection to the Lockean view that it classifies *person* as a phase sortal.[7]

To return to the Two-Objection to the Lockean view: there are at least four responses to this objection.

1. We could deny that *B* is ever (identical with) a self-conscious subject of experience. Rather, *B* is a subject only in the sense that she shares her matter with a subject, namely, *A* (prior to t_2) and *C* (after t_3).

This is a possible response, but it is apt to seem *ad hoc*, and it contradicts the plausible thought that *B* herself – at t_1 and t_3 – is a subject of self-conscious mental states in her own right, and not merely derivatively. After all, *B* (at t_1) is the possessor of a normally functioning human brain and CNS; so why deny that *B* is (identical with) a subject of the mental life that this biological system supports?[8]

[6] For a slightly more on this, see (Garrett, 1985).

[7] However, if *person* is considered a phase sortal, other problems remain. If *person* is a phase sortal, then I am not essentially a person. But neither am I essentially an animal if, e.g., preservation of personal identity through total bionic replacement is a possibility. But then *what* am I essentially?

[8] This sentence may rest on a confusion. Could one not argue, on analogous grounds, that the lump of gold is (identical to) a statue? Hence, there could be a Two-Statue Objection to the non-identity thesis.

Perhaps the mistake is to think that a judgement about identity can be made purely synchronically. This is not so: an object can be identical to a statue only if any of its possible futures is a possible future for a statue. And this is not true of a lump of gold. Response 1 may, after all, be tenable.

2. We could opt for Wiggins's solution and hold that $A = B$, that is, that *person* and *animal* yield a unitary criterion of identity and persistence, and that person A and animal B are one and the same entity.

However, this is simply not a plausible description of the brain-zap example. Its implausibility derives, in part, from the implausibility of Wiggins's definition of personhood. In addition, if we accept plausible descriptions of more fantastic thought-experiments such as brain-transplantation and teletransportation, then a person can persist, yet any animal with which he might plausibly be identified has either ceased to exist or is clearly not identical with the original person.[9]

3. A more subtle response is to argue that the consequence that two persons occupy a single body at the same time is absurd only if we assume a three-dimensional view of ordinary continuants. If we accept a four-dimensional metaphysics, according to which continuants have temporal as well as spatial parts, the absurdity disappears.

On a three-dimensional view, persons are "wholly present" at all times at which they exist (much as a universal is said to be "wholly present" in each instantiations). On this view, persons have only spatial parts (no temporal parts), and so the exact spatial coincidence of persons may seem an absurdity.

If instead we regard persons as four-dimensional objects, with temporal as well as spatial parts, the exact spatial coincidence of two persons ought to be conceptually unremarkable. All such coincidence amounts to is the fact that two persons may have temporal parts in common (as A and B do, prior to t_1). But this is not more absurd than the fact that two people (for example, Siamese twins) may have spatial parts in common. Hence, we appear to have a satisfying response to the Two-Person Objection, which neither sacrifices Locke's definition of personhood nor denies that B-before-t_1 is a person.[10]

---

[9] Suppose that X's body is riddled with cancer, and that he is offered the chance of having his brain transplanted into a very similar, but non-cancerous, body. Furthermore, X will be conscious throughout the (pain-free) operation. Suppose X accepts the surgeon's offer, and that the operation is a success. Call the resulting person'Y'. Since X and Y are psychologically fully connected (e.g., Y believes that he is X and is psychologically just like X), it is overwhelmingly plausible to judge that $X = Y$. Yet, it is plausible to believe, the animal that X shared his matter with is not identical with the animal that $Y (= X)$ now shares his matter with. It follows that a person and the animal he shares his matter with cannot be identical. More controversially, in *Star Trek*-style teletransportation, many believe that the person who enters the departure chamber is identical with the person who materialises on the planet's surface. But in the absence of any continuity of matter, the effect of teletransportation is to destroy one animal and create another (out of new matter). If so, a person cannot be identical to the animal with whom he shares his matter.

[10] There are independently good reasons to accept the four-dimensional view. For example, such a metaphysics avoids the apparent incompatibility between Leibniz's Law and the possibility of change that besets the traditional version of the three-dimensional view. Further, in jettisoning the relation of identity over time in favour of some transtemporal 'counterpart' relation, the four-dimensionalist avoids additional difficulties that beset a believer in identity over time. For example, there are grounds for thinking that the relation of identity over time can admit of vagueness or indeterminacy; yet the supposition that the identity relation might be vague is, arguably,

However, there may still be grounds for discontent. The four-dimensionalist allows us to accept with equanimity the possibility that distinct persons (things of the same kind) might have temporal parts in common. But even on that, it ought to be absurd to suppose that two persons might share all and only the same temporal parts. This would be analogous, on the three-dimensional view, to two objects sharing all and only the spatial parts.

But the Two-Person Objection can be made to yield just such a consequence. Imagine a race of animal persons who typically come into existence fully formed (physically and psychologically), and simply vanish at death. In the normal case, there is no time at which an animal (say, X) exists, but the person sharing matter with him (say, Y) does not exist, or *vice-versa*. There is just as much reason to maintain that X and Y are distinct, as there is to maintain that A and B, in our original case, are distinct. (After all, the case of X and Y could have been abnormal.) Yet X and Y share all and only the same temporal parts. This result seems absurd. If so, the shift to a four-dimensional metaphysics will not deflect instances of the Two-Person Objection to the Lockean view.

4. We could reject the assumption, shared by both Wiggins and Locke, that *person* is a genuine sortal concept and that persons are genuine objects (whether three-dimensional or four-dimensional). If we do, the question of whether person A is identical with an object (such as animal B) will not even arise.

Though sketchy, this response has much to recommend it. It is natural to suppose that the property of personhood supervenes upon other properties, such as rationality and self-consciousness. (Hence, if two creatures are psychologically identical, and one is a person, the other must be too.) And then it becomes tempting to think of persons as being realised or instantiated in living human bodies, much as colours and shapes are instantiated in material bodies.

This view should not be confused with the view (associated with Arnold Zuboff (1990)) according to which there exists only one person who has multiple concrete instantiations (just as a single colour is multiply instantiated). The fourth response enjoins no such downward revision in our estimate of the number of persons in existence. (We should, however, be careful to distinguish the colloquial use of personal proper names to refer to concrete instantiations, and the strict use of such names to refer to universals.)

It is worth noting that response 4 – the denial of the thesis that *person* is a genuine sortal concept – is consistent with a different (non-universalist) conception of persons: the episodic conception. On this view, a person is neither a continuant (that is, material object) nor a universal, but is rather a lengthy event or episode in the history or career of an animal. Although universalist and episodic conceptions are of interest, they both need further development and I mention them only as formal possibilities.

---

demonstrably false. In contrast, there appears to be no analogous incoherence in the supposition that some transtemporal counterpart relation might be vague.

17.4 Conclusion

There are difficulties with all four of the responses canvassed above. However, my present concern is not to argue for any particular solution. My aim has merely been to highlight the following tension in our thought about the relation between persons and human beings: there are good reasons for thinking that a person and the animal he shares his matter with are numerically distinct, reasons stemming from Locke's definition of personhood and our best descriptions of certain thought-experiments (zapping, brain-transplantation, and the like); yet there are also reasons for holding a person to be identical to the animal he shares his matter with, reasons stemming from the Two-Person Objection.

References

Carter, W. R. (1989). How to change your mind. *Canadian Journal of Philosophy, 19*(1), 1–14.
Garrett, B. (1985). Noonan, best candidate theories, and the ship of theseus. *Analysis, 45*(4), 212–15.
Locke, J. (1694/1975). Of identity and diversity. In P. Nidditch (Ed.), *An essay concerning human understanding*, 2nd edn. Oxford: Oxford University Press.
Snowdon, P. (1990). Persons, animals, and ourselves. In C. Gill (Ed.), *The person and the human animal*. Oxford: Oxford University Press.
Wiggins, D. (1980). *Sameness and substance*. Cambridge: Harvard University Press.
Zuboff, A. (1990). One self: The logic of experience. *Inquiry, 33*(1), 39–69.

Chapter 18
The Story of 'I': Comments on Rudder Baker's Constitution View of Persons

Abstract In this chapter, I discuss Lynne Rudder Baker's Constitution View of persons that she presented in her book, *Persons and Bodies: A Constitution View*. I raise several concerns about her view. In particular, I show that her view faces problems accounting for 'self-conscious' thoughts and the first-person perspective.

18.1 Introduction

In her thorough and comprehensive study *Persons and Bodies*, Lynne Rudder Baker argues for what she calls the Constitution View of persons. This view comprises two strands. According to one strand, persons are constituted by, but not identical with, their bodies. According to the other strand, persons are essentially self-conscious beings with a distinctively first-person perspective on the world. The book is basically an elucidation and defence of these two strands.

I am pretty much in agreement with Rudder Baker on both strands. I agree, *contra* the Animalists, that persons are not identical with their bodies/brains, but reject Dualism; so I agree that the relation between a person and his body is constitution-without-identity. And I agree that persons are distinctively and uniquely self-conscious beings, with a first-person perspective on themselves and the world.[1]

However, I found it a bit odd that both these strands were described as comprising the Constitution View, as if the two strands formed a unified view. I would have thought that "Constitution View" is really only a name for the first, metaphysical, strand; after all, many different metaphysical conceptions of the relation between a person and his body could agree that there is an intimate link between personhood and self-consciousness. But this may just be a book-keeping point. What of more substantial issues? I have no intention of discussing every issues Rudder Baker

[1] My own views on these matters are set out in my short 1998 book, *Personal Identity and Self-Consciousness*.

B. Garrett, *Time, Identity and the Self: Essays on Metaphysics*, Synthese Library 442, https://doi.org/10.1007/978-3-030-85517-8_18

raises, and will confine my comments largely to claims made in Chaps. 3, 5 and 9 of her work.

18.2 Rudder Baker on Self-Consciousness and the First-Person

Rudder Baker begins her discussion of self-consciousness by distinguishing "two grades of first-person phenomena: weak and strong" (Rudder Baker, 2000, 61). Only subjects of strong first-person phenomena have a first-person perspective (and are self-conscious). Why draw this distinction? Because many creatures (animals, infants, etc.) have an egocentric perspective on the world, and much of their behaviour can only be explained from that perspective. As Rudder Baker puts it: if a dog could speak, he might say, "There's a bone buried there in front of me, and I want it" (Rudder Baker 2000, 61). Yet they nonetheless lack a first-person concept and are not self-conscious (not persons). Creatures who exhibit weak first-person phenomena can distinguish between first and third person standpoints, but cannot conceptualise that distinction, i.e., they cannot "conceive of oneself as oneself" (Rudder Baker, 2000, 61).

The distinction between weak and strong first-person phenomena can also be characterised linguistically: subjects of weak first-person phenomena can make first-person attributions ("I am tall"), whereas subjects of strong first-person phenomena can also attribute first-person reference to themselves ("I believe that I am tall"). The latter kind of sentence Rudder Baker, drawing on ideas of Hèctor-Neri Castañeda, calls an 'I*' sentence. Thus thinking "I think that I* am *F*" "is an indication that one is entertaining an I* thought" (Rudder Baker, 2000, 65) and hence has a first-person perspective. On this view, 'I' and 'I*' express different concepts – a toddler, for example, may possess the former but not the latter. "For a being without a concept of itself as itself*, 'I' is just a marker of perspective. Acquisition of a first-person perspective brings with it a genuine self-concept" (Rudder Baker, 2000, 69).

Now I'm not totally unsympathetic to the spirit of this, but let me make a couple of comments. First, even on her own terms, I don't see the need for Rudder Baker to invoke the '*' terminology. Nor am I sure I understand what "I think that I* am *F*" is supposed to mean if it means anything other than "I think that I am F". Why didn't Rudder Baker just put her point this way: beings with just a weak first-person perspective can think basic or non-iterated 'I'-thoughts ("I am *F*"), whereas beings with a strong first-person perspective (self-conscious beings, persons) can also think iterated 'I'-thoughts ("I think that I am *F*"). So being able to think iterated 'I'-thoughts is the hallmark of self-consciousness, and there is no need to make any Castañeda-style comment on, or supplement to, the second occurrence of 'I' in such iterations.

Perhaps I can fill out this point. When Castañeda introduced the '*' terminology he did so with respect to the pronoun 'he' (not 'I'). And for good reason. A sentence like "John believes that he is bald" is at least three-ways ambiguous. It could mean that John believes that Bill is bald (because 'he' refers to Bill in that context); or it could mean that John believes that John is bald (without realising that he is the John in question); or finally it could be that John is having a fully self-conscious thought about himself, that we would express perspicuously by saying: John believes that he himself is bald. Castañeda's '*' just marks the 'himself' spot, indicating a fully self-conscious thought. Now here the '*' terminology has a point and marks a contrast. But there simply is no such contrast to be drawn in the case of 'I': 'I' could not but be 'I*', so to speak. Could Rudder Baker re-phrase her point in terms of 'he*'? What would her concession to animals and toddlers be then: the dog believes that he* is about to be attacked? But then how would the dog contrast with us? She could say: no, all we can say is that the dog believes that he is about to be attacked. But how do we now characterise the low-grade first-person perspective allegedly had by the dog? (That is, what now makes it worth calling a first-person phenomenon?)

Second, I want to disagree with Rudder Baker's starting point here. I don't think beings who have perspectives on the world, and can modify their behaviour in response to the input from their environment, should thereby be attributed 'I'-thoughts. Rather, my view would be: there is a simple connection between having 'I'-thoughts and being self-conscious, viz., a being is self-conscious (has a first-person perspective) if and only if that being has, or is capable of having, 'I'-thoughts. Animals and toddlers don't have 'I'-thoughts (even though they have some sort of egocentric perspective on the world); hence they're not self-conscious.

Why prefer my account to Rudder Baker's? First, I would not want to attribute 'I'-thoughts to any old thing that has a perspective on the world and is capable of adjusting its behaviour to fits its goals. Doubtless certain kinds of missile have in-built maps with themselves as origin and can modify their speed and direction in sophisticated ways. But missiles don't have 'I'-thoughts. This point is hardly knock-down, but the onus is now on Rudder Baker to say how she can treat missiles differently, in this respect, from animals and toddlers. Second, it's not obvious to me why a being who can have non-iterated 'I'-thoughts is not also capable of having iterated 'I'-thoughts. If a thinker can think "I think that *p*" why can't he also think "I think that I think that *p*"? Rudder Baker would have to insist that iteration involves a massive and qualitative conceptual leap. The trouble is that it doesn't seem to at all. Third, it seems to make sense to attribute a being present-tense 'I'-thoughts ("I am *F*") only if it also makes sense to attribute to that being past and future (and maybe counterfactual) 'I'-thoughts ("I was *F*", "I will be *F*", "I might have been *F*"). But it's surely implausible to attribute the latter types of thought to animals and toddlers; so it's also implausible to attribute to them simple present-tense 'I'-thoughts.

In sum, I don't think that the difference between subjective perspective and self-consciousness is usefully understood in terms of a distinction between basic and iterated 'I'-thoughts.

18.3 Rudder Baker on the First-Person Perspective

Rudder Baker then makes some comments about some features of the first-person perspective (Rudder Baker, 2000, 69–76). I agree with her that all uses of 'I' are immune to reference-failure. However, I don't think that Wittgenstein meant to imply that "as object" uses of 'I' are not so immune (if that's what Baker thinks). The distinction between "as subject" and "as object" uses was, I think, meant to be an epistemic distinction, corresponding to features of different ways of knowing truths about oneself.[2]

Rudder Baker then defends an argument to show that the first-person perspective is relational in a certain sense (Rudder Baker, 2000, 72–76). I would have liked more discussion of premise (2) of that argument ("*x* can think of herself as herself* only if *x* has concepts that can apply to things different from *x*"). This is presumably supposed to be a necessary truth, but is it obvious that it is? The fact that developmental psychologists accept it is hardly relevant to the question of its necessity. Is it metaphysically or logically impossible for there to be a Solitary Egotistical God? (Issues to do with private language bear here too.)

Further on, Rudder Baker argues for the indispensability of the first-person perspective (Rudder Baker, 2000, 76–79). The first sort of ineliminability concerns language: "First-person reference is not eliminable from I* sentences, whether it is eliminable from simple, direct-discourse 'I' sentences or not" (Rudder Baker, 2000, 76). Leaving to one side my earlier qualms about the '*' notation, I agree with this remark. But Rudder Baker is willing to give some credence to the Russell-Geach view that first-person reference is eliminable in direct discourse. I am not (and our disagreement here doubtless leads back to Rudder Baker's willingness to attribute basic 'I'-thoughts to animals and infants). There are (at least) two ways in which the 'I' in "I am *F*" might be eliminated: 'I' might be replaced by a name or 'I' might be replaced by a quantifier, yielding "there is *F*" (as in the Russell-Geach proposal).

The first way strikes me as implausible. If ever there was a reason for believing in referential opacity, it's in the case of indexicals. I can surely think "I am *F*" but not think "Garrett is *F*" (because I'm amnesiac, say). But then, with Frege, we should think that "I am *F*" (uttered by me) and "Garrett is *F*" (uttered by anyone) do not have the same content; so the former cannot be eliminated in favour of the latter. The Russell-Geach proposal is open to a different worry. Suppose I am thinking of Paris and you are thinking of Vienna. It would not be enough to re-write these indexical truths as "there is thinking of Paris" and "there is thinking of Vienna", for this would leave out the fact that I was thinking of Paris and you were thinking of Vienna. So the quantified sentences would need to be relativised to persons. So my thought "I am thinking of Paris" would be rendered either "there is thinking of Paris (me)" or "there is thinking of Paris (Garrett)". If the first, we seem to have simply another way of writing "I am thinking of Paris" (so 'I' has not been eliminated). If the second,

[2] Again see Chapters 7 and 8 of (Garrett, 1998), and references therein to Evans's work.

the earlier opacity objection re-surfaces: "there is thinking of Paris (Garrett)" simply does not capture what I think when I think "I am thinking of Paris".

So all 'I'-sentences are ineliminable, in my view. This makes them indispensable in one sense: viz., if someone is thinking an 'I'-thought, and we want to give a complete inventory of their mind, we must include that very 'I'-thought in our inventory. But equally, if someone thinks "Tully is *F*" and "Cicero is *G*", we must cite those very thoughts in our inventory (at least for those of us, like myself, who believe in opacity quite generally). So there's nothing special about 'I'-thoughts in this regard. Given all this, I obviously agree with Rudder Baker about her second way in which first-person reference is indispensable: for psychological explanation.

18.4 A General Worry About Rudder Baker's View

I had a general worry about Rudder Baker's account of self-consciousness, but I'm not sure it's much of an objection. There is something unsatisfying about it, as if, at the end of it, we still don't know what self-consciousness really amounts to. She drew some reasonable and familiar distinctions, and laid down some plausible constraints that any account of the concept of self-consciousness must respect, but I didn't feel that the concept of self-consciousness had been mined particularly deeply. The reason this may not be an objection is that it's not clear that there is much to be said. It's not that I think that only a reductive analysis can be satisfying (I don't). Indeed, it's pretty clear that the concept of self-consciousness cannot be given any reductive analysis. That is, we cannot analyse 'self-consciousness' as "consciousness $+X$", where X can be characterised independently of the concept of self-consciousness. I take this to be one moral of Anscombe's example of the '*A*'-users in her thoughtful 1981 article "The First Person". (I assume that in the present discussion we're talking only of the concept of self-consciousness, not the property that it's a concept of. That property presumably is some kind of neural property (in us). It's only the concept that's irreducible.)

It's something to be told that self-consciousness consists in having a first-person perspective which, in turn, consists in being able to entertain 'I'-thoughts. Some light is cast. But then the question arises: what is it to have 'I'-thoughts? Merely distinguishing 'I' thoughts from other kinds of thought, thus showing that 'I' thoughts are unique and ineliminable, somehow does not provide much of an answer. Still, this is not an objection to Rudder Baker if no one can do any better. I think a bit more can be said about the concept of self-consciousness and its link with the "as subject" use of 'I' (see Chapters 7 and 8 of (Garrett, 1998)), but I agree I don't say much.

18.5 Rudder Baker on Personal Identity

In Chap. 5, Rudder Baker discusses the traditional question of personal identity over time. Her own view is that personal identity over time is not analysable in terms of anything more basic. She motivates this view by considering attempts at such analyses, and showing how they fail. She considers a number of familiar criteria of personal identity – sameness of body, sameness of living organism, sameness of brain, psychological continuity, and sameness of soul – and finds them all wanting.

I agree with many of the points she makes against these criteria. One additional point I would make is that the sameness of living organism criterion really has no advantage over the sameness of body criterion. One objection to the sameness of body criterion is that, according to it and absurdly, I am identical with my corpse. This absurdity is supposed to be avoided if we identify the person with the living organism, rather than the body. But is it? The following question now comes to the fore: is the organism when alive identical with the organism when dead? If 'yes', there is no advantage over the body criterion. If 'no' (on the grounds that there is no organism after death), then my body now is not identical with my human organism (since my body does exist after death). But that seems an absurd duplication. Either way, no advantage is gained by moving to the living organism criterion.

Rudder Baker objects to the psychological criterion that it cannot handle cases of branching in a satisfactory way. I have argued that it can (see (Garrett, 1998, ch. 4)), but will not press the point here. One point worth making is that the criteria of personal identity that Rudder Baker criticises do not exhaust the field. She looks at purely physical criteria and at purely psychological criteria, without looking at mixed criteria of the sort advocated by myself and (I think) Derek Parfit (1984). The view I endorse, for example, says that *A* at one time, t_1 is the same person as *B* at another time, t_2 if and only *A* and *B* stand to each other in the relation of non-branching psychological continuity, where the cause of the continuity is either normal or physically continuous with the normal cause. Rudder Baker will not like this way of avoiding the duplication objection, but it's at least worth considering mixed views in general.

On another point, Rudder Baker seems to think that the various criteria she criticises are intended as reductive accounts of personal identity. I don't see them that way, at least not in the first instance. In my criterion above, for example, '*A*' and '*B*' occur in the right-hand side of the analysis, and these names are introduced via the sortal *person*. There is nothing reductive about the criterion as stated. Of course, if Parfit is right, it may be possible to eliminate reference to persons in the right-hand side of the analysis, but that is a further, and controversial, claim.

Are non-reductive criteria not open to the charge of circularity? Yes, but this is not necessarily an objection. There are circles, and there are *circles*. A circular analysis can still be illuminating, provided it makes vivid the connections between the target concept and some other range of concepts. For example, it's circular and useless to be told, as an analysis of the concept *red*: x is red if and only if x is red. But it is circular and illuminating (if true) to be told: x is red if and only if x looks red to normal human observers in normal lighting conditions. This is circular because 'red' appears in the right-hand side of the analysis, but illuminating because it links *red* with other concepts (*normal human observer*, *normal lighting conditions*).[3] Anyway, Rudder Baker's objection to the criteria she criticises is not that they are circular, but subject to more straightforward faults.

Now Rudder Baker concludes from her critique of standard views that the concept of personal identity is unanalysable or primitive. One cannot "give informative sufficient conditions for sameness of person over time without presupposing sameness of person" (Rudder Baker, 2000, 119). However, and following on from her discussion of the first-person perspective, Rudder Baker does feel she can say: P_1 at t_1 is the same person as P_2 at t_2 if and only if P_1 and P_2 have the same first-person perspective, though she concedes that this condition is not terribly informative.

However, it soon becomes clear that Rudder Baker's view of personal identity is very radical indeed. (She insists on calling it the Constitution View. Fair enough, it's a free country. But nothing she says in this chapter of her book (i.e., Chap. 5) draws on the metaphysical account of the constitution relation she outlines elsewhere. So it just seems misleading to me.) She seems to think there are no *a priori* constraints on personal identity over time (i.e., on identity of first-person perspective). In a case of fission, for example, Rudder Baker thinks that I could be identical with one of the off-shoots, or to the other, or to neither (even though all other facts remain the same in these three possible scenarios).

She also says that if either off-shoot had my first-person perspective, I would know it (Rudder Baker, 2000, 139). But how? Both off-shoots would think they were me, and neither would have information the other lacked. How could one know and the other not? Both would believe they were me, and one would be wrong. (I found a number of Rudder Baker's comments puzzling, appearing to confuse the synchronic triviality that for any person P at t_1, P knows at t_1 that he is himself, with some non-trivial diachronic identity claim. There is transparency in the synchronic case, but surely not in the diachronic case. See below.)

Now Rudder Baker's no-constraints view is very radical (though she has an ally in Colin McGinn, see (McGinn, 1996, ch. 6)), and does not follow from her rejection of the standard criteria of personal identity. Let's take the second point first. Consider an analogy with knowledge. Let's agree that there is no neat set of necessary and sufficient conditions for "S knows that P" (i.e., there is no reductive analysis of propositional knowledge). All the standard accounts are open to counterexamples. Does it follow that there is no sufficient condition (however weak) for "S knows that P" specifiable without using the concept of knowledge? Well, no, or not obviously. Isn't it plausible that (necessarily) if a subject, S has a justified true belief, reliably caused in a certain way, counterfactually sensitive to a proposition, P's truth-value in other worlds (add in your favourite condition [...]) then S knows that P? That seems plausible to me; or at least, its falsity does not

[3] David Wiggins drives home a more general point; see (Wiggins, 1980, 49–55).

follow simply from the concession that there is no set of necessary and sufficient conditions for “*S* knows that *P*”. And I would make exactly the same point against Rudder Baker: from the failure of attempts to give informative conditions necessary and sufficient for “*A* at t_1 is the same person as *B* at t_2” it doesn’t follow that there is no set of sufficient conditions.

And now the first point. Rudder Baker’s view (like McGinn’s) is so radical as to be unacceptable. To start with, it just seems pretty obvious that there is a (weak) sufficient condition for my identity over time: if my brain, body, and psychological stream continue as normal, and there’s no duplication, fission, fusion, teletransportation, etc., then I will occupy this body tomorrow. But Rudder Baker has to deny this, otherwise she would be embracing an informative sufficient condition for personal identity over time. She must think that a different first-person perspective (different person) could occupy my body tomorrow, even though everything else just continues as normal. This strikes me as bizarre.

The bizarreness shows up epistemically. On Rudder Baker’s view, in a case of fission, I could be *B* or *C* or neither. Suppose I’m *B*. Since, *ex hypothesi*, everything is the same from the perspectives of *B* and *C*, neither would know that they were me. Moreover, the fact that I am *B* would be completely unknowable (by anyone): no one could ever know it. (*B* would know that he is himself, but that is a triviality.) You might say: so what, maybe some truths are unknowable? (Rudder Baker, 2000, 134) But the trouble is that the scepticism generalises. Even in a normal everyday case, how is a person supposed to know at t_2 that he existed in the same body at t_1? He can know that if he knows that the same first-person perspective persisted in the same body from t_1 to t_2. But how is he supposed to know that, given that he has no privileged access to identity of first-person perspective over time, and given that identity of first-person perspective is not fixed by the facts he does have access to (sameness of body/brain and psychological continuity)? This is an objection to Rudder Baker’s view since we do not feel any sceptical qualms when we regularly re-identify our friends and acquaintances. (Remember this discussion is not taking place in the context of Cartesian scepticism.)

To re-iterate an earlier point: Rudder Baker makes it seem that there is no epistemological problem here, but only, I think, by projecting features of synchronic self-identification (criterionless, no identification of a subject, etc.) onto diachronic self-identifications (which do not have these features). For example, she writes: “The following seem to me to be incontrovertible facts, easily discernible from a first-person perspective: Every morning when I wake up, I know that I am still existing – without consulting my mirror, my memory, or anything else. I can tell.” (Rudder Baker, 2000, 136). But, given Rudder Baker’s no-constraints view of the first-person perspective, how can she tell? Remember we’re not concerned with the synchronic, indexical triviality that any person can say the sentence “I am me” and thereby speak the truth (cf. “I am here” and “the time is now”). So Rudder Baker must be saying that she can tell now (in the morning) that the same first-person perspective has persisted through the night. But how can she tell, on her view? On that view, all the psychological facts (memory, etc.) and physical facts (identity of brain/body) do not fix identity of first-person perspective. Nothing fixes the latter, for Rudder Baker, so how can it's persistence be known (immediately or otherwise)?

18.6 Rudder Baker on the Determinacy of Personal Identity

Rudder Baker thinks it's an advantage of her view that it does not allow for indeterminacy in personal identity over time. But it's unclear to me both why this would be an advantage and why her view doesn't allow for indeterminacy. Take the second issue first. What one would expect is that the necessity of such determinacy would flow from the nature of the first-person perspective. But, as noted earlier, Rudder Baker doesn't really say much about the first-person perspective, so the requirement of determinacy just looks like a stipulation on her part. If we think of a case in the middle of Parfit's Combined Spectrum, where I have half of my cells removed and replaced, and have many of my psychological states altered radically, it's far from obvious to me that it would be wrong to say: it's vague or indeterminate whether one and the same first-person perspective has survived. Why would this be an absurd thing to say?

As to the first issue, I don't see why it's a defect in a criterion of personal identity that it allows for indeterminate cases. A belief, quite generally, in the possibility of indeterminate cases arises from the most benign of motives. One simply judges that certain small changes would not destroy the identity of an F, whereas other, bigger, changes would, and so concludes that in cases in the middle range it is indeterminate whether the same F persists. (The only alternative description is that there is a sharp cut-off point. But, like many, I find the idea that a small change could make the difference between identity and non-identity implausible.) For example: I know that changing one plank will not destroy a ship, but that changing all but one plank will. (I'll then have dismantled one ship, and rebuilt another.) So in cases in the middle, the sentence "The earlier ship is the later ship" is indeterminate in truth-value. (It's controversial what the source of this indeterminacy is – language or the world – but that's a different issue.)

I think it's unfair of Rudder Baker to characterise the indeterminacy theorist as saying: the resulting ship (person) is partly one ship (person), partly another. A belief in indeterminacy does not involve that kind of incoherence. (Even in the case of colours it would be wrong to describe grey as "partly white, partly black". Grey is a new colour which results from combining white and black. Something is "partly white, partly black" if and only if it has a white part and a black part.) So I don't see that it's a point against a theory of personal identity that it allows for indeterminate cases.[4]

18.7 Rudder Baker on Human Persons

Rudder Baker is offering us a sufficient condition for sameness of human person over time. But since she (and I) thinks that 'person' and 'human' are sortals associated with different criteria of identity, the phrase "same human person" sounds a bit odd. The only way I can understand "*x* is the same human person as *y*" is with one or other of the sortals as dominant. That is, either "*x* is the same human person as *y*" is true if and only if *x* is the same person as *y* and both are human or "*x* is the same human person as *y*" is true if and only if *x* is the same human being as *y* and both are persons. Now we've been assuming that the truth-condition of "*x* is same human as *y*" is not problematic, and Rudder Baker has been telling us what she thinks can be said about the truth-condition of "*x* is the same person as *y*", so what new issue is being raised in these pages?

Rudder Baker says that "although human persons are not essentially human (they may have [i.e., survive in] inorganic bodies), anything that begins existence as a human person is essentially embodied" (Rudder Baker, 2000, 214). But (on her view) why? We are referred to Chap. 4, presumably principle (T6) of that chapter, but I couldn't see what the argument for this principle was supposed to be. The reason I'm mentioning this is that I would have thought that anyone with Rudder Baker's views would reject, or at least not endorse, (T6). According to Rudder Baker, what makes for personal identity over time is the continuation of the (primitive, unanalysable) first-person perspective. This can continue in non-human bodies, or silicon bodies, or what have you. Fine. But if immaterial souls are a logical possibility, why should it not be logically possible for my first-person perspective to continue in an immaterial soul? I can't see why Rudder Baker would deny this possibility, given her views. Of course, if she thinks that immaterial substances in general are logically impossible (I don't get the impression she does), that's obviously a reason to deny that my first-person perspective could continue in an immaterial soul. Even then, though, this denial wouldn't be a consequence of her theory of personal identity, but of more general views about immaterial substances. Anyway, if immaterial substances are a logical possibility (as even many materialists think), then Rudder Baker should not be endorsing (T6).

Finally, can I just observe that I find Rudder Baker's conditions for failing "to take persons seriously" (Rudder Baker, 2000, 218–222) somewhat idiosyncratic. To take persons seriously, I would have thought, is to agree that persons are valuable

[4] Although it may not be worth mentioning, I really didn't follow Rudder Baker's discussion in (Rudder Baker, 2000, 138–140), and couldn't see what the point of condition (T) was supposed to be.

beings, whose lives are typically to be valued much more than those of other animals or material possessions. Someone who believes that we are not essentially persons can still take persons seriously, in this sense of the phrase. And if Rudder Baker also wants to understand "taking persons seriously" as "regarding persons as irreducible, ineliminable elements of the universe", then Reductionists, like Parfit, should just turn round and denounce that idiosyncratic sense too.

References

Anscombe, G. E. M. (1981). The first person. In *Metaphysics and the philosophy of mind*. Oxford: Blackwell.

Garrett, B. (1998). *Personal identity and self-consciousness*. London: Routledge.

McGinn, C. (1996). *The character of mind: An introduction to the philosophy of mind*. Oxford: Oxford University Press.

Parfit, D. (1984). *Reasons and persons*. Oxford: Oxford University Press.

Rudder Baker, L. (2000). *Persons and bodies: A constitution view*. Cambridge: Cambridge University Press.

Wiggins, D. (1980). *Sameness and substance*. Cambridge: Harvard University Press.

Chapter 19
Personal Identity and Extrinsicness

Abstract In this discussion, I defend the best-candidate theories of personal identity from the charge that their commitment to the extrisicness of identity leads to absurd consequences. I show that such commitment can be accepted without absurdity.

19.1 Introduction

On one familiar and very broad view of personal identity, the continued existence of a person over time admits of analysis in terms of relations of non-branching physical and/or psychological continuity.[1] (One version of this view is the Psychological Criterion, according to which A at t_1 is identical to B at t_2 if and only if A and B stand to each other in the relation of non-branching psychological continuity.)

The need for a non-branching or no-competitors clause is occasioned by the most plausible description of the division or fission of persons, a situation in which one individual stands to each of two later individuals in qualitatively identical relations of physical and psychological continuity. The inclusion of such a clause is necessary in order to avoid the consequence that the earlier person is identical with both resulting persons.

The inclusion of a non-branching component in theories of personal identity over time has been thought to incur the charge of absurdity. The charge can be pressed as follows: any best-candidate theory of personal identity, which incorporates a non-branching component, violates a necessary constraint which governs our concept of strict numerical identity and – absurdly – implies, in a sense to be characterised, that the identity of a person over time can be extrinsically determined. Consequently, any best-candidate theory of personal identity over time is untenable.

[1] See, e.g., Derek Parfit's statement of the Physical and Psychological Criteria in (Parfit, 1984, 204; 207) and in Shoemaker and Swinburne (1984, 198).

B. Garrett, *Time, Identity and the Self: Essays on Metaphysics*, Synthese Library 442, https://doi.org/10.1007/978-3-030-85517-8_19

If so, it follows that we must re-describe the transtemporal identities which hold in a case of division, e.g., along the lines suggested by David Lewis (1976), John Perry (1972), and Harold Noonan (1985) (according to which the distinct post-division persons both occupy the single pre-division body), or else give up entirely the attempt to analyse the identity of a person over time in terms of physical and/or psychological continuity (and embrace instead, e.g., Cartesian dualism).[2] However, my ultimate aim in this paper is to show how commitment to the extrinsicness of identity on the part of best-candidate theorists can be accepted without absurdity.

19.2 Wiggins on the Case of Division

First, however, I shall consider the question of whether division really is a genuine metaphysical possibility for persons. If it is not, there is no need for the inclusion of a non-branching component in the analysis of a person's identity over time, and commitment to the extrinsicness of personal identity is thereby avoided.

David Wiggins has argued that the division of persons is not genuinely possible: although we can describe cases of division at a purely causal level, in terms of movement of organic matter, etc., division is not a metaphysical possibility for persons (Wiggins, 1980, ch. 6, sec. 7 & 8). Despite appearances to the contrary, the concept *person* loses all application in such a situation.

Prima facie, this is a desperately implausible position. Nothing in our concept of a person appears to exclude imaginary dividing creatures – possessing all the relatively sophisticated psychological properties that make for personhood – from the category of persons. Yet Wiggins is forced to say that such creatures, though "epistemic counterparts" of persons, are not themselves persons.

However, Wiggins would concede that nothing in our concept of a person excludes the possibility of division: the impossibility of dividing persons may be a truth which no amount of *a priori* reflection can reveal. It is, rather, a consequence of the purported fact that all persons are animals, combined with an essentialist view of natural kinds, delivering up *a posteriori* metaphysical necessities of the sort associated with Saul Kripke and Hilary Putnam.

If this combination of views is correct, then,

> we should not count ... as genuinely conceivable any narrative in which persons undergo changes that violate the lawlike regularities constituting the actual nomological foundations for the delimitation of the kind we denominate as that of persons.[3] (Wiggins, 1980, 170)

[2] This disjunction follows on the assumption, defended below, that division is a genuine metaphysical possibility for persons.

[3] Wiggins actually prefixes his sentence with: "the sense of the sortal predicate 'person' will exempt us from counting as genuinely conceivable any". But this cannot be right: it is not the sense of the predicate 'person' which yields the purported *a posteriori* impossibility of division (any more than it is the sense of 'water' which implies that, necessarily, water is H_2O).

Thus, if Wiggins is correct to incorporate animalhood in his theory of persons, certain laws of development – which may exclude the possibility of division – will be *a posteriori* essential to persons, in much the same way that, e.g., having its actual internal structure, is (purportedly) *a posteriori* essential to gold.

Wiggins's argument has the following two premises: first, that all persons are animals (or equivalently, that person is an animal kind concept); second, that if all persons are animals, the division of persons is not a genuine metaphysical possibility. Both premises can, I think, be questioned. The first premise, to start with, requires qualification. *Person* is not an animal kind concept in the sense that there is some one animal kind (e.g., *Homo sapiens*) to which all persons belong. The existence of non-human persons, if not actual, is surely metaphysically possible. Wiggins himself concedes that the extension of the concept person could conceivably "give hospitality" to such creatures as chimpanzees, dolphins or parrots, "in exchange for suitably amazing behaviour" (Wiggins, 1980, 171).

We can easily imagine that there are, or might have been, animals with a different genetic origin from that of human beings, and with a different internal constitution, who nonetheless possess the properties of rationality and self-consciousness distinctive of persons. Hence, the thesis that person is an animal kind concept must be understood as the thesis that, for any actual or possible person, there is some animal kind of which that person is a member, and not as the stronger thesis that there is one animal kind (e.g., *Homo sapiens*) of which all persons are members.

Even so, the thesis is very implausible. Those people who believe in the existence of supernatural persons (God, Satan, the angels, disembodied spirits engaged in astral travel, etc.), and – less contentiously – those who believe in the possibility of robot persons, do not appear to violate any *a priori* constraint governing the concept person. As noted, Wiggins must rest the argument for his thesis on the premise that animality is a necessary *a posteriori* constraint upon the possession of a mental life or, less stringently, on the premise that animality is a necessary *a posteriori* constraint upon possession of the sophisticated mental life characteristic of persons. But, in that case, Wiggins' argument rests upon a controversial thesis in the philosophy of mind, for which he gives no good argument.

However, even if Wiggins's first premise were correct, his second premise – that if all persons are animals, division is metaphysically impossible for persons – cannot, I think, be sustained. Christopher Peacocke has pointed out the following disanalogy between the concepts *gold* and *human being*, a disanalogy which yields a line of support for the thesis that division is metaphysically possible for human beings (Peacocke, 1978, 458–459).

The laws of development governing members of biological natural kinds such as human beings do not play a role analogous to that of the atomic properties of a non-biological natural kind such as gold. How an organism develops depends, *inter alia*, upon its environment, and radical changes in the environment may produce genetic changes over generations which allow future persons to divide like amoebae.

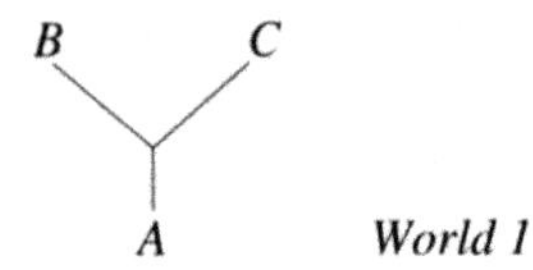

Fig. 19.1 The case of division

(Further, we can easily imagine that we might have had two brains running in parallel: evolution does, after all, favour such fail-safe devices (e.g., kidneys).)[4]

However, the most damaging consideration against Wiggins's second premise is that certain imaginary cases of the division of persons appear to be nomologically possible for actual, present-day, human beings. Even if amoeba-style splitting is nomologically impossible for all known persons, the impossibility of hemisphere bisection and transplantation appears to be "merely technical". Imagine that the equipollent upper hemispheres of the brain of person A are separated and placed in two bodies – exactly similar to A's body – from which the upper hemispheres have been removed. The effect of the operation is, *prima facie*, to bring into existence two persons, B and C, both of whom are fully psychologically continuous, and partly physically continuous, with A. (See Fig. 19.1.)

Whatever the correct description of the transtemporal identities in this scenario, the possibility of division of this sort does not appear to undermine the nomological foundations for the delimitation of the kind we denominate as that of human beings. Division by hemisphere transplantation appears to be a nomological, hence metaphysical, possibility for human beings.

The two premises of Wiggins's argument thus stand in need of urgent defence. In the absence of a better argument, any theory of the identity of persons over time must acknowledge, and be sensitive to, the metaphysical possibility of the division of persons.

19.3 The Challenge of Division

How best ought we to describe the above case of the division of persons, depicted as follows:

Since B and C are perfectly symmetrically related to A in respect of physical and psychological continuities, no Continuity Theorist – who endorses the general view that the identity of a person over time admits of analysis in terms of relations of physical and/or psychological continuity – could countenance the intelligibility of descriptions of world 1 according to which either $A = B$ and $A \neq C$ or $A \neq B$ and $A = C$. Moreover, any view which entertains the possibility of such asymmetrical descriptions of division faces severe epistemological and metaphysical difficulties. Hence, for any Continuity Theorist, either $A = B$ and $A = C$ or $A \neq B$ and $A \neq C$.

[4] This point is due to Galen Strawson.

However, some Continuity Theorists, such as Lewis, Perry, and Noonan, would claim that my labelling of the persons who exist in world 1 is incomplete and misleading. Lewis believes that before division two persons (B and C) occupy the A-body; Perry and Noonan believe that three people (A, B, and C) occupy the single pre-division body. On such views, B and C exist prior to division, but become spatially distinct only after division has occurred.

However, the view that more than one person occupies the A-body before division involves such a distortion of our concept of a person that it is hard to take seriously. The idea that distinct persons might occupy exactly the same space at the same time, if not incoherent, is bizarre. Even more odd is the consequence that whether it is correct to believe that only one person occupies 'my' body, depends upon whether, at any future time, 'I' divide.[5] There is also the further difficulty of how, on this view, we can account for the coherence of the 'I'-thoughts of the (apparently single) locus of reflective mental life which occupies the A-body. For these reasons, therefore, we should be sceptical of theories which maintain that B and C occupy the A-body prior to division.

Any Continuity Theorist, who accepts that only one person occupies the A-body prior to division, must hold that either $A = B$ and $A = C$ or that $A \neq B$ and $A \neq C$. If it were held that $A = B$ and $A = C$, then, by the transitivity of identity, it would follow that B and C are one and the same person. But this, like the Lewis/Perry view, would grossly distort our concept of a person.

Though initially exactly similar, B and C possess distinct *loci* of mental life and occupy different bodies at different, perhaps causally unconnected, spatial locations. *Prima facie*, they ought to count as numerically distinct persons (as opposed, e.g., to being counted as distinct (sub-personal) parts of A, or as distinct instantiations of the concrete universal A, or as the very same person). This judgement is reinforced when we imagine B and C acquiring different physical and psychological characteristics; then it becomes intolerable to regard them as anything but distinct persons.

Further, no theorist could plausibly maintain that A exists after division 'composed' of the numerically distinct persons, B and C (just as the Pope's three crowns comprise one crown).[6] Hence, on the most plausible description of A's division, B and C are distinct persons who exist only after division has occurred, and A is identical to neither resulting person.

Can we give a further explanation of why it is that, e.g., A is not the same person as B? Is it because A and B do not possess the same body? Is it because they do

[5] This consequence seems as absurd as the best-candidate theorist's commitment to the extrinsicness of identity. If so, belief in the absurdity of the latter commitment will not provide a compelling reason for accepting the Lewis/Perry description of division.

[6] Parfit points out more particular absurdities in regard larger person: e.g., if B and C fight a duel and C kills B, are there two acts here – one of murder and one of suicide – or just one? (Parfit 1984, 257.)

not possess the same (whole) brain? These are bad reasons.[7] The best explanation of why *A* is not *B* is simply that there is another, equally good, candidate for identity with *A*. Consequently, the most plausible theory of personal identity over time must incorporate a non-branching or no-competitors clause, and is therefore a best-candidate theory.

19.4 Best-Candidate Theories and the *"Only a and b"* Condition

Why should the presence of such a component be thought objection- able? A number of philosophers have claimed that inclusion of the non- branching restriction violates a necessary *a priori* constraint which governs our concept of strict numerical identity. This constraint has been characterised in a number of ways. Wiggins writes:

> What we need, if identity is what we want to elucidate, is that for a relation *R* to be constitutive of the identity of *a* and *b*, such that objects distinct from *a* and *b* are irrelevant as to whether *a* has *R* to *b*. (Wiggins, 1980, 96)

Noonan writes:

> whether a later individual is identical with an earlier individual cannot ever merely depend upon whether there are, at the later time, any better [or equally good] candidates for identity with the earlier individual. (Noonan, 1986, 79)

Finally, Parfit ascribes to Williams the following requirement:

> Whether a future person will be me must depend upon the intrinsic features of the relation between us. It cannot depend upon what happens to other people.[8] (Parfit, 1984, 267)

Following Wiggins, I shall call this constraint on any candidate identity relation the *Only a and b* condition.

The *Only a and b* condition states that a relation *R* can constitute the identity of *a* and *b* only if the holding of *R* between *a* and *b* (however the objects are described) does not depend upon the existence or non-existence of any other object. The *Only a and b* condition is thus one attempt to characterise the requirement that

[7] It is plausible to suppose that neither sameness of body nor sameness of (whole) brain is necessary for the identity of a person over time. Many people would regard brain-transplantation as identity-preserving: if my whole brain were transplanted into a new body, it is plausible to suppose that I survive in the new body. For example, Parfit writes: "Receiving a new skull and a new body is just the limiting case of receiving a new heart, new lungs, new arms, and so on" (Parfit, 1984, 253). Similarly, Robert Nozick claims that we can imagine brain-transplant operations becoming "a standard medical technique to prolong life" (Nozick, 1981, 38). Sameness of body cannot plausibly be thought a necessary condition of personal identity over time.

[8] This principle is certainly assumed in Bernard Williams's "Guy Fawkes" argument against the Psychological Criterion (Williams, 1982, 8–9).

identity over time can be only intrinsically determined. (It should be noted that the truth of the *Only a and b* condition is quite consistent with the contingency of, e.g., "Jones is identical with the sole heir to his father's fortune". Whether the individual denoted by the name 'Jones' is identical with the individual denoted by the definite description "the sole heir to his father's fortune" does not depend upon whether, e.g., Jones has an elder brother; though whether Jones satisfies the definite description does so depend.)

Thus understood, the plausibility of the *Only a and b* condition should be manifest: whether x at t_1 is identical with y at t_2 cannot depend upon the existence or non-existence of some other object z. If it did, then it could be true that, e.g., x is not identical with y, but had z not existed, x would have been identical with y. This consequence is plainly incompatible with the thesis of the necessity of identity (the thesis that all identity statements containing only rigid designators are, if true, necessarily true, and, if false, necessarily false).[9] Hence, the *Only a and b* condition does indeed serve to characterise a genuine constraint on any relation which purports to be that of identity over time: to violate this constraint is just to violate the necessity of identity.

Why should best-candidate theories of personal identity over time be thought to violate the constraint embodied in the *Only a and b* condition?[10] Consider the world in which A's upper hemispheres are transplanted, resulting in the creation of persons B and C. On the most plausible theory, A is not the same person as B. But, it is reasonable to suppose, had C not 'taken' (e.g., had the surgeon accidentally dropped the C-hemisphere before inserting it in the C-skull), branching of the relevant sort would not have occurred and A would then have been identical with B.[11] Call the world in which C does not 'take', world 2. (Note: I assume that a functioning hemisphere is not a person, and hence that the short-lived C-hemisphere in world 2 is not a candidate for identity with A.) Thus: although A is not identical with B, had C not existed, as in world 2, A would have been identical to B. But this consequence directly contravenes the *Only a and b* condition and the necessity of identity.

One possible response which may be made to this charge is to claim that worlds 1 and 2, as I have characterised them, are not mutually accessible (i.e., not possible relative to each other). From the perspective of world 1, it might be argued, there is no accessible possible world in which A has only one surviving off-shoot. In a sole survivor world, A does not exist, though someone exactly similar to A, A', there occupies A's body, and is identical with the surviving off-shoot. If world 2 is not a

[9] A proof of the necessity of identity appears in, e.g., (Kripke, 1971).

[10] Richard Gale believes that best-candidate theories show the *Only a and b* condition to be "patently false" (Gale, 1984). I think the condition is patently true, and that best-candidate theories do not violate it.

[11] The grounds for accepting the judgement that had C not 'taken', A would have continued to exist and have occupied the B-body, are just the grounds for holding that sameness of body or whole brain is unnecessary for sameness of person over time (see note 7 above). These are thus precisely the grounds for thinking that the correct explanation of why A is not the same person as B is a best-candidate explanation.

possible world relative to world 1, it will not be true that had C not existed, A would have been identical with B.

However, this is not a plausible strategy of reply. There appears to be no reason to believe that worlds 1 and 2 are mutually inaccessible, other than a desire to avoid commitment to the counterfactual that, had C not existed, A would have been B. The strategy thus appears *ad hoc*. Worse still, the stipulation that worlds 1 and 2 are mutually inaccessible is counter-intuitive. If A is about to undergo division, it is natural to characterise the sense in which the future is 'open' for A, by claiming that there is a range of mutually accessible possible worlds (containing A) which are indistinguishable until A's division, but differ thereafter. (In worlds in which only one candidate survives, A continues to exist; in other worlds, A dies.) If so, worlds 1 and 2 cannot reasonably be regarded as mutually inaccessible.

A similar reply can be made to the response, not that worlds 1 and 2 are mutually inaccessible, but that world 2 is too 'distant' in Lewis's terminology (Lewis, 1973, 32–36) from world 1 to license the truth of the counterfactual: had C not existed, A would have been identical with B, just as, e.g., the existence of a possible world in which the non-wearing of safety-belts is accompanied by a radical suspension of the laws of nature is too distant to license the truth of the counterfactual: had X not been wearing a safety-belt, X would not have been killed.[12] However, world 2 seems sufficiently close to world 1, and there appears to be no way in which a best-candidate theorist might non-question-beggingly have a reason to suppose them to be too distant from each other.

However, the most natural response for a best-candidate theorist to make to the charge that his preferred analysis of personal identity over time violates the *Only a and b* condition is to insist – in a way that is not question-begging – that world 2, as described, is an impossible world, relative to world 1. We have no right to suppose that the person occupying B's body in world 2 is B. To avoid prejudging the issue, call the person occupying B's body in world 2, B'. The best-candidate theorist will argue that, since $A \neq B$ in world 1 and $A = B'$ in world 2, it follows, by the necessity and transitivity of identity, that $B \neq B'$. Given that $A \neq B$ and $A = B'$, we must, on pain of inconsistency, regard B and B' as distinct persons.

If $B \neq B'$, the best-candidate theorist should deny that B and C are candidates for identity with A in the sense that there is a possible world in which, e.g., $A = B$. The candidates are rather the B-body person and the C-body person (where these designators are non-rigid): the B-body person is a candidate for being A, and in worlds in which C does not 'take', the B-body person is A. (At the sub-personal level, we can also regard the hunks of matter which constitute B and C as candidates for being, in different possible worlds, the hunks of matter which constitute A.)

If $B \neq B'$, the *Only a and b* condition has not been violated. Whether A is identical with B does not depend upon whether C exists. World 2 is not a world in which A is identical with B; *a fortiori*, it is not a world in which A is identical with B in virtue of the non-existence of C. What is true, of course, is that whether A

[12] This example is used by Crispin Wright (1983, 173).

is the B-body person (where, to repeat, the latter designator functions non-rigidly) depends upon whether C exists: if C does exist, together with B, (as in world 1), A is not the B-body person; if C does not exist (as in world 2), A is the B-body person. But, *prima facie*, the contingency of "A is the B-body person" ought not to seem paradoxical: identity statements containing non-rigid designators are, by definition, contingent in truth value.

19.5 Extrinsicness of Personal Identity

This manoeuvre, however, does not settle the issue. In arguing that $B \neq B'$, the best-candidate theorist does not violate the *Only a and b* condition, thus avoiding one horn of a dilemma, but is impaled – so the argument runs – on the other horn. If $B \neq B'$, in virtue of the existence of C, the best-candidate theorist is still, but in a different way, committed to the extrinsicness of identity.

If $B \neq B'$, in virtue of the existence of C, it is true that, but for the existence of C, B would not have existed at all. Consequently, B can truly say: "Thank goodness C didn't fail to 'take', otherwise I wouldn't have existed". This consequence appears absurd: how can B's existence depend upon whether C exists, given that B and C exert no causal influence upon each other? (The qualification is crucial: the fact that, but for the existence of my father, I would not have existed, is obviously not paradoxical.)

Similarly: if $B \neq B'$, in virtue of the existence of C, then whether A is the B-body person depends upon whether C exists. That is, whether A continues to exist depends upon what happens to another person: A continues to exist in the B-body if C (who exerts no causal influence upon B) does not exist. Is this not manifestly absurd?

The "air of paradox" surrounding these consequences cannot be dispelled simply by noting the general fact that identity statements containing non-rigid designators are (non-paradoxically) contingent. It is precisely the contingency of "A is the B-body person", in this context, which yields the seemingly paradoxical consequences. The contingency of "Jones is the sole heir to his father's fortune", in contrast, has no such paradoxical consequence. Whether Jones continues to exist does not – in the absence of any causal connection – depend upon whether his brother exists.[13]

Penelope Mackie has recently argued that the best-candidate theorist's commitment to the extrinsicness of identity is not absurd on the grounds that B and C are not causally isolated: they are causally connected with each other, indirectly, in virtue of their individual causal connections with A (Mackie, 1987, 173). This

[13] It might be thought that on a four-dimensional conception of continuants such as persons, commitment to extrinsicness is less paradoxical than on the three-dimensional conception, since it will not then be the identity relation which is extrinsically determined. Equally, it may still be thought absurd to suppose that whether the temporal slice A-at-t_1 is part of the same (four-dimensional) person as B-at-t_2 can depend upon extrinsic, causally otiose factors.

is an interesting proposal, but I do not believe it can work, and I have criticised it elsewhere (Garrett, 1988).[14]

In *Reasons and Persons*, Derek Parfit outlines an alternative explanation of why we are wrong to regard the intrinsicness requirement as a genuine constraint on the identity of persons over time, and hence why commitment to the extrinsicness of identity is not, after all, absurd (Parfit, 1984, ch. 12, sec. 91). (Parfit does not distinguish violations of the *Only a and b* condition from violations of the intrinsicness of identity. I shall therefore represent Parfit's argument as a defence of theories of personal identity over time which violate the intrinsicness constraint.)

Parfit concedes that "no plausible criterion of identity" can satisfy the following requirement:

(1) Whether a person, X, continues to exist can only be determined intrinsically, it cannot depend upon what happens to individuals who exert no causal influence upon X.

However, the following requirement is not flouted by best-candidate theories:

(2) Whether X stands to some future person in the relation that matters can depend only upon intrinsic features of X's relation to that future person.

The argument which Parfit's discussion suggests is this. It is because we accept (2), but falsely believe that identity is what matters, that (1) – the requirement that identity be intrinsic – seems compelling at all. Consequently, if we accept that the relation which matters in a person's continued existence is not identity (but rather, e.g., psychological continuity and/or connectedness), the consequence that the identity of a person over time might be determined extrinsically ought not to seem absurd.

However, this is not necessarily the correct diagnosis of our antipathy towards extrinsic identity. We may believe that the identity of a person over time can be only intrinsically determined, whether or not we believe that identity is what matters. That is, perhaps it ought to be of no great concern to A, facing the prospect of division, whether both off-shoots survive, provided that there is at least one future person with whom he is strongly psychologically connected. Nonetheless, it may still be absurd to suppose that whether A is identical with the B-body person can depend upon the existence of a person who exercises no causal influence upon the B-body person.[15] Hence, even if identity is not the relation that matters in the survival of a person over time, and people falsely believe that it is, it does not follow that the inability of a theory to satisfy requirement (1) thereby ceases to be absurd.

Parfit may reply that he was claiming only that if we relinquish the belief that identity is what matters, the consequence that the identity of a person over time can

[14] See Chap. 9 of this volume.

[15] As Noonan writes, "Why can it not be the case that something is, from a practical point of view, of no significance whatsoever, and yet the truth about it still be obvious? Surely this is very often the case" (Noonan, 1986, 209).

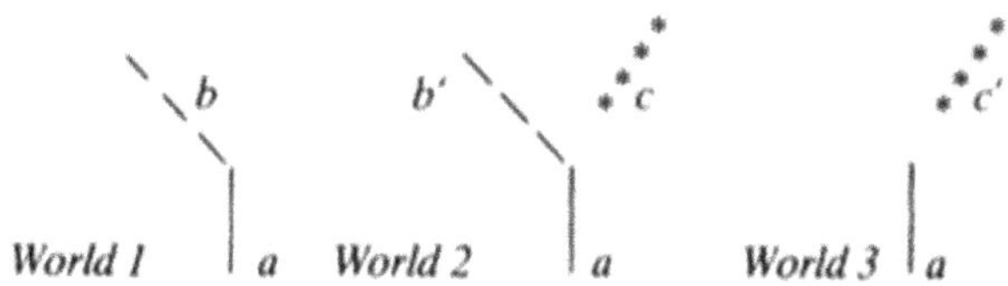

Fig. 19.2 Three possibilities of the Ship of Theseus

be extrinsically determined ought to meet with less resistance, even if it is still hard to accept. However, consideration of certain possible histories of the Ship of Theseus appears to undermine Parfit's explanation – conceived as a general explanation – of why the belief that identity over time can be only intrinsically determined is so widely held. Consider the following three possible histories of the Ship of Theseus. (See Fig. 19.2.) In all three worlds, 'a' denotes Theseus's original ship. In world 1, 'b' denotes the continuously repaired ship. In world 2 (the situation described by Hobbes), 'b'' denotes the continuously repaired ship and 'c' denotes the plank-hoarder's ship, reconstructed from a's original planks. In world 3, the ship reconstituted from a's original planks is denoted by 'c''. Given that we regard spatio-temporal continuity (under a sortal) as the dominant criterion of artefact identity, outweighing the identity-of-original-parts criterion, but acknowledge the fact that an artefact can survive dismantlement and reassembly, the common-sense description of worlds 1–3 is as follows: in world 1, $a = b$; in world 2, $a = b'$ and $a \neq c$; and in world 3, $a = c'$. Hence, by the necessity and transitivity of identity, c is not the same ship as c' (even though c and c' are materially and qualitatively identical).

The structure of this common-sense theory is that of a best-candidate theory: in world 2, the continuously repaired ship and the plank-hoarder's ship (where the definite descriptions function non-rigidly) are both candidates for identity with Theseus's ship, though the former ship has the stronger claim; in world 3, the reconstructed ship is the best candidate for identity with Theseus's ship.

The common-sense description of worlds 1–3 implies that the identity over time of ships can be extrinsically determined. However, we should note an important difference between the commitments of our common-sense theory of ship identity and the commitments of best-candidate theories of personal identity.[16] Since ship a is identical to one of the two candidates in world 2, the common-sense description of worlds 1–3 does not license the counterfactual: had b' not existed, c would not have existed at all, since world 3 is not a world in which $b' (= a)$ does not exist. In general, best-candidate theories of identity over time will entail an extrinsicness counterfactual of the form: if x had not existed, y would not have existed, only if

[16] Note that the *Only a and b* condition would not be violated even if c and c' were the same ship. Whether a is c (even if $c = c'$), does not depend upon what happens to any entity distinct from a or c: the continuously repaired ship in world 2 is a. This reinforces the claim, made above, that the *Only a and b* condition does not adequately delineate the intrinsicness constraint.

the candidates (x and y) are both distinct from the earlier individual (e.g., if x and y are equally good candidates).

However, the common-sense description of worlds 1–3 does imply that the identity of ships over time can be extrinsically determined. The implication manifests itself in our commitment to the truth of the following extrinsicness counterfactual: had Theseus's original ship (a) not been continuously repaired, c would not have existed at all.[17] Given that the events which constitute the replacement of a's planks exert no causal influence upon the events which occur in c's spatial location, commitment to this extrinsicness counterfactual is as absurd as the best-candidate theorist's commitment to an analogous extrinsicness counterfactual in the case of personal identity.

However – to return to the question of the adequacy of Parfit's explanation – the reason why we are inclined to believe that the identity of ships over time can be only intrinsically determined cannot be that we believe that identity is what matters (to us) in the continued existence of ships over time, and that this belief is false. Antiquarian interests aside, no one believes that identity is what matters in the survival of ships over time: if I were a ship owner, it would make no difference to me if my ship were destroyed and replaced with an exactly similar – but numerically distinct – replica.[18] Any attitudes I may have to my original ship can simply be transferred to the replica, since there is perfect replication of function, structure and appearance. Hence, Parfit's explanation of the grounds for our belief that identity over time can be only intrinsically determined cannot, in general, be correct.

Parfit may reply that he was concerned only to show how the consequence that the relation of personal identity over time is extrinsically determinable can avoid, in whole or in part, the charge of absurdity; his explanation was not intended to constitute a general defence of extrinsic identity.

However, philosophers who object to the consequence that the identity of a person over time can be extrinsically determined, typically do so because they believe that violation of the intrinsicness requirement constitutes violation of a necessary constraint on the identity relation per se (whatever the *relata*). They do not believe that there is any special absurdity involved in jettisoning the intrinsicness requirement as a constraint on the identity of persons over time, even if the absurdity is illustrated most forcefully in the personal case. If so, Parfit has not succeeded in explaining away or ameliorating the (apparent) absurdity inherent in the best-candidate theorist's commitment to the extrinsicness of identity.

[17] Even if it were thought that the identity-of-original-parts criterion outweighed the spatio-temporal continuity criterion – and, hence, that $a = c$ in world 2 – it would not affect the commitment to the extrinsicness of ship identity. A different subjunctive conditional would evince that commitment: it would then be true that, had the discarded planks not been used to build a ship, b' would not have existed at all. For an example, due to David Kaplan, which appears to count in favour of the identity-of- original-parts criterion, see (Salmon, 1981, 221).

[18] The same may not be true of, e.g., works of art and wedding rings.

19.6 Concluding Remarks

How then ought we to reply to the charge that best-candidate theories are untenable since they are committed – absurdly – to the consequence that the identity of a person over time may be extrinsically determined? The beginning of a reply consists in noting that the charge of absurdity has simply not been made out. Once we appreciate that violation of the intrinsicness constraint does not entail violation of the *Only a and b* condition or the necessity of identity, it is unclear why commitment to the extrinsicness of identity should be thought absurd; *ipso facto*, it is far from obvious that the commitment to extrinsicness can straightforwardly feature in a successful *reductio* of best-candidate theories of personal identity over time.

The best-candidate theorist's commitment to the extrinsicness of identity implies that a predicate such as "being occupied by person B" denotes an extrinsic (hence, relational) property of the B-body: an account of what it is for a particular body or hunk of matter to be occupied by B will involve reference to the existence of another person (in this case, C), who exerts no causal influence upon B.

Why is this consequence absurd? The property *being occupied by person B* does not appear to be a causal property of the B-body (i.e., does not contribute to the causal powers of the B-body).[19] In general, if a property P does not contribute to the causal powers of an object X, it should come as no surprise if its possession by X can depend upon what happens to objects which exercise no causal influence on X (think of the property *being a war widow*). Hence, there appear to be independent grounds for believing that *being occupied by person B* should be counted an extrinsic property.

The fact that the property *being occupied by person B* is non-causal is neutral with respect to the question of whether such a property is a genuine property of the B-body. Those who are impressed by the "causal powers" criterion of genuine propertyhood, according to which the only genuine properties are causal properties, will conclude that "being occupied by person B" does not denote a genuine property of the B-body.[20] However, this is a further, and separate, issue.

Thus: the inclusion of a no-competitors clause in the analysis of the identity of a person over time implies that the possession of a property such as being occupied by person B can be determined extrinsically. This is not a consequence which we ought to find counter-intuitive, and is precisely what would be expected given the non-causal character of such a property. Thus, the charge that commitment to the extrinsicness of identity reduces best-candidate theories to absurdity has simply not been made out.

---

[19] Note that the property *being identical with B* also appears to be non-causal in character. However, unlike the property *being occupied by person B*, its possession – by B – cannot "depend upon" what happens elsewhere, since this would imply that being identical with B is a contingent property of B.

[20] Shoemaker (1985) advocates the "causal powers" criterion of genuine propertyhood. However, later, in (Shoemaker, 1988), he defends a more temperate line.

In conclusion: I have argued that division is a genuine metaphysical possibility for persons, and that this fact necessitates the inclusion of a non-branching component in any plausible theory of personal identity over time. On any such theory, the identity of a person over time can be extrinsically determined. However, I claimed that neither this consequence, nor anything it implies, is absurd, and cannot feature in a successful *reductio* of theories.

References

Gale, R. (1984). Wiggins' Thesis $D(x)$. *Philosophical Studies, 45*(2), 239–245.
Garrett, B. (1988). Vagueness and identity. *Analysis, 48*(3), 130–134.
Kripke, S. (1971). Identity and necessity. In M. Munitz (Ed.), *Identity and individuation*. New York: New York University Press.
Lewis, D. (1973). *Counterfactuals*. Oxford: Basil Blackwell.
Lewis, D. (1976). Survival and identity. In A. O. Rorty (Ed.), *The identities of persons*. Los Angeles, University of California Press.
Mackie, P. (1987). Essence, origin, and bare identity. *Mind, 96*(382), 173–201.
Noonan, H. (1985). The closest continuer theory of identity. *Inquiry, 28*, 195–229.
Noonan, H. (1986). Reply to Garrett. *Analysis, 46*(4), 79–85.
Nozick, R. (1981). *Philosophical explanations*. Cambridge: Harvard University Press.
Parfit, D. (1984). *Reasons and persons*. Oxford: Oxford University Press.
Peacocke, C. (1978). Review of A. O. Rorty (ed.), *The identities of persons. Philosophical Review, 87*(3), 456–460.
Perry, J. (1972). Can the self divide? *Journal of Philosophy, 69*(16), 463–488.
Salmon, N. (1981). *Reference and essence*. New Jersey: Princeton University Press.
Shoemaker, S. (1985). Causality and properties. In *Identity, cause and mind*. Cambridge: Cambridge University Press.
Shoemaker, S. (1988). On what there are. *Philosophical Topics, 16*(1), 201–223.
Shoemaker, S., & Swinburne, R. (1984). Personal identity: A materialist's account. In *Personal identity*. Oxford: Blackwell.
Wiggins, D. (1980). *Sameness and substance*. Cambridge: Harvard University Press.
Williams, B. (1982). Personal identity and individuation. In *Problems of the self*. Cambridge: Cambridge University Press.
Wright, C. (1983). Keeping track of Nozick. *Analysis, 43*(3), 134–140.

Chapter 20
Personal Identity and Reductionism

Abstract In this discussion, I examine theories that purport to provide an ontological reduction of persons. I argue that such theories are either false or fail to constitute genuine reduction.

20.1 Introduction

Suppose (as many philosophers anyway believe) that the Cartesian conception of persons is false: persons are not immaterial (i.e., non-spatial) substances. Suppose, further, that we accept the plausible view that the identity of a person over time admits of analysis in terms of relations of physical and/or psychological continuity (the Continuity Theory).[1]

One instance of the Continuity Theory is the Psychological Criterion according to which person A at time t_1 is identical with person B at time t_2 if and only if A and B stand to each other in the relation of (non-branching) psychological continuity. (Competing versions of the Psychological Criterion differ over whether the cause of the psychological continuity, if it is to be identity-preserving, must be normal – i.e., the continued existence of the brain and central nervous system – as opposed, e.g., to the operation of a *Star Trek* Teletransporter.)

Another instance of the Continuity Theory is the Physical Criterion according to which the identity of a person over time is analysable exclusively in terms of relations of physical continuity (in particular, spatio-temporal continuity of the body and/or brain) which hold between persons at different times. Yet other – Mixed – Criteria assign varying degrees of importance to both physical and psychological continuity.[2]

---

[1] Defenders of the Continuity Theory include: Derek Parfit (1984), Sydney Shoemaker and Swinburne (1984), Robert Nozick (1981), and David Lewis (1976).

[2] Nozick's "Closest Continuer" schema allows for varying degrees of 'closeness' to be assigned to physical and psychological continuities (Nozick, 1981, ch. 1).

B. Garrett, *Time, Identity and the Self: Essays on Metaphysics*, Synthese Library 442, https://doi.org/10.1007/978-3-030-85517-8_20

If we reject Cartesianism and accept some version of the Continuity Theory, a crucial question which arises is this: can our preferred analysis of a person's identity over time proceed to a reductionist stage? Can we reduce persons to their bodies and experiences? This is perhaps the most difficult question in the philosophy of persons, and part of its difficulty is entirely general in character: exactly what constitutes, or suffices for, a reduction of Fs to Gs?[3]

In this paper, I characterise various attempts at an ontological reduction of persons and argue that such attempts are either false or fail to constitute a genuine reduction. I am not aware of any attempt at an ontological reduction of persons which would escape these objections. I also argue that the consequences for ethics and rationality which Derek Parfit has drawn from his reductionist conception of persons may still follow, even if we refuse to advance to a reductionist stage in our analysis of personal identity over time (Parfit, 1984, ch. 14 and 15).

20.2 What Ontological Reduction Is

Rejection of Cartesianism does not imply the truth of any reductionist view of persons: there is no incoherence in the conception of persons as entities made entirely of matter, yet not reducible to their bodies and experiences.[4] Thus I do not regard the thesis that all persons are material as, in any interesting sense, reductionist. Reduction would require a more fine-grained account of the relation between a person and his body and experiences.

Further, all instances of the Continuity Theory are, in themselves, neutral on the question of the ultimate tenability of an ontological reduction of persons. In each version there is reference to persons in the *analysans* (e.g., in the right-hand side) of the Psychological Criterion there is reference to persons A and B), and the concept person, in virtue of being a sortal concept, 'contains' the criteria of personal identity over time, precisely the criteria we are attempting to elucidate. A reductionist must therefore claim that the surface grammar of the *analysans* is misleading, and that, e.g., reference to persons is eliminable in favour of reference only to bodies and experiences.

However, the shift to a reductionist stage is far from mandatory for a Continuity Theorist. A non-reductive analysis of the concept *same person*, though circular, need

[3] It is important to distinguish eliminative from non-eliminative varieties of reductionism. The reduction of the abstract to the concrete, for example, is typically eliminative in character: the conclusion of such a reduction is simply a negative existential claim (e.g., there are no abstract directions, only concrete lines). Other versions of reductionism are non-eliminative in character (e.g., the reduction, via a theoretical identification, of water with H_20). One problem, which is the central focus of this paper, is how we are best to understand the reductionist import, if any, of non-eliminative claims about persons.

[4] Thus, Parfit is wrong to endorse Lichtenberg's belief that "because we are not separately existing entities, we could fully describe our thoughts without claiming that they have thinkers" (Parfit, 1984, 225). The fact that we are not separately existing entities (e.g., Cartesian Egos) does not imply any reductionist-sounding conclusion.

not be vicious. Provided that concepts other than the concept *person* feature in the *analysans*, a non-reductive analysis can still reveal and illuminate the interrelations between the target concept and other concepts (such as the concepts of physical and psychological continuity). As Wiggins writes, we should appreciate:

> how much can be achieved in philosophy by means of elucidations which use a concept without attempting to reduce it, and in using the concept, exhibit the connexions of the concept with other concepts that are established, genuinely collateral and independently intelligible. (Wiggins, 1980, 19)

However, despite the fact that the shift to a further reductionist stage of analysis is not compulsory, are there grounds for believing that some form of ontological reductionism about persons is nonetheless tenable? As noted, whether there are such grounds will depend, in part, upon a general account of what it is to reduce entities of a certain sort to entities of some other range. It is this broader question that I shall first discuss.

Reductionism about material objects has often been thought to consist in the existence of relations of logical equivalence between statements about material objects and statements about, e.g., sense-data. A. J. Ayer, for example, characterises phenomenalism about the external world as the thesis that physical objects are "logical constructions" out of sense-data, and takes this to be equivalent to the thesis that any physical object statement is logically equivalent to some statement or set of statements about sense-data (Ayer, 1952, 84–87). Similarly Anthony Quinton, writing about social objects, claims that:

> ontological doctrines ... can be expressed in the idiom of philosophical analysis as the thesis that statements about social objects can or cannot be reduced, are or are not logically equivalent, to statements about individuals who are members of the groups or institutions in question (Quinton, 1976, 3).

These remarks reflect one dominant thought in analytic philosophising about reductionism, viz., that it is sufficient to effect a reduction of Fs to Gs that any statement about an F is logically equivalent to some statement or set of statements about Gs.

However, it ought to be apparent that a logical equivalence between F-statements and G-statements cannot, in itself, suffice for a reduction of Fs to Gs. Crispin Wright has pointed out that the relation of logical equivalence is a symmetric relation (if P is logically equivalent to Q, Q is logically equivalent to P), yet the relation of reducibility is asymmetric (if Fs are reducible to Gs, Gs cannot be reducible to Fs) (Wright, 1983, 31–32). Hence, from the mere fact that statements about Fs are logically equivalent to statements about Gs, it appears arbitrary to conclude that Fs are reducible to Gs, rather than vice-versa.

Further, as Wright also notes, the assumption that the logical equivalence of statements about Fs with statements about Gs suffices for a reduction of Fs to Gs leads to manifestly absurd consequences (Wright, 1983, 32–35). F. P. Ramsey pointed out that any statement which is intuitively 'about' a certain individual, predicating a certain property of it, can always be regarded instead as being about that property and predicating something of it, viz., that it is instantiated by the individual in question.

For example, the sentence "Leo is a tiger" could be regarded as being about Leo, predicating the property *being a tiger* of him, or it could be construed as being about the concept *tiger*, claiming of it that it is Leo-instantiated. (On the latter construal, 'Leo' functions, not as a singular term, but as an adverb expressing a mode of instantiation.) But the idea that in virtue of equivalences such as that between "Leo is a tiger" and "Tiger is Leo-instantiated", we ought to regard reference to ordinary concrete particulars as illusory and embrace an exclusively Platonic ontology, seems absurd. A reductionist strategy which proceeds via a logical equivalence thesis is thus, not just arbitrary, but also unsound.[5]

Of course, it may be true that in certain purportedly reducing biconditionals – e.g., $Da = Db$ if and only if $a//b$ (where the definite descriptions 'Da' and 'Db' refer to abstract objects: directions, 'a' and 'b' refer to concrete lines, and '$//$' represents the relation of parallelism between lines) – the right hand side of the analysis has epistemic priority over the left hand side. That is, it may be that the meaning of direction-sentences is explained in terms of the meaning of line-sentences, and that the identity conditions for directions are given in terms of the relation of parallelism between lines. But it does not follow from this that the right hand side has ontological priority over the left hand side. Why not regard the biconditional as, in effect, nullifying any such claim to ontological priority?

However, even if every statement about Fs is logically equivalent to some statement or set of statements about Gs, it is clear what might nonetheless motivate a reduction of Fs to Gs, rather than vice-versa, viz., if it is not true that every statement about Gs is logically equivalent to some statement or set of statements about Fs. However, this potential asymmetry is irrelevant here, since I shall argue that statements about persons are not logically equivalent to statements or sets of statements about bodies, brains and experiences. In particular, I shall argue against the existence of any entailment of the latter class to statements of the former.[6]

---

[5] It is worth noting that Ramsey's argument is not compromised by the fact that what a statement is 'about' may not be a matter of logic, ontology or epistemology, but of "conversational pragmatics". To use an example of P. F. Strawson's, the sentence "Rubber is elastic" could be 'about' rubber (if rubber and its properties were the focus of conversational interest) or it could be 'about' elasticity (if the property of elasticity, and its incidence, were the focus of interest). Even so, I claim, Ramsey's objection can still be pressed. Imagine a context in which "Leo is a tiger" is uttered, and in which it is clear that Leo is the focus of conversational interest. It would surely be absurd to suppose, in virtue of the logical equivalence between "Leo is a tiger" and "*Tiger* is Leo-instantiated", that reference to the concrete individual Leo is illusory. (Further, as Don Gustafson has pointed out, it is not clear that a reduction along these lines is possible in the first place: can we really understand the phrase 'Leo-instantiated' without grasping the ordinary use of 'Leo' as a singular term referring to a concrete object?)

[6] It should be noted that I am not concerned with the claim that the existence of a functioning brain and body, and interrelated stream of mental and physical events, entails the existence of a person (where this entailment does not exclude the possibility of numerically distinct persons

20.3 Ontological Reduction of Persons

As a point of entry, consider the reductionist proposal embodied in the Impersonality Thesis put forward by Derek Parfit in Part Three of *Reasons and Persons*. (This proposal, in effect, attempts a contemporary articulation of Hume's "Bundle Theory" of the self.)

The central claim of the Impersonality Thesis is that all reference to persons is eliminable in favour of reference to bodies and experiences: reality can be completely and impersonally described.[7]

Parfit characterises the Impersonality Thesis as follows:

(1) the fact of a person's identity over time just consists in the holding of certain more particular facts;
(2) these facts can be described without either presupposing the identity of this person, or explicitly claiming that the experiences in this person's life are had by this person, or even explicitly claiming that this person exists. These facts can be described in an impersonal way;
(3) though persons exist, we could give a complete description of reality without claiming that persons exist.[8] (Parfit, 1984, 210–212)

How are we to understand conditions (1)-(3)? According to Parfit, a complete and impersonal description of reality is possible if:

(4) there exists a particular brain and body, and a particular series of interrelated mental and physical events

and

(5) there exists a particular person

are either two ways of presenting the same fact (just as, e.g., "Tully is *F*" and "Cicero is *F*" are two ways of presenting the same fact) or, less stringently, if

---

occupying the same body in different possible worlds). It is hard to see how this claim expresses any interesting reductionist thought. Only a "Featureless Cartesian" would deny it.

[7] In formulating his Impersonality Thesis, Parfit explicitly acknowledges his debt to the following remarks of Kripke:

> Although the statement that England fought Germany in 1943 perhaps cannot be reduced to any statement about individuals, nevertheless in some sense it is not a fact "over and above" the collection of all facts about persons, and their behaviour over history. The sense in which these facts about nations are not facts "over and above" those about persons can be expressed in the observation that a description of the world mentioning all facts about persons but omitting those about nations can be a complete description of the world, from which facts about nations follow. (Kripke, 1980, 50)

[8] Of course, if experiences can be identified and individuated only by reference to a personal subject of experience, the reductionist aspirations of the Impersonality Thesis would immediately be dashed.

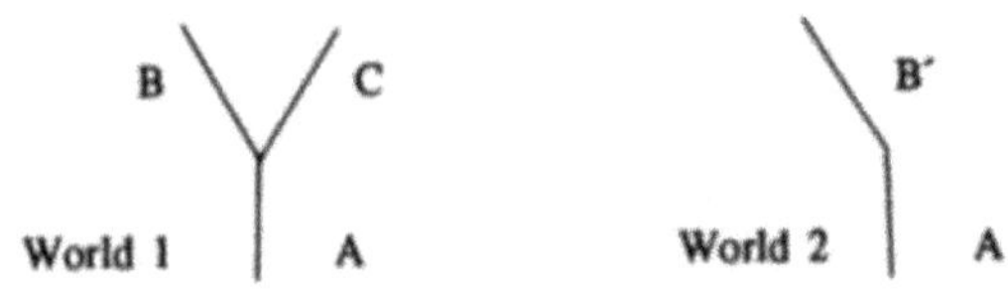

Fig. 20.1 Branching and non-branching worlds

(4) entails (5). Parfit's belief is that reality can be completely and impersonally described.

Consider the weaker claim (if this is false, so is the stronger claim). Does (4) entail (5)? Does the existence of a particular brain, body and interrelated stream of mental and physical events entail the existence of a particular person? No: the following example shows that (4) does not entail (5). (See Fig. 20.1.)

In world 1, A's brain is divided and each (equipollent) upper hemisphere is placed in a new body, exactly similar to A's body, resulting in a creation of two persons, B and C, both of whom are fully psychologically continuous with A. In world 2, the same operation is carried out, but the surgeon accidentally drops the C-hemisphere and C fails to 'take'. (I assume that, in world 2, no person exists composed only of the C-hemisphere; hence, personal branching does not occur in that world.)

Since there are two equally good candidates for identity with A in world 1, the best description of this world is that A is numerically identical with neither B nor C. However, given that – arguably – sameness of body or whole brain is unnecessary for the sameness of person over time, there is one, sufficiently good, candidate for identity with A in world 2.[9] The most plausible description of this world, therefore, is that A is identical with the person there occupying B's body. Call this person, B'. If A is B' in world 2, and A is not B in world 1, it follows, by the necessity and transitivity of identity, that B and B' are distinct persons. Yet B and B' possess the same brain and body, and are 'associated' with the same stream of interrelated mental and physical events. Hence, the existence of the left side body, brain and stream of consciousness does not entail the existence of any particular person (e.g., B). Consequently, (4) does not entail (5) (*a fortiori*, (4) and (5) cannot be different presentations of one and the same fact).

At one point in his discussion, Parfit suggests a different, epistemic construal of the Impersonality Thesis. The Impersonality Thesis will be true, he writes, if:

> given our understanding of the concept of a person, if we know that [(4)] is true, we shall know that [(5)] is true. (Parfit, 1984, 213)

However, the example of worlds 1 and 2 also refutes this proposal. If I consider the functioning human brain and body which exists in both worlds after A's operation (the B-body), my knowledge that there exists a particular brain and body, and a particular series of interrelated mental and physical events, does not enable

[9] See, e.g., (Parfit, 1984, 253; 269), for arguments for the view that sameness of body or whole brain is unnecessary for sameness of person over time.

me to know that a particular person (e.g., B) exists. I will know this only if I also know that the other off-shoot, C, exists.

In order to avoid these objections, Parfit might modify his Impersonality Thesis as follows. A complete and impersonal description of reality is possible just in case if all the impersonal facts in two possible worlds are identical, all the personal facts in those two worlds are identical. Thus, any world which contains the same functioning brains and bodies, and the same streams of interrelated mental and physical events, as the actual world, must contain the very same persons. This Modified Impersonality Thesis is quite consistent with the non-identity of B and B' in worlds 1 and 2 since the impersonal facts in those worlds are not the same (e.g., there are facts about the brain, body and stream of consciousness of C in world 1 which will not feature in a complete description of world 2).

The Modified Impersonality Thesis, thus understood, will be false if there can be 'bare' or 'ungrounded' transworld statements of personal non-identity; that is, if two possible worlds might differ only in their personal facts. The possibility of bare transworld non-identities is, however, a consequence of the weakest and least contentious version of the contingency of origin thesis. From the highly plausible principle that an object such as a person or a ship might have been made of slightly different matter (e.g., just one atom or molecule different), together with a plausible transworld non-identity assumption, it follows that there can be bare transworld non-identities.

The proof for this due to Nathan Salmon, and can be stated as follows (Salmon, 1981, appendix 1, sec.29). Suppose, for the sake of simplicity, that artefacts of a certain kind K are composed of just three parts, and that any particular K could have originated composed of – at most – one different part (the weak contingency of origin assumption). Suppose that X in W_1 is a K originally composed of parts a, b and c, and that Y in W_2 is a K originally composed of parts a, b and d. Assume that X is not identical to Y (only a very implausible sufficiency condition for transworld identity would preclude such an assumption). By the weak contingency of origin assumption, there is a world, W_3, in which X is originally composed of parts a, c and d. But, by the same assumption, there is a world, W_4, in which Y is also originally composed of parts a, c and d. Since $X \neq Y$, it follows that X in $W_3 \neq Y$ in W_4. Everything else in worlds 3 and 4 may be held constant: e.g., let X and Y be constructed by the same artisan.[10]

This transworld non-identity is bare; nothing grounds the non-identity between X and Y in worlds 3 and 4. An analogous argument can, without much difficulty, be generated for persons. Thus, from the most minimal of assumptions, we can derive bare transworld non-identities between persons. Hence, given the plausibility of the initial transworld non-identity assumption and the weak version of the contingency

[10] I should point out that Salmon does not accept this proof on the grounds that we have been given no reason to suppose that W_4 is possible relative to either W_1 or W_3. But since we have no independent grounds to deny that all four worlds are mutually accessible, I believe we should accept the proof as valid.

of origin thesis, it follows – for perfectly general reasons – that the Modified Impersonality Thesis is false.

However, the central difficulty with the Modified Impersonality Thesis is that, even if it were true, it is not evident why it should be thought to embody any reductionist conception of persons. The truth of the Modified Impersonality Thesis would be doubted only by a Featureless Cartesian (who believes that two possible worlds, alike in all physical and psychological respects, could nonetheless differ in the identity of the immaterial souls existing in those worlds) or, more generally, by someone who believes (rightly, in my opinion) that statements of transworld personal identity or non-identity can be bare or ungrounded.[11] One could reject either of these views without endorsing any reductionist conception of persons.

Theses analogous to the Modified Impersonality Thesis may be true in other areas of philosophy. It may be true that two possible worlds which agree in their physical facts agree in their mental facts; or that two worlds which agree in their natural facts agree in their moral facts; or that two worlds which agree in their atomic facts agree in their molecular facts. But if such theses were true, would it simply follow that some reductionist thesis about mentality, morality and molecularity must be true? Arguably not: one can recognise the existence of constraints on the relation between, e.g., natural facts and moral facts, without thereby reducing the moral to the natural. (It is too much to demand of a non-reductionist about morality that he make no play with any constraints of the natural upon the moral.) Thus, I am not convinced that the Modified Impersonality Thesis, even if it were true, would serve to delineate any genuinely reductionist conception of persons.

It may be objected – cf. the Kripke quote above – that the Impersonality Thesis is simply one attempt to give content to the claim that persons are nothing "over and above" their bodies and experiences, in much the way that nations are said to be nothing "over and above" their citizens and territory. If persons are nothing "over and above" their bodies and experiences, must not some form of reductionism about persons be true?

However, in the sense in which the thesis that a person is nothing "over and above" his body and experiences is true, it serves merely to emphasise the fact that persons are not Cartesian Egos and that the identity of a person over time is analysable in terms of relations of physical and/or psychological continuity (the *relata* of which are persons at different times). And – to repeat – neither rejection of the Cartesian view nor endorsement of the Continuity Theory implies that persons are, in any interesting sense, reducible to entities or events of some other kind.[12]

---

[11] The term "Featureless Cartesian" is Parfit's, see (Parfit, 1984, 228).

[12] It should be noted that endorsement of the ontological irreducibility of persons is compatible with accepting Parfit's argument based upon the mind-splitting example of *My Physics Exam* (Parfit 1984, 245–252) which attempts to show that the phenomenon of the "unity of consciousness" is not to be explained in terms of ownership by a subject. If Parfit's argument is sound, there is a sense in which we ought to be "explanatory reductionists" about persons: reference to persons will not feature in an explanation of the unity of consciousness. But such an explanatory reduction does not, in itself, imply any ontological reduction of persons. (Analogously, the 'reduction' of biology

Can any reductionist account of social objects, such as nations, be sustained? David Hillel-Ruben has argued persuasively for the ontological irreducibility of nations. He argues that an assertion such as "France is a charter member of the UN" is not logically equivalent to any assertion which does not require the existence of France for its truth, and that there is no candidate (e.g., geographical area, particular sets or groups of people, etc.) with which France might be reductively identified (Hillel-Ruben, 1982).

Of course, it is true that a nation is nothing "over and above" its citizens and territory. But the content which can legitimately be given to this claim is, predictably enough, just the following: nations are not immaterial entities which might exist apart from any citizens and territory, and the identity over time of a nation is analysable in terms of the identity over time of its citizens and territory. This thesis is compatible with the ontological irreducibility of nations. (There is, I think, no sense in which it is true that a nation is nothing "over and above" its citizens and territory, and in which it is not also true that a person is nothing "over and above" his body and experiences.)[13]

A natural thought at this stage is the following: if the combined effect of the above arguments is to endorse Hume's famous analogy between persons and nations, has the spirit of the Humean view not been vindicated, even if the label 'reductionist' may no longer be deemed appropriate?[14] Some remarks of Parfit suggest that this may be so:

> I claim that a person is not like a Cartesian Ego, a being whose existence must be all-or-nothing. A person is like a nation ... In my claims about Reductionism and identity, I may have made mistakes ... But my main claim is that persons are like nations, not Cartesian Egos. If this claim is true, it would not be undermined by my mistakes. In the account that makes no mistakes, persons and nations would still go together. (Parfit, 1984, 275)

However, if Parfit's thesis is that a person is like a nation only in the sense that neither is an immaterial substance, this is a thesis which any Continuity Theorist – reductionist or non-reductionist – can and ought to accept. But Parfit claimed more than this: he claimed that some particular version of ontological reductionism about persons is true, viz., the Impersonality Thesis. But I criticised this further claim in the above discussion.

The spirit of the Humean view will be vindicated only if we ought to be reductionists about both persons and nations. Unless this is true, Hume's analogy

---

to physics and chemistry, if it could be completed, would imply only that the laws of biology are, at a fundamental level, explanatorily redundant. It would not follow from this that the objects of biological theory (heart, liver, lungs, etc.) do not exist or are otherwise reducible to their molecular or atomic constituents.)

[13] Raziel Abelson has pointed out that there is an important disanalogy between persons and nations. The citizens of a nation may continue to exist whether or not nations continue to exist, but any experience must be the experience of some subject. The precise import of this disanalogy is unclear, but – presumably – its effect would be to tell against reductionism about persons.

[14] David Hume writes: "I cannot compare the soul more properly to anything than to a republic or commonwealth" (Hume, 1978).

between persons and nations will have been robbed of its intended deflationary metaphysical import. The crucial question cannot be – simply – whether persons are like nations.

20.4 Reductionism and What Matters

Even if we are non-reductionists about personal identity, the consequences for rationality and ethics which Parfit has drawn from his metaphysical conception of persons may still follow. Parfit argued that theories of personal identity have significant implications for issues in rationality and morality: in particular, for the self-interest principle, personal commitments, punishment, the scope of distributive principles, and the weight which should be assigned to such principles.

In *Reasons and Persons*, Parfit outlines the implications of his reductionist conception of persons for these issues (Parfit, 1984, ch. 14 and 15). In all of these cases – except that concerning the weight which ought to be assigned to distributive principles – the implications hold in virtue of the (purported) fact that "what matters" to an ideally rational person contemplating his own future is not identity, but rather relations of psychological continuity and connectedness, relations which are not logically one-one, and which can hold to varying degrees.

The thesis that identity is not what matters should thus be understood as the thesis that pure, self-interested concern for one's own future is irrational: it is irrational of me to have any special concern for some future person just because that person is me. However, this thesis is not one which only a reductionist (Parfitian or otherwise) could – or should – endorse. This can be seen from a brief review of the two central arguments for the thesis that identity is not what matters: the Argument from Division and the Argument from Extrinsicness.

The Argument from Division can be stated as follows.[15] Suppose that I am about to divide. It would be absurd if I were to regard the prospect of division with the same horror that I would regard the prospect of my immediate death. There is surely a vast difference between my stream of consciousness ending forever, and its continuing in two streams. Since the prospect of division is as good as that of ordinary survival, I stand to my off-shoots in the relation that matters. However, on any plausible description of division, I am numerically identical with neither off-shoot. Consequently, identity cannot be the relation that matters.

The Argument from Extrinsicness runs as follows. On any plausible version of the Continuity Theory, the analysis of a person's identity over time will incorporate a non-branching component. (This is the most plausible way to avoid the consequence that, in a case of division, the original person is identical with both resulting persons.) The presence of a non-branching component implies that the identity

[15] The Argument from Division is the central argument which Parfit endorses for the thesis that identity is not what matters (Parfit, 1984, 261–66).

of a person over time can be extrinsically determined.[16] But whether I stand to some future individual in the relation that matters, it is plausible to suppose, cannot be extrinsically determined. (Whether I ought to care especially about the fate of my left-hemisphere off-shoot surely cannot depend upon what happens to the right hemisphere elsewhere in the hospital.) Consequently, identity cannot be the relation that matters.

Whatever the merits of these arguments, their success evidently does not require any reductionist assumptions. Consequently, all the practical implications for rationality and morality which flow from the thesis that identity is not what matters may still hold, even if we refuse to advance to a reductionist stage in our analysis of the identity of a person over time. Hence, theses about the nature of personal identity (in particular, reductionist proposals), and theses about the importance of personal identity (e.g., "identity is not what matters") are separately evaluable.

Matters are less straightforward with respect to the question of the weight which ought to be assigned to distributive principles. Parfit has argued that, if reductionism is true, the fact of the "separateness of persons" is "less deep", and hence less weight ought to be assigned to distributive principles (Parfit, 1984, 329–345). The reductionist conception of persons thus lends support to Utilitarianism. (Utilitarians assign no weight to distributive principles: they aim simply to maximise the net sum of benefits over burdens, whatever their distribution.) It might appear, therefore, that non-reductionist conceptions of persons will not imply that distributive principles ought to receive less (or no) weight.

However, consider again the analogy between persons and nations. The fact that, e.g., France and Britain are distinct nations does not appear to be a morally significant fact, and it remains morally insignificant even if we refuse to endorse a reductionist conception of nations. But if the ontological irreducibility of nations does not compromise the moral insignificance of the "separateness of nations", the ontological irreducibility of persons may constitute no essential barrier to regarding the boundaries between persons as, similarly, morally insignificant. If persons are like nations – even if we are reductionists about neither sort of entity – then it is still plausible:

> to claim that, just as we are right to ignore whether persons come from the same or different nations, we are right to ignore whether experiences come from the same or different lives. (Parfit, 1984, 341)

Hence, it appears that all the implications for issues in rationality and morality which flow from a reductionist conception of persons may still hold, even if we refuse to embrace reductionism. This point is important since many philosophers who refuse to countenance any reductionist conception of persons may assume that this blocks the implications for rationality and morality which Parfit has delineated. If the arguments of this section have been sound, this assumption is false.

[16] For more on the issue of extrinsic identity, see (Garrett, 1990), reprinted here as Chapter 19.

References

Ayer, A. J. (1952). *Language, truth and logic*, 2nd edn. London: Dover Publications.
Garrett, B. (1990). Personal identity and extrinsicness. *Philosophical Studies, 59*, 177–94.
Hillel-Ruben, D. (1982). The existence of social entities. *Philosophical Quarterly, 32*(129), 295–310.
Hume, D. (1739/1978). *A treatise of human nature*. Oxford: Oxford University Press.
Kripke, S. (1980). *Naming and necessity*. Cambridge: Harvard University Press.
Lewis, D. (1976). The paradoxes of time travel. *American Philosophical Quarterly, 13*(1), 145–152.
Nozick, R. (1981). *Philosophical explanations*. Cambridge: Harvard University Press.
Parfit, D. (1984). *Reasons and persons*. Oxford: Oxford University Press.
Quinton, A. (1976). Social objects. *Proceedings of the Aristotelian Society, 76*, 1–27.
Salmon, N. (1981). *Reference and essence*. New Jersey: Princeton University Press.
Shoemaker, S. & Swinburne, R. (1984). Personal identity: A materialist's account. In *Personal Identity*. Oxford: Blackwell.
Wiggins, D. (1980). *Sameness and substance*. Cambridge: Harvard University Press.
Wright, C. (1983). Keeping track of Nozick. *Analysis, 43*(3), 134–140.

Chapter 21
Bermúdez on Self-Consciousness

Abstract In this discussion, I argue that José Luis Bermúdez has not shown that there is a paradox in our concept of self-consciousness. The deflationary theory is an implausible theory of self-consciousness. A more plausible theory, "the simple theory", is not paradoxical. However, I do think there is a puzzle about the connection between self-consciousness and 'I'-thoughts.

21.1 Introduction

José Luis Bermúdez believes that in our notion of self-consciousness there is a paradox, which he attempts to delineate in (Chapter 1 of) his 1998 book, *The Paradox of Consciousness*. But is there really a paradox? What considerations about self-consciousness are supposed to generate the paradox? I shall summarise Bermúdez's reasoning, then offer a critique.

21.2 Self-Consciousness, 'I'-Thoughts, and the Deflationary Theory

The capacity for self-consciousness is clearly linked to the capacity to entertain a range of 'I'-thoughts (as opposed, for example, to the view of self-consciousness as introspective awareness of one's self, a view which is objectionable for familiar Humean reasons). 'I'-thoughts involve self-reference, but in a familiarly, distinctive manner – this is a view made by John Perry (1979). Bermúdez neatly elucidates this "distinctive type of self-reference", and concludes with the following definition:

> An 'I'-thought is a thought whose content can only be specified directly by means of the first-person pronoun 'I' or indirectly by means of the indirect reflexive pronoun 'he*'. (Bermúdez, 1998, 3–4)

The terminology of 'he*' derives from Héctor-Neri Castañeda (1967). 'He*' indicates that 'he' is functioning as a 'quasi-indicator'. The idea is that "*X* believes

B. Garrett, *Time, Identity and the Self: Essays on Metaphysics*, Synthese Library 442, https://doi.org/10.1007/978-3-030-85517-8_21

that he* is F" is true if and only if X is self-consciously aware that he is the person who is F. In such a case, we could capture this more colloquially by saying "X believes that he himself is F".

Bermúdez then introduces a well known distinction between two types of 'I'-thought, the distinction Wittgenstein characterised as that between "as subject" and "as object" uses of 'I' (Wittgenstein, 1972, 66–67). Examples Wittgenstein gave of the former type were "I think it will rain" and "I have toothache"; examples of the latter, "My arm is broken" and "I have grown six inches". Bermúdez characterises this distinction epistemically, in terms of 'grounds'. A judgement "I am F" is "as object" if and only if it is logically reconstructable as the result of conjoining two thoughts "A is F" and "I am A". The former is a predication component, the latter an identification component.[1] 'I'-judgements which are not decomposable in this way are "as subject".

This characterisation fits with another way in which Wittgenstein's distinction has been glossed, that was offered by Sydney Shoemaker. Shoemaker characterised "as object" uses of 'I' as those occurring in 'I'-judgements which are liable to error through misidentification of the subject; occurrences immune to such error are "as subject". Shoemaker defined the liability to the error, quite generally, as follows:

> To say that a statement "a is F" is subject to error through misidentification relative to the term 'a' means that the following is possible: the speaker knows some particular thing to be F, but makes the mistake of asserting "a is F" because, and only because, he mistakenly thinks that the thing he knows to be F is what 'a' refers to. Shoemaker (1982, 7–8)

Bermúdez regards the appeal to knowledge in Shoemaker's definition as too restrictive, and offers his own version, with "is warranted in believing" replacing 'knows' (Bermúdez, 1998, 7).

Bermúdez takes it that this characterisation fits with the previous one, 'I'-judgements which have an identification component can be subject to error through misidentification of the subject. So for him the two characterisations are equivalent.

Bermúdez also sees an asymmetry here: the "as object" use, as he has defined it, presupposes the "as subject" use, whereas the "as subject" use does not presuppose the "as object" use. (Any "as object" 'I'-judgement will have an identification component. This component is either itself "as object", or else "as subject"; if "as object" it will have an identification component. On pain of infinite regress, this sequence must terminate in an identification-free component.) This asymmetry suggests a sense in which the "as subject" use is prior to the "as object" use, and perhaps more fundamental to self-consciousness (Bermúdez, 1998, 7).

Bermúdez notes the difficulty in giving a positive account of the "as subject" use (i.e., one that does not involve negative terms such as, e.g., 'criterionless' or 'identification-free' or 'non-inferential') (Bermúdez, 1998, 6–ff). However, he offers the following suggestion:

---

[1] The terminology is from Gareth Evans, see (Evans, 1982, 185).

> there is at least one good reason to think that the semantics of the first-person pronoun might hold the key to immunity to error through misidentification. This emerges when one reflects that the first-person pronoun has guaranteed reference." (Bermúdez, 1998, 9)

He then goes on to characterise the supposedly popular 'deflationary' theory of self-consciousness, according to which we are to account for self-consciousness "in terms of the capacity to think 'I'-thoughts that are immune to error through misidentification, where immunity to error through misidentification is a function of the semantics of the first-person pronoun" (Bermúdez, 1998, 10). The semantics for the first person is essentially encapsulated in the token-reflexive rule "If a person employs a token 'I', then he refers to himself in virtue of being the producer of that token" (Bermúdez, 1998, 15).

Bermúdez notes an obvious objection to this proposal. The semantics of the first person, including its consequence that uses of 'I' are immune to reference failure and misreference, applies to both uses of 'I', "as subject" and "as object". "So how can mastery of the semantics of the first-person pronoun capture what is distinctive about those first-person contents that are immune to error through misidentification (Bermúdez, 1998, 9–11).

However, Bermúdez thinks this difficulty is only apparent. As noted, he holds that all 'I'-judgements are either "as object" or "as subject", and that all "as object" judgements are decomposable into component judgements one of which – the identification component – must either be, or terminate in, an "as subject" judgement, which is immune to error through misidentification of the subject (hereafter, IEM) (Bermúdez, 1998, 11–12).

Bermúdez suggests that the deflationary theory neatly dovetails with the dominant thought-language principle, according to which "the philosophical analysis of thought can proceed only through the philosophical analysis of language" (Bermúdez, 1998, 12). This suggestion is intended to confirm the familiar and generally accepted character of the deflationary theory.

Despite its alleged dominance in our thinking, however, Bermúdez takes the deflationary theory to lead to paradox. The paradox of self-consciousness consists of two unacceptable consequences that follow from the deflationary theory: explanatory circularity and capacity circularity (Bermúdez, 1998, 15–21). As to the first kind of circularity,

> the deflationary theory of self-consciousness (and by extension, any account of self-consciousness that tries to explain what is distinctive about self-consciousness in terms of mastery of the first-person pronoun) will end up being viciously circular because mastery of the semantics of the first-person pronoun involves the capacity to think first-person thoughts. (Bermúdez, 1998, 16–17)

The latter claim Bermúdez takes to have been established by his discussion of the token-reflexive reference-fixing rule. Basically, the idea is that I can know that I refer to myself in virtue of being the producer of a given token only if I know that I produced the token, and this is a thought with a first-person content (Bermúdez, 1998, 14–16).

As to the second kind of circularity,

> this form of circularity arises because the attempt is being made [by defenders of the deflationary theory] to explain one capacity (the capacity to think thoughts with first-person contents) in terms of another capacity (mastery of the semantics of the first-person pronoun). (Bermúdez, 1998, 18)

Yet the latter capacity presupposes the former; so, Bermúdez concludes, "it is natural to describe this as an instance of capacity circularity" (Bermúdez, 1998, 18). Given these consequences, we are invited to reject the deflationary theory and its (supposed) corollary, the thought-language principle.

21.3 Critique

I shall offer four criticisms of Bermúdez's discussion, in order of increasing severity. First, is Bermúdez right to characterise a judgement "I am *F*" as "as object' if it is the result of conjoining two thoughts "*A* is *F*" and "I am *A*"? Not obviously. Suppose I arrive at an 'I'-judgement by engaging in an act of 'outer' perception (e.g., I look down and judge "I am wearing a yellow tie" or "I have five fingers"). Such judgements are clearly not IEM. Yet should such judgements be thought of as inferential in the way just described, e.g., the result of conjoining "This body has five fingers/wears a yellow tie" and "I am this body"? Does my body wear a yellow tie? What if, for familiar philosophical reasons, I am not identical with my body?

If the inferentialist explanation is found wanting, the only option is to alter the definition of the "as object" use to include those 'I'-judgements which, though not (consciously or unconsciously) inferential, are nonetheless grounded in acts of 'outer' perception. This consequence has the potential to frustrate the reasoning behind Bermúdez asymmetry thesis (Bermúdez, 1998, 7), since some "as object" uses will not now depend on "as subject" uses on pain of infinite regress.

Second, Bermúdez asked the question, "How can mastery of the semantics of the first-person pronoun capture what is distinctive about those first-person contents that are immune to error through misidentification?", and answered it by saying that any "as object" 'I'-judgement is decomposable into component judgements, the 'I'-judgement of which is "as subject".

But it is hard to be satisfied with this answer. "As object" 'I'-judgements are governed by the token-reflexive rule, and so possess guaranteed reference, yet they are not IEM. How then can the semantics of the first person explain IEM? Moreover, given the first criticism above, it is not true that all "as object" 'I'-judgements decompose in the manner suggested by Bermúdez.

Third, since the idea that the semantics of the first person can explain IEM is built into the deflationary theory, my second criticism suggests that this theory is not the natural and plausible account Bermúdez presents it as being. It is controversial, and, I have just argued, false. Of course, Bermúdez too wants to reject the theory because it leads to paradox. But its falsity ought to have been evident from the outset.

Bermúdez breaks the deflationary theory into the following three claims:

1. once we have an account of what it is to be capable of thinking ‘I’-thoughts, we shall have explained everything distinctive about self-consciousness;
2. once we have an account of what it is to be capable of thinking thoughts that are [IEM], we shall have explained everything distinctive about the capacity to think ‘I’-thoughts’;
3. (a) once we have explained what it is to master the semantics of the first-person pronoun, we shall have explained everything distinctive about the capacity to think [IEM] thoughts.

Both of the latter two claims should be rejected: 3(a) for the reason given in the second criticism above; and (2) because the capacity to think of thoughts that are IEM cannot explain everything distinctive about the capacity to think ‘I’-thoughts, since we plainly can think ‘I’-thoughts which are not thus immune.

If this is right,then Bermúdez’s project falters at the outset. He claims to entangle the deflationary theory in paradox. But this would be an interesting result only if the deflationary theory were a plausible theory to begin with. A paradox, after all, is supposed to be an unacceptable or absurd consequence drawn from a pool of plausible premises. Deriving an absurd conclusion from implausible premises is not a paradox, though it may not be entirely without interest. Moreover, since the reasons just given for rejecting the deflationary theory in no way call into question the thought-language principle, it is hard to see how this principle can be a serious component of the deflationary theory.

Finally, fourth, what of the paradox? The interest of this question has somewhat diminished now, but it does seem that the deflationary theory, as Bermúdez characterises it, is viciously circular in the ways he indicates. The circularity arises, naturally enough, because the deflationary theory purports to offer an explanation of self-consciousness in terms of mastery of the first person pronoun.

However, there is another more plausible theory in the neighbourhood – I shall call it “the simple theory” – which captures the key insight of the deflationary theory without imploding in vicious circularity. The simple theory does not attempt to explain self-consciousness in terms the mastery of the first person, but rather elucidates the concept of self-consciousness by identifying the phenomenon of self-consciousness with mastery of the first person. If neither phenomenon is held to be explanatorily prior to the other, there can be no charge of explanatory circularity.

Similarly, on the simple theory, there is no capacity circularity. If coming to be self-conscious just is coming to master the first-person pronoun, then there can be no question of acquiring one capacity before acquiring the other. But there is nothing mysterious, or even awkward, about this.

Bermúdez lists six propositions which he takes to generate the paradox of self-consciousness. By endorsing the simple theory, I am committed to denying proposition (5): “A non-circular account of self-consciousness is possible” (Bermúdez, 1998, 24). Bermúdez attempts to defend this proposition by suggesting that if we reject it, “it follows that the capacity to think ‘I’-thoughts is unanalysable, which is a highly undesirable result” (Bermúdez, 1998, 25). But this is confused. A group of concepts $\{A, B, C, D\}$ may form a circle, each analysable in terms of the others. The concept A is analysable in terms of B, C, and D, and these concepts are analysable, *inter alia*, in terms of A. Plainly there is no incoherence here; so circularity is not incompatible with analysis. Of course, circularity is incompatible with reductive analysis, but I see no reason to suppose the concept of self-consciousness has to be or is, susceptible to reductive analysis. In other words, there is no immediate prospect of an analysis of self-consciousness along the lines: "self-consciousness = consciousness $+X$", where ingredient X can be understood independently of the concept of self-consciousness.

It may be objected that a circular group of concepts could not be learnt. But this is also a confusion. Obviously, to revert to the previous example, one could not first fully grasp A, then fully grasp B, and so on. But that does not mean that concepts cannot be acquired. Rather, light dawns gradually over the whole, until a full understanding of all four concepts is achieved.

21.4 Conclusion and Further Work

So, in sum, the deflationary theory, as Bermúdez states it, is not a theory which ought to command immediate assent. Since it is a false theory, it is unsurprising that it should have implausible or absurd consequences. However, there is a much more plausible theory, the simple theory, which captures the genuine insight in the deflationary theory, yet does not involve any vicious circularity, and in no way threatens the thought-language principle.

Nevertheless, I think there is still a puzzle about our concept of self-consciousness. On the one hand, we take it that all 'I'-judgements exhibit self-consciousness. On the other hand, we take it that only "as subject" 'I'-judgements stand in a special intimate connection with self-consciousness. The puzzle is how we are to reconcile these two commitments.

The latter commitment is neatly illustrated by G. E. M. Anscombe's example of the '*A*'-users (Anscombe, 1981, 21–37). In her imaginary community '*A*' is the name each person uses to refer to himself, and that name is stamped on each person's wrist. Reports on one's own actions, which one gives straight off from observation, are made using the name on the wrist.[2] What is striking about the '*A*'-users is precisely their total lack of self-consciousness. Since they have no device of self-reference with "as subject" characteristics, it is natural to conclude that the "as subject" use is essential for self-consciousness.

[2] However, there is something (especially) odd about the '*A*'-users. Anscombe writes as if they were like us in having thoughts, sensations, etc. But if an '*A*'-user has a pain, he cannot utter "*A* is in pain" simply in virtue of feeling the pain. Rather, he must first observe pain-like behaviour, notice that it is exhibited by the body whose '*A*'-inscribed wrist he can see, and then judge "*A* is in pain" (Anscombe, 1981, 24). But does this make any sense? If he can feel pain, why can he not ascribe it to himself on that basis? Or should the '*A*'-users be understood as insensate zombies?

Perhaps we could resolve the puzzle by refusing to see "as object" uses of 'I' as expressive of self-consciousness. But even an utterance of "I am six feet tall", made upon measuring myself, seems expressive of self-consciousness, and does not express the same thought as that expressed by an utterance of "Such and such a body is six feet tall". A puzzle thus remains.

References

Anscombe, G. E. M. (1981). The first person. In *Metaphysics and the philosophy of mind*. Oxford: Blackwell.

Bermúdez, J. L. (1998). *The paradox of consciousness*. Boston: MIT Press.

Castañeda, H. (1967). Indicators and quasi-indicators. *American Philosophical Quarterly, 9*, 85–100.

Evans, G. (1982). *The varieties of reference*. Oxford: Clarendon Press.

Perry, J. (1979). The Essential indexical. *Noûs, 3*, 3–21.

Shoemaker, S. (1982). Self-reference and self-awareness. In *Identity, cause, and mind*. Cambridge: Cambridge University Press.

Wittgenstein, L. (1972). *The blue and brown books*. Oxford: Blackwell.

Chapter 22
Anscombe on 'I'

Abstract In "The First Person", G. E. M. Anscombe argues against the common-sense view that 'I' is a referring expression. My aim in this discussion is to show that her arguments for this claim are problematic.

22.1 Introduction

The common-sense view of 'I' has two components: the referential view and the indexical view. According to the referential view, 'I' is a referring term, as much as proper names like 'Clinton' and 'Nixon'. According to the indexical view, the reference of a particular utterance of 'I' gets fixed by virtue of the following self-reference rule: a given token of 'I' refers to whoever produced it. Thus, the common-sense view holds that 'I' is a singular term, and it explains how the reference of particular tokens of 'I' gets fixed.

In "The First Person", G. E. M. Anscombe attempts to undermine the common-sense view. She writes: "'I' is neither a name nor another kind of referring expression whose logical role is to make a reference, at all" (Anscombe, 1981, 32). By this she does not mean that 'I' is an empty referring term (like 'Odysseus' or 'Hamlet'). She means that it does not belong to the category of singular terms. It is analogous rather to "feature-placing" occurrences of 'it' (as in "it is raining" or "it is snowing").

Anscombe's paper contains two main arguments against the common-sense view of 'I'. Her first argument attacks the indexical view. Her second argument attempts to counter the referential view. The first argument, which I shall call "Ancombe's Challenge", alleges that the indexical view fails to explain what is special about 'I', namely, that its competent use in judgement manifests self-consciousness. The second argument, which I shall call "The Tank Argument", concludes that "if 'I' is a referring expression, then Descartes was right about what the referent was" (Anscombe, 1981, 31). That is, if 'I' refers, it refers to an immaterial Cartesian Ego. This is to be a *reductio* of the view that 'I' is a referring term.

B. Garrett, *Time, Identity and the Self: Essays on Metaphysics*, Synthese Library 442, https://doi.org/10.1007/978-3-030-85517-8_22

22.2 Anscombe's Challenge

Anscombe invites us to:

> Imagine a society in which everyone is labelled with two names. One appears on their backs and at the top of their chests, and these names, which their bearers cannot see are various: '*B*' to '*Z*' let us say. The other, '*A*', is stamped on the inside of their wrists and is the same for everyone. In making reports on people's actions everyone uses the name on their chests or backs if he can see these names or is used to seeing them. Everyone also learns to respond to utterances of the name on his own chest and back in the way and sort of circumstances in which we tend to respond to utterances of our names. Reports on one's own actions, which one gives straight off from are made using the name on the wrist. (Anscombe, 1981, 24)

Each person in this imaginary community has two proper names: one that is unique, and one that is shared ('*A*'). These names are the only devices of "self-reference" in this community. Reports on one's own actions are made on the basis of using the name '*A*' on one's wrist, and on the basis of inference, including inferences from the testimony of others.

It is difficult to overestimate the extent of the differences between the '*A*'-users and ourselves. When an '*A*'-user says "*A* is *F*', his judgement is always based on third-person or publicly accessible grounds, e.g., observation of his behaviour or bodily condition, or inference from the testimony of others (on hearing "*B* is *F*", *B* can infer "*A* is *F*" given that he accepts "*A* is *B*"). Even the '*A*'-users' "self-ascriptions" of pain will have to be based on behavioural data. In short, as Anscombe observes, "our description does not include self-consciousness on the part of people who use the name '*A*' (Anscombe, 1981, 24).

In this thought-experiment, we have described a singular term ('*A*') which, it seems, we can substitute for '*I*' in the self-reference rule, *salva veritate*. In the case of our imagined community, '*A*' is the name that each person uses to refer to himself. From this, Anscombe infers that '*A*' is governed by the self-reference rule. Yet, *ex hypothesi*, uses of '*A*' in judgement fail to manifest self-consciousness. Hence, the indexical view can make no space for the incontrovertible fact that our 'I'-judgements manifest self-consciousness.

However, even if we were to grant Anscombe her premise that '*A*' is governed by the self-reference rule, it would not follow that the indexical view is untenable. We must distinguish two conclusions: the weak conclusion that the indexical view fails to explain the evident fact that 'I'-judgements manifest self-consciousness, and the strong conclusion that the indexical view is incompatible with that evident fact. Anscombe needs the strong conclusion in order to refute the indexical view, but her argument, if successful, supports only the weak conclusion. The weak conclusion would tell against the indexical view on the assumption that the view, if true, must explain the link between first-person judgement and self-consciousness. But why assume that the indexical view incurs this explanatory obligation?

However, the weak conclusion does not follow. Anscombe's key premise is false: '*A*' is not governed by the self-reference rule. Unlike 'I', '*A*' is based on criteria. Certain observational conditions must be satisfied in order for an '*A*'-user to refer using '*A*'. That is, '*A*' is not used simply as a device of self-reference. It is not an indexical. Consequently, Anscombe's Challenge is unsuccessful.

Perhaps her example was merely infelicitous. Can we not imagine that the '*A*'-users might introduce into their language a singular term '$A*$', which, as a matter of convention, is deemed to refer to its utterer? The application of such a term is not based on observational criteria. In fact, '$A*$' is governed by the rule that governs 'I'. Yet uses of '$A*$' in judgement fail to manifest self-consciousness.

This example supports the weak conclusion. The fact that a term is governed by the self-reference rule does not imply that it features in self-conscious judgements. But, as noted, the weak conclusion does not undermine the indexical view.

Further, we can distinguish 'I' from '$A*$' in the following way: although both terms are governed by the self-reference rule, uses of 'I' conform to that rule in an immediate or criterionless way, whereas uses of '$A*$' do not. An '$A*$'-user must first establish that he is the producer of his token of '$A*$' in order to use that token in judgement. In contrast, an 'I'-user does not have to establish that he is the producer of his token of 'I' in order to use that token in judgement: that knowledge is direct and basic. (This is not to claim any sort of infallibility. One can be mistaken about whether one is the producer of a given token of 'I'.)

22.3 The Tank Argument

Anscombe's second argument starts out with the following question:

> Let us waive the question about the sense of 'I' and ask only how reference to the right object could be guaranteed... this reference could only be sure-fire if the referent of 'I' were both freshly defined with each use of 'I', and also remained in view so long as something was taken to be I... it seems to follow that what 'I' stands for must be a Cartesian Ego. (Anscombe, 1981, 30)

This line of reasoning is underwritten by the Tank Argument:

> Imagine that I get into a state of "sensory deprivation" (i.e., no input from and no bodily feeling) I tell myself "I won't let this happen again!". If the object meant by 'I' is this body, this human being, then in these circumstances present to my senses; and how else can it be "present to" me? Am I reduced to, as it were, "referring in absence'? I have not lost my "self-consciousness"; nor can what I mean by 'I' be an object no longer present to me. (Anscombe, 1981, 31)

In other words: if 'I' refers, what I mean by 'I' is an object that is always "present to" me. In a sensorially deprived state, no material object (e.g., human body or human being) is "present to" me. Since I remain a competent 'I'-user whilst sensorially deprived, what is "present to" me must be something immaterial, a Cartesian Ego. But the Cartesian view is absurd. Hence, we should reject the assumption that led to this result, and conclude that 'I' is not a referring expression.

Anscombe makes two questionable assumptions in the course of this argument. First, she assumes that if the use of 'I' were to refer to my body, then the referent of

‘I’ would have to ‘present’ itself to me as a body. However, why assume that if the self were something bodily, and were perceived introspectively, it would have to be perceived as something bodily? An analogy suggests otherwise: if pains are neural events, it does not follow that when I feel a pain, I feel it as a neural event.

Second, Anscombe assumes, more generally, that if ‘I’ refers, its object must be “present to” the subject. But the thesis that self-reference requires self-presentation has little to recommend it. It is quite consistent to endorse the referential view of ‘I’ and to concede, with Hume, that there is no distinctive introspective phenomenology of the self.

The two assumptions which support the Tank Argument have a deeper source. Anscombe’s guiding thought is that if ‘I’ refers, it must be a device of demonstrative reference, rather than of indexical reference. If ‘I’ were a referring term, it would function as an ‘inner’ demonstrative (proxy for, e.g., “this self”). That being so, any token ‘I’-thought would require that its thinker be in receipt of information deriving from the object demonstrated. (This premise – that demonstrative reference always requires appropriate information links – is also in need of clarification and defence.) In the tank, only an immaterial Ego could serve as the source of such information. Hence, if ‘I’ refers in the tank, it refers to an Ego, and so much the worse for the view that ‘I’ refers. However, since we have no reason to accept Anscombe’s guiding thought, the Tank Argument is without force.

22.4 Supporting the Referential View

The referential view of ‘I’ has emerged unscathed. Further, as Anscombe is aware, two considerations strongly favour this view. First, ‘I’ has the same “syntactical place” as a referring expression (Anscombe, 1981, 29). Second, an occurrence of ‘I’ in a sentence “I am *F*”, uttered by *X*, can be replaced *salva veritate* by the name ‘*X*’. Both considerations make a powerful case for the referentiality of ‘I’.

Anscombe is not convinced. She objects to the first consideration on the grounds that it is ‘absurd’ to argue from syntax to reference – no one thinks that “it is raining” contains a referring expression, ‘it’ (Anscombe, 1981, 30). But the analogy is lame. The non-referential character of such uses of ‘it’ is manifested in other ways. For example, we cannot infer “Something is raining” from “it is raining”. But we can infer “Someone is in pain” from “I am in pain”. Or again, parenthetical qualification of the subject is possible in the case of ‘I’ (as in, e.g., “I, the person speaking to you now, am Scottish”). But parenthetical qualification makes no sense in the case of feature-placing uses of ‘it’ (e.g., “it, the sky above you, is raining”).

Anscombe objects to the second consideration on the grounds that the biconditional “If *X* asserts something with ‘I’ as subject, his assertion will be true if and only if what he asserts is true of *X*” is perfectly correct, it is not a “sufficient account” of ‘I’, since it does not distinguish between ‘I’ and ‘*A*’. However, as we have seen, ‘I’ and ‘*A*’ can be distinguished in other ways – in particular, ‘*A*’ is not governed by the self-reference rule. Moreover, the above biconditional is not true with '*A*' in place of 'I'. If an '*A*'-user (say, *B*) were to mistake *C*'s wrist for his own, he might truly assert "*A* is *F*", yet fail to assert something true of himself. In such a case, *B*'s use of '*A*' would refer to *C*.

To conclude: Anscombe's arguments against the common-sense view of 'I' are flawed, and there are positive reasons why we should regard 'I' as a referring term.

Reference

Anscombe, G. E. M. (1981). The first person. In *Metaphysics and the philosophy of mind*. Oxford: Blackwell.

Chapter 23
Wittgenstein on the First-Person

Abstract What is the link between 'I'-judgements and self-consciousness? What are we to make of Wittgenstein's cryptic remarks in the *Blue Book* about the "as subject" use of 'I'? Are the salient characteristics of the "as subject" use peculiar to 'I'? Do they illuminate the nature of self-consciousness? These questions are addressed in this discussion.

23.1 The Problem with 'I'-Judgements

Lichtenberg, famously, remarked that Descartes was not entitled to his dictum "I think, therefore I am". All that would remain after the application of the Method of Doubt was "there is thinking, therefore there is a momentary thinker" or "this is thought, therefore at least one thought is being thought". As a corollary, Lichtenberg suggested that instead of "I think", one ought to say "it's thinking", on an analogy with forms of words such as "it's raining" and "it's snowing'.

What was the point of Lichtenberg's remark? It is normally thought that Lichtenberg was endorsing the view that an occurrence of 'I' in "I think" is non-referential, comparable to the occurrence of 'it' in "it is raining".[1] Whether or not this is exegetically accurate, it should be apparent that "I think" and "it's raining" are not analogous in relevant respects. First, it is a mark of the referentiality of a term 'a' that 'Fa' implies "Something is F". We cannot infer "Something is raining" from "it is raining", yet we can infer "Someone is in pain" from "I am in pain". Second, the following truth-value link rule governs 'I'-judgements: "I am F" said by X is true if and only if X is F. The best explanation of the correctness of this rule is the co-reference of 'I' and 'X' across the biconditional. What is the corresponding link rule for "it's raining"? Presumably: "it's raining" uttered at place p is true if and only if, at p, it's raining. However, since this rule contains feature-placing (hence

[1] However, John McDowell has suggested that Lichtenberg is best seen as offering a *reductio* of the Cartesian conception of 'consciousness' as self-contained and context-free which permits the derivation of such a bizarre conclusion (McDowell, 1997, sec. 4).

B. Garrett, *Time, Identity and the Self: Essays on Metaphysics*, Synthese Library 442, https://doi.org/10.1007/978-3-030-85517-8_23

non-referential) occurrences of 'it' on both sides of the biconditional, we cannot explain the correctness of the rule in terms of co-reference.

There is a further disanalogy. If we replace "I think" with "it thinks", and we wish to avoid solipsism, we will have to index each utterance of "it thinks" (to: "it thinks (x)", not: "it thinks (y)", etc.), if we are to avoid contradiction. Of course, we have to do likewise with utterances of "it's raining" – we index to a place of utterance. But what do we index to in the case of "it thinks"? The natural index is to persons; but then the intended point of Lichtenberg's recommendation would be lost entirely. We could no longer conceive of thinking as a subjectless occurrence, like a state of the weather, since the indexed person would be the subject. Derek Parfit suggests that we can preserve Lichtenberg's insight by relativising not to a person or subject, but to a "particular life" (Parfit, 1984, sec. 81). But Parfit never makes clear how we can intelligibly think of a particular human life as anything other than the life of a person, a subject of thought and experience.

23.2 Wittgenstein on the Two Uses of 'I'

In what follows, I assume that 'I' is a referring term, tokens of which figure in a range of true statements. In that respect, 'I' is in the same category as other personal pronouns and personal proper names. But 'I' is a peculiar personal referring term: it is governed by the indexical rule that a token of 'I' refers to the person who produced it. This rule explains why competent use of 'I' is guaranteed against both misreference and reference-failure. In addition, the austerity (or non-descriptive character) of the rule explains why one's competent use of 'I' can survive both total loss of 'objective' beliefs about oneself (e.g., beliefs about one's nature, history, and spatio-temporal location), and the acquisition of massively false beliefs about one-self (e.g., "I am Napoleon").

However, none of these features explains what is distinctive about 'I'-judgements, viz., that they are manifestations of self-consciousness. The central task of any successful philosophical account of the first person pronoun is to explain that, and why, competent use of 'I' manifests self-consciousness. How might such an account proceed? As a starting point, consider the following well-known passages from the *Blue Book*:

> Now the idea that the real I lives in my body is connected with the peculiar grammar of the word 'I', and the misunderstandings this grammar is liable to give rise to. There are two different cases in the use of the word 'I' (or 'my') which I might call "the use as object" and "the use as subject". Examples of the first kind are these: "My arm is broken", "I have grown six inches", "I have a bump on my forehead", "The wind blows my hair about". Examples of the second kind are: "I see so-and-so", "I hear so-and-so", "I try to lift my arm", "I think it will rain", "I have a toothache". One can point to the difference between these two categories by saying: The cases of the first category involve the recognition of a particular person, and there is in these cases the possibility of an error, or as I should rather put it: The possibility of an error has been provided for ... It is possible that, say in an accident, I should feel a pain in my arm, see a broken arm at my side, and think it is

mine, when really it is my neighbour's. And I could, looking into a mirror, mistake a bump on his forehead for one on mine. On the other hand, there is no question of recognising a person when I say I have a toothache. To ask "are you sure it's you who have pains?" would be nonsensical. And now this way of stating our idea suggests itself: that it is impossible that in making the statement "I have a toothache" I should have mistaken another person for myself, as it is to moan with pain by mistake, having mistaken someone else for me. To say "I have pain" is no more about a particular person than moaning is.

We feel then that in cases in which 'I' is used "as subject", we don't use it because we recognise a particular person by his bodily characteristics; and this creates the illusion that we use this word to refer to something bodiless, which, however, has its seat in our body. In fact this seems to be the real ego, the one of which it was said, "Cogito, ergo sum". (Wittgenstein, 1972, 66–67; 69)

From these passages, we can extract the following six claims:

(i) There are two different uses of the pronoun 'I', "the use as object" and "the use as subject".
(ii) Given Wittgenstein's examples, we are evidently meant to infer that "as object" uses of 'I' feature only in physical self-ascriptions, and that "as subject" uses feature only in mental self-ascriptions.
(iii) All and only "as object" uses "involve the recognition of a particular person".
(iv) Only in such uses has "the possibility of an error been provided for", viz., the error of mistaking another person for oneself.
(v) An "as subject" occurrence of 'I' (as in a typical utterance of "I am in pain") is not "about a particular person".
(vi) It is a misreading of the 'grammar' of "as subject" uses of 'I' which fuels the illusion of a Cartesian subject.[2]

Wittgenstein has latched onto an important distinction, but he has failed to draw it properly. To see this, we should focus on (ii), (iii) and (iv). The problem is that (ii) is inconsistent with (iii) and (iv).

What does Wittgenstein mean when he says that "as object" uses of 'I' "involve the recognition of a particular person" [(iii)]? What is meant by 'recognition'?[3] I take it that a judgement "I am *F*" involves the recognition of its subject if it is the result of an inference from premises "*X* is *F*' and "I am *X*", or if it is the upshot of an act of outer perception. Typical examples of such recognition occur when a person judges "I am *F*" after identifying himself with someone in a mirror or photograph.

However, (ii) and (iii) conflict. First, many occurrences of 'I' in physical self-ascriptions will count as "as subject". My judgement "I am sitting", known in the

[2] None of (i)-(vi) imply either that the "as object" use of 'I' refers to the body or that the "as subject" use is non-referential. The fifth claim might seem to imply the non-referentiality of "as subject" uses of 'I', but I take the point of (v) to be that the function of 'I' in "I am in pain" is not to describe its object (Garrett, 1993).

[3] As Gareth Evans notes, there is a trivial sense in which all singular thought involves recognition of its object (Evans, 1982, 218). When I think that x is F, I must identify the referent of 'x' in thought. This could not have been the sense which Wittgenstein had in mind.

normal way (through proprioception), is not the result of any process of subject-identifying inference or outer perception. (That is, it is not the presence of inference as such that makes for 'recognition', but only inference that involves identification of the subject.) In fact, self-ascriptions which are the result of explicit inferences (involving mirrors, photographs, etc.) are fairly rare. Second, some occurrences of 'I' in mental self-ascriptions will count as "as object". Imagine a futuristic brain-scanner which emits a certain signal whenever a person connected to it is in pain. If I am connected to the scanner, I might judge that I am in pain on the grounds that, according to the emitted signal, someone is in pain, and I believe that person to be me.[4]

Claims (ii) and (iv) are also in conflict. According to (iv), in "as object" uses of 'I' there is always the possibility of mistaking another person for oneself. In contrast, self-ascriptions incorporating "as subject" occurrences of 'I' are immune to error through misidentification of the subject. How should we understand this immunity? If we read 'misidentification' as 'misrecognition', (iv) merely becomes a variant of (iii): if there is no recognition or identification of the subject in "as subject" uses of 'I', there can be no possibility of misidentification. But there is a more interesting way of understanding this impossibility. We can say that a self-ascription "I am *F*" is immune to error through misidentification of the subject just if the question "Someone is *F*, but is it me?" makes no sense.[5]

On this reading, (iv) does not carve up "as object"/"as subject" uses in the way implied by (ii). An occurrence of 'I' in the physical self-ascription "I am sitting", known in the normal way, is immune to error through misidentification of the subject. In such a case, the question "Someone is sitting, but is it me?" makes no sense.[6] Conversely, an occurrence of 'I' in the mental self-ascription "I am in pain", arrived at via the brain-scanner, is not immune to error through misidentification of the subject. Since my belief that I am hooked up to the scanner may be false; the question "Someone is in pain, but is it me?" will make sense – at least if it is only via the scanner that I arrive at my self-ascription.

[4] It might be objected that this example is too fanciful. How could I fail to know, in the normal way, that I am in pain when I am? But even if there are two routes to knowledge in this example, and the 'inner' route is always available, it doesn't follow that I can never know that I am in pain by hearing the sound of the scanner. (I can know it's sunny by looking, even if both visual and tactual modes of sensing are relaying the information that it's sunny. On a particular occasion, the visual mode may be cognitively dominant.) Second, some philosophers have questioned the self-intimation thesis that, if I am in pain, I thereby know (by introspection) that I am in pain. For example, I may be in pain, yet not know that I am in pain, because I am distracted. In such situations, I could use the scanner to gain knowledge that I am in pain.

[5] This interpretation was first suggested, as far as I am aware, by Sydney Shoemaker (1982); it was later endorsed by Evans (1982) and Colin McGinn (1983).

[6] Of course, "I am sitting" is not incorrigible – I could be mistaken about my bodily position. But that is beside the point. The claim is only that if I know that I am sitting (through proprioception), the "Someone [. . .] ?" question makes no sense.

23.3 Analysing Wittgenstein's View

Thus, (ii) and (iii), and (ii) and (iv), are inconsistent pairs. Which should be jettisoned? I suggest that it is (ii) which should be dropped. Wittgenstein thought that whether an occurrence of 'I' is "as object" or ''as subject" depended only upon the type of proposition in which it figured. All occurrences of 'I' in tokens of "I am in pain" are "as subject"; all occurrences of 'I' in tokens of "I am sitting" are "as object". This was a mistake.[7] As (iii) and (iv) make clear, the ''as object"/"as subject" distinction is epistemological. It is a contrast between different ways of knowing truths about oneself, and it is a contrast which cuts across the distinction between physical and mental self-ascriptions.[8]

We might provisionally re-formulate the "as object"/"as subject" distinction as follows. An occurrence of 'I' in a token judgement "I am F", known in way W, is an "as subject" occurrence if and only if (a) W does not involve any subject-identifying inference or outer perception; and (b) it would make no sense to say "Someone is F, but is it me?", where knowledge of the existential component is gained by way W. An occurrence of 'I' in a self-ascription which does not have these features is "as object". Condition (a) is an elaboration of (iii); condition (b) is an elaboration of (iv). One intriguing possibility is that if we add (a) and (b) to our features listed above, we may gain some understanding of just which features of 'I' make its competent use an expression of self-consciousness.

However, we need to understand more about (a) and (b), and the relation between them. In what ways can a person gain knowledge of himself, knowledge of truths of the form "I am F"? There are (at least) three ways: inference (including inference from the testimony of others); outer perception (e.g., observation of one's physical attributes or relations); inner perception (which includes kinaesthesis, proprioception, sense of balance, of heat and cold, and of pressure). The way of knowing specified in condition (a) excludes not just knowledge by subject-identifying inference, but also knowledge by outer perception. Clearly, if all knowledge by outer perception were inferential (if my judgement "I am wearing a blue sweater" must be derived from, e.g., "this person is wearing a blue sweater" and "I am this person"), there would be no need to mention outer perception in condition (a). But that view is implausible.[9]

[7] Shoemaker made a similar mistake, see (Shoemaker, 1982, 7–9). His distinction between 'absolute' and 'circumstantial' immunity to error through misidentification is vitiated by his assumption that some mental self-ascriptions are absolutely immune to error through misidentification of the subject. That assumption is false. Immunity is always circumstantial, and not a function of judgement-type.

[8] The latter point is important. Evans cites the fact that "as subject" uses of 'I' feature in both physical and mental self-ascriptions in support of a naturalistic view of persons according to which mental properties are no more basic to personhood than physical properties. This is a close cousin of P. F. Strawson's thesis that the concept of a person is 'primitive'; it is the concept of a subject to which both mental and physical predicates can be applied (Strawson, 1959).

[9] Evans and Shoemaker point out that demonstrative knowledge (e.g., the knowledge expressed by a typical perceptual demonstrative judgement "that man is bald") is not the result of inference; yet it clearly involves outer perception.

Some commentators have pointed out that the property of identification-freedom alluded to in condition (a) is not unique to 'I'-judgements. Shoemaker noted that present-tense demonstrative judgements ("that woman is tall", "this is red", etc.) are identification-free,[10] and Evans emphasised the identification-freedom of ordinary 'here'-judgements. But neither commentator succeeds in distinguishing conditions (a) and (b), and Evans's revised definition runs them together. He writes:

> a judgement is identification-free if it is based upon a way of knowing about objects such that it does not make sense for the subject to utter "Something is *F*, but is it *a* that is *F*?", when the first component expresses knowledge which the subject does not think he has, or may have, gained in any other way. (Evans, 1982, 189–190)

Are (a) and (b) equivalent? No: (a) does not entail (b). Suppose that, unbeknownst to me, I occasionally receive information – "from the inside" – about the bodily position of someone else. I am standing; but it seems to me, "from the inside", as if I am sitting. Imagine that I become aware of my situation. Since I know that I receive the impression of sitting if and only if either I am sitting or the other person is, I can know by proprioception that someone is seated (hence condition (a) is satisfied), but sensibly doubt whether I am seated (hence condition (b) is not satisfied).

Here are two further examples. Suppose I judge "I am six feet tall" on the basis of memory. In this case, condition (a) is satisfied. Memory-based judgements do not involve any subject-identifying inference or outer perception. (No doubt my original judgement of my height, based on observation of a measurement, fails to satisfy condition (a) – but that is not relevant here.) Yet the question "Someone is six feet tall, but is it me?" makes perfectly good sense (so condition (b) is not satisfied). Next, consider a typical memory-judgement, such as "I was in pain". This judgement does not rely on subject-identifying inference or outer perception; yet the question "Someone was in pain, but was it me?" makes sense.[11] All three examples make it plain that (a) does not entail (b).

Should we alter our provisional definition of the "as subject" occurrence of 'I'? Are conditions (a) and (b) both essential to the definition of such an occurrence? The cases just discussed will help us decide. How do we want to classify my

[10] Shoemaker thinks that only present-tense demonstrative judgements are identification-free (Shoemaker, 1982, 10). Yet a past-tense demonstrative judgement, e.g., "that man was hirsute", is typically not the result of any subject-identifying inference (hence, it is identification-free).

At one point, Shoemaker unpacks the identification-freedom of present-tense demonstrative judgements in terms of the impossibility of any disparity between intended reference and actual reference (Shoemaker, 1982, 9). But that cannot be right. Since reference-failure is always a possibility for demonstrative terms that purport to refer to public objects, there is at least one way in which there can be a disparity between intended demonstrative reference and actual demonstrative reference. This yields one point of disanalogy between 'I' and 'this'. A further disanalogy is that ordinary demonstrative judgements ("that *F* is *G*") require the thinker to "keep track" of the *F*. In the case of 'I'-judgements, there is no requirement that the thinker "keep track" of himself in order to continue to self-refer using 'I'.

[11] Note the contrast here with first person judgements of intention. The question "Someone intends to *F*, but is it I who intend to *F*?", where knowledge of the existential component is gained in the normal way, does not make sense.

memory-based judgement that I am six feet tall or my memory-judgement that I was in pain? These judgements, in their respective contexts, are expressions of self-consciousness, and contain paradigm instances of the "as subject" use of 'I'. Their failure to satisfy condition (b) does nothing to undermine their title to such status. We should revise our definition as follows: an occurrence of 'I' in a judgement "I am *F*" is an "as subject" occurrence if and only if the way in which "I am *F*" is known does not involve subject-identifying inference or outer perception. It is interesting that in the case of some self-ascriptions containing "as subject" occurrences of 'I', the question "Someone is *F*, but is it me?" makes no sense. But this latter condition should not be built into the definition of the "as subject" occurrence of 'I'.

23.4 The 'I'-as-Subject and Self-Consciousness

In what sense, if any, is the "as subject" use of 'I' basic? We can distinguish two senses in which this use might be basic: the "as subject" use of 'I' might be more basic or fundamental than the "as object" use, and understanding the "as subject" aspects of 'I' might help to elucidate the sense in which 'I'-judgements are expressions of self-consciousness. I will argue that the "as subject" use is basic in both senses.

Shoemaker (1982, 12–13) and Evans (1982, 181) endorse the following argument for the conclusion that the "as subject" use of 'I' is more basic than the "as object" use. Suppose I know that I am *F*. This instance of self-knowledge is either identification-free or identification- dependent. If it is identification-dependent, it is based on the premises *X* is *F* and I am *X*. Each premise is itself either identification-free or identification-dependent. If the latter, and if we are to avoid an infinite regress, the chains of dependence must terminate in premises that are identification-free. Hence, on pain of infinite regress, every piece of self-knowledge must rest on an identification-free component. Since self-ascriptions incorporating "as subject" uses of 'I' are precisely those self-ascriptions which are identification-free, we have confirmed the first of the senses in which the "as subject" use of 'I' is basic.

It might be thought that this argument proves too much. Surely, it is possible for there to be creatures who have identification-dependent self-knowledge, but no identification-free self-knowledge. Consider Elizabeth Anscombe's example of the '*A*'-users (Anscombe, 1981, 24–25). The '*A*'-users are a community of people who lack self-consciousness. Each '*A*'-user identifies himself in a third person way, and each person uses the proper name '*A*' (printed on his wrist) to refer to himself. When an '*A*'-user judges truly that he is standing (e.g., by observing his bodily position), he possesses an item of self-knowledge which is neither identification-free, nor rests upon an identification-free premise.

However, this is not a counterexample to the regress argument. The '*A*'-users do not have self-knowledge in the sense relevant to that argument. An individual '*A*'- user knows many truths about the person who is, in fact, himself (truths he would express by saying "*A* is *F*"); but he does not possess self-conscious self-knowledge (the sort of knowledge I express by saying "I am *F*"). An '*A*'-user's assertion of "*A* is six feet tall" is based on an identification-component (e.g., it may be the conclusion of an inference from "the body of whose wrist this is a part is six feet tall" and "*A* has this body"), but it is not based on any self-identification or subject-identification. A counterexample to the regress argument would arise if a piece of self-knowledge rested on a self-identification which neither was, nor depended upon, an identification-free judgement. The example of the '*A*'-users does not enable us to construct such a counterexample.

There is another way in which the "as subject" use of 'I' is more basic than the "as object" use. Shoemaker writes:

> where '*F*' is a [material] predicate, to say that I am *F* is to say that my body is *F*. And if asked what it means to call a body "my body" I could say something like this: "My body is the body from whose eyes I see, the body whose mouth emits sounds when I speak, the body whose arm goes up when I raise my arm, the body that has something pressing against it when I feel pressure, and so on." All the uses of 'I' that occur in this explanation of the meaning of the phrase "my body" are "as subject".[12] (Shoemaker, 1982, 18)

This argument is misleading. It is no part of the definition of the "as object" use that all such occurrences of 'I' refer to the body. This is clear once we appreciate that mental self-ascriptions can contain "as object" uses of 'I'. But even if all "as object" occurrences of 'I' featured in physical self-ascriptions, it still wouldn't follow that the referent of such occurrences of 'I' is the body. It is a non-trivial metaphysical claim that a token of 'I' in, e.g., "I am six feet tall" refers to my body, in preference to a psycho-physical substance which is spatially coincident with my body. (Think of analogous debates about whether or not a gold statue is numerically identical to the lump of gold which constitutes it.) Shoemaker may simply have assumed that since we can't substitute for 'I' a description of the body in "I feel pain", so in physical self-ascriptions we can make such a substitution. That assumption is controversial; however, it is not required for the success of Shoemaker's argument.

What of the second sense in which the "as subject" use of 'I' might be thought basic? What is the link between the "as subject" use of 'I' and the concept of self-consciousness? It would be excessive to claim that our concept of self-consciousness can be exhaustively characterised in terms of the "as subject" features of 'I'. There is more to self-consciousness than that: a self-conscious being must be able to engage in reason and reflection, and consider itself as a being in time, with a past accessible in experience-memory and a future accessible in intention. But these features are possible only because of the "as subject" features of 'I'. A being whose devices of self-reference failed to satisfy condition (a) could only think of himself as one object amongst others, whose features are accessible only by subject-identifying inference or outer perception. Such a being would be incapable of the sort of direct

[12] *Contra* Shoemaker, this argument cannot in turn be used to support the (admittedly plausible) thesis that "as subject" uses of 'I' are referential. The fact that "as subject" uses of 'I' are necessary for uses of 'I' which are referential (i.e., "as object" uses) does not imply that "as subject" uses are referential.

or identification-free access to his past, present, and future that is constitutive of self-consciousness.

This is confirmed when we reflect that the best explanation of why the '*A*'-users are not self-conscious will make reference to the fact that the name '*A*' is a device of self-reference which fails to satisfy condition (a). The '*A*'-users lack identification-free self-knowledge. This observation, in turn, allows us to specify what it is for us to possess a first person perspective on ourselves.

References

Anscombe, G. E. M. (1981). The first person. In *Metaphysics and the philosophy of mind*. Oxford: Blackwell.
Evans, G. (1982). *The varieties of reference*. Oxford: Clarendon Press.
Garrett, B. (1993). Wittgenstein on solipsism and avowals. In B. Garrett & K. Mulligan (Eds.), *Themes from Wittgenstein*. Australian National University, RSSS Monograph Series no. 3., Canberra.
McDowell, J. (1997). The first person. In J. Dancy (Ed.), *Reading parfit*. Oxford: Blackwell.
McGinn, C. (1983). *The subjective view*. Oxford: Clarendon Press.
Parfit, D. (1984). *Reasons and persons*. Oxford: Oxford University Press.
Shoemaker, S. (1982). Self-reference and self-awareness. In *Identity, cause, and mind*. Cambridge: Cambridge University Press.
Strawson, P. F. (1959). *Individuals*. London: Methuen.
Wittgenstein, L. (1972). *The blue and brown books*. Oxford: Blackwell.

Chapter 24
Persons and Values

Abstract In this discussion, I want to explore the connections – if any – between theories of persons (that is, theories of the nature, individuation, and persistence, of persons) and theories of value (that is, normative theories in ethics and rationality). There might appear to be an obvious sense in which theories of persons and theories of value interconnect – in general, the value of *F*s must be a function of the nature of *F*s. (If kangaroos are valued more than trees, this is because of the different natures of kangaroos and trees.) But this general claim will not be truistic if the following condition holds: it is metaphysically possible for entities of different ontological categories to be *F*s. In that case, it is a moot question whether competing theories of the nature of *F*s will issue in divergent value judgements concerning *F*s. So, if entities of different kinds can be persons, we will require arguments to convince us that competing theories of persons yield different and conflicting value judgements. It is precisely the cogency of such arguments that I wish to consider here.

24.1 Theories of Values and the Definition of 'Person'

There is a view about the sense of the predicate 'person', on which it is natural to think that different theories of the metaphysical or ontological nature of persons will have no differential impact on value theory. Suppose we think, with Locke, that the core sense of the predicate 'person' is exhausted by the following, purely functional, definition: "a person is a thinking intelligent being, that has reason and reflection, and can consider itself as itself, the same thinking thing, in different times and places" (Locke, 1975, 335). This definition is purely functional in just this sense: it imposes no *a priori* constraints on the sort of entity (animal, spirit, machine, etc.) that can be a person. On this view, to be a person is just to possess a complex psychological profile; and it is an entirely *a posteriori* matter what kinds of entity do, or might, possess such a profile.

This definition generates a certain picture. On this picture, the value of (human) persons is entirely a consequence of the fact that typical adult humans possess the psychological profile described above. Consequently, competing theories of the ontological nature of actual persons (e.g., Cartesianism and Reductionism) will be

B. Garrett, *Time, Identity and the Self: Essays on Metaphysics*, Synthese Library 442, https://doi.org/10.1007/978-3-030-85517-8_24

unable to motivate one value theory rather than another (e.g., Consequentialist rather than Deontological theories), since the competing theories of persons do not call into question Locke's functional definition.

Note, in passing, that we may be unconcerned about modifications to Locke's definition that have the effect only of increasing or decreasing the extension of the predicate 'person'. For example, according to David Wiggins's definition of personhood, a being is a person if typical members of its kind are rational, self-conscious, etc. (Wiggins, 1980, 171). One consequence of this relational definition is that fetuses would count as persons, since they are members of a natural kind (*human being*) whose typical members are rational, self-conscious, etc. According to Locke's definition, in contrast, fetuses would not count as persons. Thus, two theories of persons differ over whether fetuses are persons, and hence differ, for example, over whether fetuses should be assigned the same rights as typical adult humans. But this is not the most philosophically interesting way in which theories of persons and theories of value have been thought to intersect.

24.2 The Case of Derek Parfit

The relevant question to ask is this: can different theories of the ontological nature of persons – whether or not they agree exactly on the extension of 'person' – motivate different value theories, in such a way that the latter theories prescribe divergent ethical and rational dictates for beings which both theories of persons unhesitatingly count as persons (e.g., normal adult humans)?

The most well-known recent attempt to engage with this question has it affirmatively: this attempt is the central of Part 3 of Derek Parfit's seminal book *Reasons and Persons* (Parfit, 1984). And to answer this question affirmatively is precisely is to subvert the Locke-inspired picture described above.

Parfit describes two conceptions of persons. On one natural and dominant conception, persons are "separately existing entities" (e.g., immaterial Cartesian Egos), only contingently linked to their physical bodies. The identity over time of Egos is necessarily determinate. On the alternative Reductionist conception, the existence of a person "just involves" the existence of a brain, body, and stream of mental and physical events, and the identity over time of a person can sometimes be vague or indeterminate. One of Parfit's central claims is that if we relinquish Cartesianism and embrace Reductionism, the identity and non-identity of persons matters less. If Reductionism is true, personal identity is not, in itself, an important relation.

24.3 Two Theses About Personal Identity and What Matters

It is necessary to distinguish diachronic from synchronic directions of implication. The diachronic thesis that the identity of a person over time is unimportant is taken to undermine the Self-interest Theory of rationality, and has implications for the tenability of transtemporal moral notions such as compensation, responsibility, and personal commitment. In addition, the diachronic thesis implies that many 'prudential' reasons for action properly belong in the realm of morality rather than in the realm of rationality.

The diachronic thesis that personal identity is unimportant implies that pure, self-interested concern is irrational. That is, it is irrational for me to be especially concerned about the fate of some future person just because that future person is me. It follows immediately that the Self-interest Theory of rationality is false. This theory states that, of all the future people I can benefit, there is only one person that it is supremely rational for me to benefit: the future person who is (identical with) me. Since the Self-interest Theory places immense weight on a relation which has no rational significance, this theory cannot be correct.

Parfit's diachronic thesis is supplemented with a positive thesis about which relation does matter. Parfit's claim is that what matters is Relation *R* (the relation of psychological continuity and/or connectedness), with any cause. The positive thesis implies that where there are only weak connections between different stages of the same life, the grounds are thereby diminished for holding the later self responsible for the crimes of the earlier self, or for compensating the latter self for burdens imposed on the earlier self, or for regarding earlier commitments as binding on the later self.

The positive thesis also implies that activities that were previously regarded as irrational (e.g., heavy smoking) may now more properly be regarded as immoral. The heavy smoker is imposing burdens on a later person who may be only weakly psychologically connected to him; hence, given that what matters is Relation *R* and not identity, the truth that the person burdened is identical with the heavy smoker is only superficial. Because of the weakened psychological connections, it is as if the smoker is imposing burdens on another person.

The synchronic thesis that the identity and distinctness of persons at a time is unimportant has been taken to imply that the fact of the "separateness of persons" is not 'deep', and that less weight should be assigned to distributive principles. The synchronic thesis thus supports (at least in part) the Utilitarian doctrine that no weight should be assigned to distributive principles: we should simply aim to maximise the net sum of benefits over burdens, whatever their distribution. The combined effect of the synchronic and diachronic theses is thus to promote a more impersonal conception of ethics and rationality.

I want to consider the central arguments for the diachronic and synchronic theses – arguments premised on the shift from Cartesianism to Reductionism. I will discuss two arguments for the diachronic thesis (the Argument from Analysis and the Argument from Division), and one argument for the synchronic thesis (the

Argument from Reductionism). My conclusion will be that these arguments are far from persuasive, and that the Locke-inspired picture described above has not been undermined. The independence of theories of persons from theories of value has not been overturned.

24.4 The Argument from Analysis

Suppose that we were once Cartesians about the self. Now we are Reductionists. For example, we might endorse the Psychological Criterion according to which the relation of personal identity over time just is the relation of non-branching psychological continuity. (The expression 'non-branching' is essential since one person may be psychologically continuous with two or more later individuals, and no potentially branching relation can be the relation of personal identity.) So we now accept the equation:

Personal identity over time = non-branching psychological continuity.

The Argument from Analysis then proceed as follows: the relation of non-branching psychological continuity is unimportant. (Why should it matter to me whether I am psychologically continuous with one future person rather than with two?) But the relation of personal identity just is this relation. Hence, personal identity is not important either.[1]

However, the Argument from Analysis makes a questionable assumption about the direction of the transmission of importance from one relation to another. It assumes that the importance or unimportance of the *analysandum* (i.e., the left hand side of the equation) is entirely determined by the importance or unimportance of its *analysans* (i.e., the right hand side of the equation). But why should we accept this assumption? What mistake is made by an ex-Cartesian convert to the Psychological Criterion who, believing personal identity to be an important relation, comes to regard the relation of non-branching psychological continuity as – thereby – equally important?

Of course, if we had good independent reasons to regard the relation of non-branching psychological continuity as unimportant, the directionality assumption would be vindicated. But I do not think there are any such reasons.[2] Hence, the shift from Cartesianism to Reductionism need not inevitably lead to any reassessment of the importance of personal identity.

---

[1] Parfit provides the materials to generate the Argument from Analysis (Parfit, 1984, sec. 90).

[2] Two subsidiary arguments – the Arguments from Extrinsicness and Triviality – attempt to show that the relation of non-branching psychological continuity is unimportant. But both arguments have implausible major premises: respectively, the premise that what matters cannot be determined extrinsically, and the premise that what matters cannot depend on a trivial fact. For criticism of these arguments, see (Sosa, 1990).

Worse still, the Argument from Analysis seems very similar to arguments that are obviously spurious. Consider the Argument for the Insignificance of Suffering: we were Dualists, but now we are Materialists. We now think of pains as patterns of neuronal activity, rather than as ghostly immaterial entities. But patterns of neuronal activity are of no intrinsic significance. Hence, physical suffering matters less if Materialism is true.[3]

This argument is hardly likely to win many votes. Why? – because if we come to believe that pain just is a pattern of neuronal activity, we shall assign to such physical patterns just the importance we presently assign to pain. The importance of the *analysandum* will simply be transferred to its *analysans*. And what reason do we have to think that analyses of personal identity are any different in this respect?[4]

24.5 The Argument from Division

The Argument from Division is perhaps Parfit's most well-known argument for the unimportance of personal identity (Parfit, 1984, ch. 12). Parfit introduces this argument by first describing the "striking evidence" yielded by split-brain patients, whose upper-hemisphere connections were severed in order to cure epilepsy. The evidence suggests that, in such patients, consciousness divided into two independent streams. There was a divided mind in a single body.

Parfit then imagines a fictional extension of these actual cases in which his own brain is divided and each (supposedly equipollent) hemisphere is placed in a new body. The resulting two people are fully psychologically continuous with Parfit (equipped with the same apparent memories, beliefs, character, etc.) and partly physically continuous. This thought-experiment certainly appears to encounter no conceptual obstacles: division seems to be a metaphysical, even nomological, possibility for human beings. How best should this case be described?

Parfit plausibly criticises the descriptions "I survive as one of the two people" and "I survive as both" (Parfit, 1984, 255–258). The first description violates plausible epistemic constraints on judgements of personal identity over time: how could it be known which of the two resulting persons is the original? The second description skewers our concept of a person by supposing that one person can have (simultaneously) two minds and two bodies. The most plausible description of division thus appears to be: "I do not survive" – I am identical with neither off-shoot.

---

[3] The analogy with pain is due to Sydney Shoemaker (1985, 451).

[4] Note that the transition to Reductionism does not involve replacing the relation of personal identity with some other relation – rather, we are being told what personal identity essentially consists in. Obviously, if the shift to Reductionism did involve such replacement, there would be no *a priori* guarantee that the new relation would inherit the value of the original.

Suppose that I am about to divide. The prospect of division is clearly not as bad as that of ordinary death. It follows that my relation to my off-shoots contains what matters. But I am not identical with either off-shoot. Hence, personal identity cannot be what matters.

The worry with this argument concerns the inference drawn from its first premise. The prospect of division is indeed not as bad as that of ordinary death. But what grounds this premise is simply the fact that, given a choice between these two options, virtually everyone would choose division. And it is not hard to see why: in division, unlike in ordinary death, there will be people around (causally linked to my present self) who can complete my projects, look after my family, etc. In short, there are obvious practical advantages to division, which are not present in cases of ordinary death. But if the thesis that my relation to my off-shoots contains what matters amounts only to the thesis that division is (in this way) better than ordinary death, it is innocuous and uncontentious. Presumably, then, this cannot be what Parfit intends; but where are the materials to generate a stronger result?

It may be useful to invoke John Perry's distinction between 'private' and 'non-private' projects (Perry, 1976). My non-private projects are those someone else could in principle complete (e.g., finishing my book or teaching my class). My private projects are those in the completion of which I feature essentially (e.g., my project of avoiding pain: this project is not fulfilled by anyone other than me avoiding pain).

The thesis that identity is not what matters appears to imply that I ought to have "strong concern" for the private projects (e.g., pain-avoidance) of my off-shoots, whether or not they interfere with the completion my non-private projects. But nothing this strong follows from the datum that most people would prefer division to ordinary death. This preference need only reflect concern for the completion of one's non-private projects.

24.6 The Argument from Reductionism

The Argument from Reductionism attempts to show that, if Reductionism is true, the fact of the "separateness of persons" (e.g., the fact that you and I are distinct persons) is not deep or significant, and hence that less weight should be assigned to distributive principles.

According to Parfit's Reductionism, reality can be completely described without reference to persons (Parfit, 1984, 210–213). If so, the following question arises: how can the boundaries between persons be important if reality can be completely described in a wholly impersonal way? Failing an answer to this question, the Argument from Reductionism concludes that the boundaries between persons are not morally significant.

The general thought underlying the Argument from Reductionism appears to be this: if reality can be completely described without referring to Fs (e.g., if all the

F-truths are implied by some set of non-F-truths), then the boundaries between Fs cannot be of any importance.

Clearly, if this general thought is to avoid triviality, the reduction in question must be non-eliminative in character: obviously the boundaries between Fs cannot be important if Fs do not exist. Fortunately, Parfit's brand of Reductionism is non-eliminative: persons do exist, but are nothing "over and above" their bodies and experiences.

On the non-eliminativist reading, the general thought ceases to be trivial; however, it also ceases to be plausible. Consider the following analogy. Suppose that we once accepted the Hegelian view of nations (that nations are "more real" than the citizens and territory which compose them). We now accept (non-eliminative) Reductionism about nations: nations exist, but are nothing "over and above" their citizens and territory. Must we thereby think that the boundaries between nations are of no moral significance, and that no weight should be assigned to distributive principles governing the allocation of resources between nations?

This is hardly plausible: many of us are Reductionists about nations and yet also hold that distributive principles do apply to nations (e.g., that we should give more money to a Third World country than to a First World country, even if this does not maximise the net sum of benefits over burdens).[5] But if the boundaries between nations do not become less significant once we become nation-reductionists, why should the "separateness of persons" become less significant if we accept Reductionism about persons?[6]

24.7 Conclusion

I conclude that the Locke-inspired picture of the independence of theories of value from theories of persons has not been undermined. We may justifiably regard the value of persons as invariant under competing ontologies of the self.

References

Adams, R. M. (1990). Should ethics be more impersonal? critical notice of Derek Parfit's *Reasons and persons*. *The Philosophical Review, 98*(4), 439–484.

Locke, J. (1694/1975). Of identity and diversity. In P. Nidditch (Ed.), *An essay concerning human understanding*, 2nd edn. Oxford: Oxford University Press.

Parfit, D. (1984). *Reasons and persons*. Oxford: Oxford University Press.

[5] As Robert Adams has pointed out: "hardly anyone holds a Non-Reductionist View about nations and other institutions, but most of us think that they can be deserving, guilty, and compensated. Our legal system reflects this belief" (Adams, 1990, 98).

[6] The question of the tenability of Parfit's Reductionism is explored in Chap. 20 of this volume.

Perry, J. (1976). The importance of personal identity. In A. O. Rorty (Ed.), *The identities of persons*. Los Angeles: University of California Press.

Shoemaker, S. (1985). Causality and properties. In *Identity, cause and mind*. Cambridge: Cambridge University Press.

Sosa, E. (1990). Surviving matters. *Noûs, 24*(2), 297–322.

Wiggins, D. (1980). *Sameness and substance*. Cambridge: Harvard University Press.

Part IV
Afterthoughts

Chapter 25
About Time

Abstract In this discussion, we trace the current form of the philosophical debate about the nature of time deriving from McTaggart's original presentation. We tackle the nuances of McTaggart's arguments and assess their plausibility.

JEREMIAH JOVEN JOAQUIN: The current philosophical debate about the nature of time seems to involve two sorts of questions. The first is about the nature of time itself: whether it 'flows' in one unique direction or whether it is just one another dimension of space-time. The second is about the ontological status of the past, the present, and the future: whether they are all equally real. Is this a fair assessment of the present state of things?

BRIAN GARRETT: Yes, I think that's fair. But I guess we need to go back to McTaggart who inaugurated the whole contemporary debate on the nature of time.

JJ: You mean the Cambridge philosopher, J. M. E. McTaggart (1866–1925)?

BG: Yes – *that* McTaggart. In his most famous paper "The Unreality of Time", McTaggart distinguished two ways of ordering events in time. He writes,

> Positions in time, as time appears to us *prima facie*, are distinguished in two ways. Each position is Earlier than some and Later than some of the other positions [. . .] In the second place, each position is either Past, Present or Future. The distinctions of the former class are permanent, while those of the later are not. If M is ever earlier than N, it is always earlier. But an event, which is now present, was future, and will be past. (McTaggart, 1908, 458)

JJ: Ah! I know this one. The first series of positions is what McTaggart labels the B series, the second the A series.

BG: That's right. For McTaggart, B-series positions are permanent in a way that A-series positions are not. We could see this in the unchanging truth value of B-series attributions. For example, since I was born in 1961, it always was and always will be true that my birth was earlier than 1970. That is, the truth value of the sentence "My birth is earlier than 1970" never changes. In contrast, A-series attributions are temporary rather than permanent. For

B. Garrett, *Time, Identity and the Self: Essays on Metaphysics*, Synthese Library 442, https://doi.org/10.1007/978-3-030-85517-8_25

a time, my birth was still in the future; then was fleetingly present; and is now past for ever more. That is, the truth value of the sentence "My birth is future" changed from true to false. Similarly, the truth value of the sentence "My birth is past" changed from false to true.

JJ: We could say, then, that in the A-series, an event E changes since it was once past, is now present, and will be future. In contrast, in the B-series, E has a fixed position. In relation to some other event E*, E might be before or after, or even be simultaneous with E* and those B series relations never change.

BG: Yes. That's the distinction.

JJ: But what's the philosophical issue here? Surely, we could describe events in terms of the A-series or the B-series much like we could describe temperature in terms of degree Celsius or Fahrenheit. Since there seems to only be a notational, and not a substantive, difference when we state that the boiling point of water as 100° C or as 212° F, there seems to be a notational, and not a substantive, difference when we describe your birth as now for ever more past or that it came after World War II.

BG: Well, that's one possible view, but it isn't McTaggart's. For McTaggart, the substantive philosophical question here is which of these two descriptions is more fundamental to time.

JJ: And by 'fundamental' you mean which of the two is necessary and sufficient for time?

BG: Quite right. Since the A and B series could be seen as both essential (or necessary) for time, the question is which of them is sufficient.

JJ: It seems that there are four possible views regarding this. On the one hand, there's the view that the A series but not the B series is fundamental (i.e., both necessary and sufficient) to time. On the other hand, there's the view that the B series but not the A series is fundamental. There's also the view that both series are fundamental. Finally, there's the view that neither series is fundamental.

BG: Yes. A defender of the first view is an A theorist. A defender of the second is a B theorist. A defender of the fourth view – like the one you sketched a while ago – thinks that the debate has been misconceived: there are two languages of time but only one time series, which can be described in different ways. Unfortunately, I don't know of anyone who holds the third view.

JJ: So, what's McTaggart's view?

BG: McTaggart's ultimate view is that time is unreal, and he has a two-step argument for this. First, he shows that the A series is fundamental to time. Second, he argues that since the A series is contradictory, time is unreal.

JJ: Let's unpack these two arguments. Let's start with McTaggart's argument for the conclusion that the A series is more fundamental than the B series.

BG: That's the right way to go.

JJ: So, what's McTaggart's argument for this?

BG: We could label this as *the argument from change*. It proceeds as follows:

1. Time necessarily involves change.
2. Change is only possible in the A series.
3. So, time fundamentally involves the A series.

Now, if you accept this argument's premises, you have to accept that the A series is fundamental to time and the B series is not.

JJ: Well, we could surely question the first premise. If Sydney Shoemaker is right that time without change is possible, then McTaggart's first premise is false (Shoemaker, 1969).

BG: You're right. But McTaggart counts the mere passage of time – pure becoming – as change. So, he intends the first premise to be a truism and offers no support for it. You may complain that this begs the question against the B theorist. But here's the thing: McTaggart doesn't really need the first premise for his conclusion. The truth of the second premise already suffices to show the superiority of the A series over the B series.

JJ: But does McTaggart offer support for the second premise?

BG: Yes, he does. He appeals to the permanency of B series locations and relations. As we've discussed, events never change their B series locations or relations. For example, it always was and always will be true that my birth occurred in 1961, and it always was and always will be true that my birth happened later than World War II. This, for McTaggart, shows that the B series doesn't allow for change.

JJ: Hmm. Let's grant that B series can't allow for change. But does this show that A series is fundamental?

BG: For McTaggart, yes, it does. The only respect in which an event can change is when it 'moves' from one temporal location to another. For example, my birth was once an event in the far future. Then it became present. Then it became past, and, as time chugs along, it will become more past. McTaggart concludes from this that change is only possible on the A series, and so the A series is fundamental to time.

JJ: But doesn't this still beg the question against the B theorist? Since McTaggart defines change as a movement from one temporal location to another, doesn't he already presuppose the A series? Moreover, B theorists could surely offer an account of change in their own terms.

BG: Ah! yes. Bertrand Russell did offer a B-theoretic account of change. According to Russell, change is an object's having different and incompatible properties at different times. As he says,

> Change is the difference, in respect of truth or falsehood, between a proposition concerning an entity and the time T, and a proposition concerning the same entity and the time T*, provided that these propositions differ only by the fact that T occurs in the one where T* occurs in the other. (Russell, 1937, 442)

Thus, according to Russell, there's change if, for example, the proposition "At time T, my poker is hot" is true, and the proposition "At time T* my poker is hot" is false. That is, change happens when my poker is hot at one time and not hot at some other time. As you can see, this notion of change only requires the B series and nothing else.

JJ: Surely, McTaggart has a ready reply to Russell.

BG: Yes – that Russell's account is not an account of change at all. For McTaggart, the proposition "At time T, my poker is hot", if true, is always true, and the proposition "At time T* my poker is hot", if false, is always false. For McTaggart, this permanency in truth value implies that there is no change in the poker.

JJ: It seems, then, that we are being offered two quite different accounts of change. On the one hand, we have McTaggart's view that change occurs only when an event alters its A series position. On the other hand, we have Russell's view that change occurs whenever an object has incompatible properties at different times. But who's right here?

BG: *Prima facie*, Russell's view seems to fare better than McTaggart's. We ordinarily think of change in terms of the very same object having different properties at different times rather than in terms of a once future event (or fact) becoming present, and then becoming past for ever more.

JJ: Are you, then, going for Russell's view over McTaggart's? If you are, then you also think that McTaggart's support for his second premise fails.

BG: So be it.

JJ: But what of the second step in McTaggart's overall argument, viz., the argument that the A series is contradictory?

BG: Ah! That argument – an ingenious one I think – is what philosophers now call "McTaggart's Paradox". Here's how it goes. We've described an event – say my birth – in the A series as once future, then present, and then past. These A series changes prompted McTaggart to propose the following argument:

1. Every event is past, present and future.
2. No event can be past, present and future.
3. So: the A series is contradictory.

The thought behind the first premise is that no event escapes the passage of time: any event is future, then fleetingly present, then past for ever more. In effect, the first premise states that every event occupies every A series position.

JJ: Surely this is not true of all events! If there is a first event, then it has no past. If there is a last event, then it has no future.

BG: Very good. But this doesn't really affect McTaggart's argument. The first event would still be present and past, and the last event future and present, and these determinations are still incompatible. So, we can put these two exceptions to one side.

JJ: But how should we understand the second premise?

BG: It just tells us that if an event is past, it is not present or future; if it is present, it is not past or future; and if it is future, it is not past or present. So, no event is past, present, and future since nothing can possess incompatible characteristics.

JJ: Ah! Now I understand the paradox. The A series is contradictory since events occupy incompatible positions in the A series.

BG: That's McTaggart's view.

JJ: I wonder whether an A theorist can avoid the contradiction by saying that events do not occupy different A series positions at the same time. Instead of saying that an event *is* past, present, and future, we say that it *was* once in the far future, then it *will* become present, and later it *will* be past for ever more.

BG: McTaggart did consider that reply. The thought behind it is that "the characteristics are only incompatible when they are simultaneous, and there is no contradiction to this in the fact that each term has all of them successively" (McTaggart, 1908, 48). So, we escape the paradox, the reply goes, if we treat events as past, present, and future successively and not simultaneously.

JJ: Does that reply work?

BG: Well, no! McTaggart has a response to it. Here's the idea. The reply implies that we can avoid the charge of contradiction in the three ground-level A series positions by invoking three second-level A series positions. As you said, instead of an event being past, present, and future, it was past, is present, and will be future.

JJ: With you so far.

BG: If you grant this, then there are nine A series positions in this second-level series; viz., is past, is present, is future, was past, was present, was future, will be past, will be present, will be future. And, according to the first premise, every event occupies each of these A series positions.

JJ: I see where this is going. Some combinations of these nine positions will be incompatible (e.g., is present and is past).

BG: Now you're getting it. To avoid the contradictions at the second level, we need to move up to a third level of A series positions. And some of these twenty-seven positions will be incompatible. To avoid contradiction, we must move up to a fourth level, and so on.

JJ: So this is the real McTaggart's paradox. We can escape the contradictory nature of the A series by moving up a level, but at every level a contradiction remains. I see now why this paradox is a hard nut to crack.

BG: Yes, and to quote McTaggart, "since this continues infinitely, the first set of terms never escapes from contradiction at all" (McTaggart, 1908, 49).

JJ: So, what do you think of McTaggart's paradox?

BG: I think the A theorist (who is the intended target of the paradox) can still defend his position. For example, Michael Dummett suggests that McTaggart implicitly assumes that a consistent and complete description of reality is, in principle, possible (Dummett, 1960).

JJ: What does this assumption amount to?

BG: The thought is that, irrespective of one's position in time, it's possible to give a description of reality which is consistent and includes all truths.

JJ: But what does that have to do with the paradox?

BG: According to Dummett, McTaggart's paradox only reveals that the A theory is incompatible with this assumption. When we try to specify all the A series truths, as opposed to specifying those which are true from one's current perspective, we end up in a contradiction. Thus, if the A theory is true, a complete and consistent description of reality is impossible. Given the assumption that such a description is possible, however, McTaggart concluded that the A series is contradictory.

JJ: But does an A theorist have to accept McTaggart's assumption that a complete and consistent description of reality is, in principle, possible?

BG: Well, he must accept the consistency requirement. But should he accept the completeness requirement (i.e., the requirement that reality can be completely described, independently of one's temporal perspective)? The answer seems clearly 'no'.

JJ: Why is that?

BG: Well, think of it this way. The essence of the A theory is that the fundamental temporal facts (i.e., the tensed facts which record an event's position in the A series) change as time passes.

JJ: Yes. That's what A theory is all about.

BG: So, if you're an A theorist, you have to think that reality is constantly being (re)partitioned. Facts that are future, become present; facts that are present become past; facts that are past become more past. For an A theorist, then, reality is constantly changing.

JJ: Ah! So, if it is now 2021, I can state the facts as they are from that perspective including, e.g., the fact that my death is future. In 2121, a statement of the facts will include the fact that my death is past.

BG: Right. And there is only a contradiction if we assume that there is some perspective-neutral description that includes both facts. An A theorist should deny that there can be any such description. Thus, any consistent description of temporal reality, from within time, is necessarily incomplete.

JJ: So, an A theorist can escape McTaggart's paradox if he denies the implicit assumption that a consistent and complete description of reality is, in principle, possible.

BG: Yes. That's Dummett's idea.[1]

JJ: Let's summarise what we have discussed so far. We have described two temporal series, the A series and the B series, and we have said that there are two competing theories of time, the A theory and the B theory. According to the A theory, the A series is fundamental to time. According to the B theory, the B series is fundamental. McTaggart presented two arguments: the first against the B theory (claiming that the B series could not account for change), and the second against the A theory (claiming that the A series is contradictory). So, at least for McTaggart, since both theories of time have fatal flaws, time is unreal.

BG: Excellent summary. But didn't we find both of McTaggart's arguments unconvincing?

JJ: Yes, we did.

---

[1] See Chap. 5 of this volume.

References

Dummett, M. A. E. (1960). A defense of McTaggart's proof of the unreality of time. *The Philosophical Review, 69*(4), 497–504.
McTaggart, J. M. E. (1908). The unreality of time. *Mind, 17*(68), 457–474.
Russell, B. (1937). *Principles of mathematics*, 2nd edn. London: Allen & Unwin.
Shoemaker, S. (1969). Time without change. *The Journal of Philosophy, 66*(12), 363–381.

Chapter 26
Affecting the Past

Abstract In this discussion, we outline an epistemic puzzle that arises for any possible world that contains both backwards causal chains and agents who initiate such chains.

JEREMIAH JOVEN JOAQUIN: Some philosophers agree that even if it doesn't actually occur, backwards causation is logically and metaphysically possible, and that the standard bilking argument to the contrary fails.[1] But you still find a problem with this. What exactly is this problem?

BRIAN GARRETT: Well, I think there might be an epistemic problem with the possibility of backwards causation.

JJ: Could you elaborate on this a bit more?

BG: Let's imagine a world pretty much like ours except that there are backwards causal chains which we can manipulate. In particular, we can initiate such chains in order to bring about events in the past.

JJ: Yes, I can't see any *prima facie* objection to such a world. If backwards causation is possible, presumably it can occur in worlds with agents who make use of backwards causal chains for their own ends, just as we do with forwards causal chains.

BG: Exactly.

JJ: So, what's the puzzle?

BG: Imagine a world in which we have excellent evidence that pressing a certain red button on a Saturday causes an explosion to have happened the previous Wednesday.

[1] For an argument for the possibility of backward causation, see Dummett (1964); for a statement of the bilking argument, see Black (1956); and, for a reply to this latter argument, see Garrett (2020a) (reprinted here as Chapter 3).

B. Garrett, *Time, Identity and the Self: Essays on Metaphysics*, Synthese Library 442, https://doi.org/10.1007/978-3-030-85517-8_26

JJ: I could imagine that. But what constitutes "excellent evidence"?

BG: The usual factors: perfect correlation to date between button-pressings and explosions, no other apparent explanation for the explosions, no apparent common cause of both types of event, etc.

JJ: Those would certainly be good grounds for believing in a backwards causal link.

BG: Right. Now suppose that I am put in charge of the button. You know I like explosions! Suppose, further, that on many occasions I have pressed the red button and brought about an explosion on the previous Wednesday.

JJ: Am I there too?

BG: If you like. You can be an observer. Now here's the puzzle, and it's a puzzle which has no correlate in more familiar cases of forwards causation. Suppose it's a Wednesday. Looking out of my window I see the usual Wednesday explosion. But now the following question occurs to me: do I have any reason to press the red button on Saturday?

JJ: So the presence of the word 'reason' makes the puzzle epistemic?

BG: Yes.

JJ: Why is it a puzzle?

BG: Well, there are only two possible answers to our question – Yes or No – and there are problems with both.

JJ: Fine, go on.

BG: Suppose I say "Yes, I do have a reason to press the button". Doesn't that answer seem odd to you? After all, I've just seen the explosion happen. You've seen it too. It even makes the news. My failing to press the button on Saturday cannot make the explosion 'unhappen', whatever that could mean. But if the explosion has occurred whether or not I press the red button on Saturday, I can hardly have a reason to press the button. I don't care whether I am the cause of them or not. No such egocentric reasons are in play. Overall, then, 'Yes' cannot be the right answer.

JJ: That sounds plausible.

BG: So the right answer must be "No, I have no reason to press the button". But that, in a different way, is a strange answer. We began with the assumption of a backwards causal link between button-pressings and explosions. Now, in general, if I know that X causes Y; I want to bring about Y; X is within my power; I thereby have a reason to do X. That seems to capture a non-negotiable internal connection between reasons and causes. But in answering 'No' we are denying that connection. We presuppose a causal link between button-pressings and explosions, and a desire for explosions, yet we deny any reason to press the button.

JJ: Hmm. I see. So neither answer is satisfying?

BG: That's how it seems to me. 'Yes' cannot be the right answer if the explosion has occurred whether or not I later press the button. 'No' cannot be the right answer either since we thereby deny an intuitive connection between reasons and causes.

JJ: Actually, I think the situation is worse than you imagine.

BG: Oh really, how?

JJ: In your example, you knew that the explosion occurred.[2] But is such knowledge necessary for the puzzle? Suppose it's a Thursday, but you didn't look out the window or watch the news. You have no idea whether an explosion occurred the day before or not.

BG: With you so far.

JJ: Why not then reason:

> Either the explosion occurred yesterday or it didn't. If it did, I have no reason to press the button, since pressing the button would be superfluous (for just the reasons you gave in your criticism of the 'Yes' answer). But if it didn't happen, I would still have no reason to press the button, since pressing the button would be ineffective (you can't bring about what didn't happen). Either way, you have no reason to press the red button.

BG: Hang on a minute. That sounds suspiciously like a past-tense analogue of a typical fatalist argument. For example, a certain type of fatalist reasons:

> Either you'll be killed on your next car trip or you won't. If you will, wearing your seat-belt is superfluous; if you won't, it's unnecessary. Either way, you have no reason to wear a seat belt.

JJ: Yes, I quite agree. It does sound like a fatalist argument, and of course we could roundly reject such arguments. But let me note two differences between the fatalist argument and my argument. First, there is a way of replying to the fatalist's argument which is not remotely plausible in the case of my argument: viz., deny the first premise (perhaps, but not only, on grounds concerning the nature of time). Second, the fatalist's last premise ("if you won't be killed, wearing a seat belt is unnecessary") is unconvincing. Quite possibly, you won't be killed because you'll wear a seat-belt; so, wearing a seat-belt is not unnecessary. If so, it's not true that you'll be killed whether or not you wear a seat-belt. In contrast, it is true that the explosion has occurred whether or not you later press the button.

BG: Yes, I can see those differences.

---

[2] This assumption is denied, most implausibly, by Dummett (1964). For a detailed critique, see Garrett (2020b) (reprinted here as Chapter 4).

JJ: Anyway, the more important question is: where did I go wrong in my argument? That argument is just a natural extension of your argument.

BG: Well, to start with, I wasn't putting forward an argument. I was outlining a puzzle. The puzzle is that there seems to be no good answer to a perfectly good question, viz., do I have a reason to press the button? If I have an argument here, it's an argument for the conclusion that we have no good answer to a good question. You are arguing for a slightly different conclusion, viz., that I have no reason to press the button (whether I know an explosion occurred or not).

JJ: I agree there is that difference. My point is that your puzzle seems to provide the ingredients to generate my argument. Or do you disagree with that?

BG: No, I agree. If my puzzle is a good puzzle, then your argument would seem to be a good argument.

JJ: So, where does that leave us?

BG: Well, in the case of my puzzle I think we would like some way of answering 'Yes' to our question. We want the result that we can rationally engage in means-end reasoning with respect to backwards causal chains, just as we do with forwards causal chains. But I can't yet see the way to such a result. Now your argument adds fuel to the fire and seems to show that the 'Yes' answer is not available: I can have no reason to press the red button. Your argument, as we noted, is fatalist in form, yet it seems to avoid the standard objections to the fatalist's argument. I can't see where it goes wrong, and it does seem to be a natural extension of my puzzle.

JJ: Why can't we just accept its conclusion? Maybe there is just no reason to press the red button.

BG: Well, then we would have to give up the internal connection between reasons and causes, and acceptance of that connection seems compulsory. Of course, nothing we have said implies that backwards causation is metaphysically impossible. For example, our reasoning has no implications for the possibility or otherwise of backwards causation in agentless worlds. However, our discussion does suggest that there is a problem making sense of worlds in which we have backwards causal chains and agents who deliberately initiate such chains.

References

Black, M. (1956). Why cannot an effect precede its cause? *Analysis, 16*(3), 49–58.
Dummett, M. A. E. (1964). Bringing about the past. *The Philosophical Review, 73*(3), 338–359.

Garrett, B. (2020a). Max black and backwards causation. *Argumenta*. https://doi.org/10.14275/2465-2334/20200.gar.

Garrett, B. (2020b). Michael dummett, reasons to act, and bringing about the past. *Philosophia, 48*, 547–556.

Chapter 27
Of Identity

Abstract In this discussion, we delve into the concept of identity and some of the philosophical puzzles surrounding it.

JEREMIAH JOVEN JOAQUIN: Our target philosophical concept in this discussion is the concept of identity. Perhaps, we should start by saying what this concept means.[1]

BRIAN GARRETT: Alright. Please do the honours.

JJ: I think that the concept of identity is best captured by the logical symbol '='.

BG: How do you mean?

JJ: What I mean is that '=' captures Leibniz's Law and the transitivity principle. Leibniz's Law tells us that if $a = b$, then if a and b have exactly the same properties. On the other hand, the transitivity principle tells us that if $a = b$ and $b = c$, then, $a = c$. Aren't these the main features of identity?

BG: Perhaps. But we need first to distinguish between the numerical and the qualitative senses of identity. While the former kind of identity may conform to the features you've mentioned, the latter doesn't.

JJ: So, what's the distinction between these two senses of identity?

BG: Numerical identity is the sense of 'identity' expressed in sentences such as "Water is H_2O", "Superman is Clark Kent", "2 is the positive square root of 4". Each of these sentences concerns just one entity, variously described or named. Identity, in this sense, conforms to Leibniz's Law. That is, if A is numerically identical to B, then they share exactly the same properties

JJ: And what of the qualitative sense of identity?

---

[1] The foregoing discussion follows (Garrett, 2017, chap. 11).

B. Garrett, *Time, Identity and the Self: Essays on Metaphysics*, Synthese Library 442, https://doi.org/10.1007/978-3-030-85517-8_27

BG: Qualitative identity is the sense of 'identity' expressed in sentences such as "They are identical twins" and "We both drive the same car". The latter sentence concerns two cars not one, and they are 'identical' in the sense that both are the same model, colour, etc. Identity, in this sense, doesn't conform to Leibniz's law. Clearly, identical twins do not have the same properties (they differ in their spatial location, for example). You know of Fred and George, the twins in Harry Potter, right?

JJ: Yes! Despite the fact that their mother couldn't tell them apart, they're still two different people. I didn't know that you're into that stuff.

BG: I'm not but I know you are.

JJ: Well, alright. Back to our discussion then. When I said that '=' best captures the concept of identity, what I really meant was it captures the concept of numerical identity.

BG: Yes. But the numerical sense of identity gives rise to various puzzles.

JJ: What sort of puzzles?

BG: We can focus on two: the Statue and the Lump puzzle and the related Goliath and Lumpl puzzle.

JJ: You don't want to get into the Ship of Theseus puzzle?

BG: I think that I have said enough about that puzzle already.[2]

JJ: Alright. Let's start with the Statue and the Lump puzzle then.

BG: This puzzle can be traced back to Aristotle. Here's one version of it. On Monday, a sculptor buys a lump of clay. By Friday, he has sculpted it into a statue of the Biblical king, David. Let's call the lump of clay 'Lump' and the statue 'David'. Given Leibniz's Law, since Lump existed before David, Lump is not identical to David. But this seems strange since, on Friday, Lump and David occupy the very same space and are composed of the same matter. The question now is: How can two distinct objects occupy the same space at the same time?

JJ: I'm familiar with this puzzle. It hinges on how we conceive ordinary objects and their identity at a time and over time.

BG: That's right. And how we respond to this puzzle may depend on the theory of persistence – i.e., the theory of identity over time – that we subscribe to.

JJ: Are you talking about the endurantist and perdurantist theories here?

BG: Yes. In recent years, these theories have emerged as the leading theories of persistence.

[2] See Chaps. 9, 10, and 11 of this volume.

JJ: Before we discuss these theories further, could you tell us something about the Goliath and Lumpl case.

BG: This is a puzzle developed in the 1970s by the American philosopher, Allan Gibbard (1975). Here's how it goes. Imagine a sculptor creating a statue of the Biblical giant, Goliath. The sculptor fuses two pieces of clay to form a new lump of clay and in doing so simultaneously creates the statue of Goliath. The following day he blows up the statue, destroying both statue and lump. Let us call the statue 'Goliath' and the lump of clay 'Lumpl'. Now what's your intuition about this case?

JJ: Hmm. Lumpl and Goliath existed for the same period of time and were composed at all times of the very same molecules. Unlike in the puzzle about David and Lump, this complete spatio-temporal coincidence gives us strong grounds to judge that Lumpl and Goliath are numerically identical.

BG: Ah! But here's the crucial twist in Gibbard's puzzle. Lumpl and Goliath differ in their modal properties. What is possible for Lumpl is not possible for Goliath. For example, Lumpl might have been squeezed into a ball and not destroyed, but that is not a possibility for Goliath. Statues have their shapes essentially; lumps of clay do not. Given Leibniz's Law, if Lumpl and Goliath differ in their properties, they can't be identical.

JJ: So, the puzzle is: we have reason to think that Lumpl is identical to Goliath and reason to think that Lumpl is numerically distinct from Goliath.

BG: Right, and obviously we cannot accept both. We have to choose between them.

JJ: How should we choose?

BG: Well, the answer will depend on which the theory of persistence we endorse.

JJ: Let's dive into these theories shall we? Let's start with the perdurantist theory.

BG: Very well. According to perdurantists, ordinary objects, such as people, trees, cars and stars, are four-dimensional entities. Aside from their spatial parts, objects have temporal parts as well. As such, a spatio-temporal object persists through time by having different temporal parts (suitably related to each other) at different times. These temporal parts will themselves typically be composed of smaller temporal parts, and so on, until we reach instantaneous three-dimensional slices.

JJ: How about the endurantist view? What theory of persistence does it give us?

BG: On the endurantist view, ordinary objects have no temporal parts and are "wholly present" at all times at which they exist. This table in front of us exists wholly today, and it existed wholly yesterday, and it will (hopefully!) exist wholly tomorrow. That is, the table today is numerically identical to the table yesterday because a single three-dimensional object has endured through time.

JJ: Endurantists and perdurantists offer two radically different views of persistence. For endurantists, objects persist by being wholly present at each time at which they exist. I'm the same person I was yesterday because I was wholly present yesterday, and I am wholly present today. On the other hand, for perdurantists, objects persist by having different temporal parts at different times. I'm the same person I was yesterday because I have different but suitably related temporal parts at each of those times. Good. So, how would perdurantists and endurantists deal with our puzzles?

BG: Well, the cases of David and Lump, and of Lumpl and Goliath, commit us to the apparently unacceptable consequence that numerically distinct objects occupy the same space at the same time. The challenge is to show either that there is no such consequence or that the consequence is not as absurd as it at first seems. In the case of David and Lump, everyone agrees that since Lump existed before David, they cannot be numerically identical. So, both endurantist and perdurantist agree that Lump is not David.

JJ: But how would perdurantists explain how David and Lump occupy the same space on Friday?

BG: Perdurantists would explain this spatial coincidence in terms of the overlap in the temporal parts of David and Lump. David and Lump don't share all temporal parts but they do share some. So perdurantist could say that two distinct objects – David and Lump – occupy the same space at the same time since the Friday part of David overlaps with the Friday part of Lump.

JJ: Isn't it this a weird thing to say?

BG: The perdurantist will insist that this is no weirder than the familiar cases of spatial overlap (for example, conjoined twins sharing a torso). The David/Lump case is simply a temporal version of the case of Siamese twins.

JJ: Let's now turn to the endurantist theory. How would it account for the David/Lump puzzle?

BG: Well, endurantists simply accept the result that David and Lump are spatially coincident on Friday, despite being numerically distinct.

JJ: But how would endurantists account for the spatial coincidence?

BG: Endurantists might simply say that there's nothing wrong with this kind of coincidence. John Locke (1975) thought that distinct objects can spatially coincide provided they are of different kinds. So, two statues could not occupy exactly the same space at the same time, but a statue and a lump – things of different kinds – could. And David and Lump are things of different kinds.

JJ: But aren't David and Lump made of the same stuff?

BG: Well, yes. But according to Locke, despite being made of the same stuff, the criterion of identity for statues is different from the criterion of identity for lumps.

JJ: I see. So, given the Lockean Principle, endurantists would give the same verdict in the Goliath and Lumpl case? They would say that Goliath isn't Lumpl because they are things of different kinds (differing in their modal properties)?

BG: Yes, they would. Endurantists will regard Lumpl/Goliath as a limiting case of David/Lump. If David and Lump can be wholly present yet numerically distinct, the same should hold for Lumpl and Goliath. The difference between the two cases is that David and Lump's coincidence is temporary while Goliath and Lumpl's is permanent.

JJ: I wonder how perdurantists would account for Gibbard's puzzle. Since Lumpl and Goliath share exactly the same spatio-temporal parts, perdurantists hold that Goliath is identical to Lumpl. (This is an instance of the perdurantist's mereological principle that if A and B have exactly the same spatial and temporal parts, then A = B.) But since Lumpl and Goliath differ in their modal properties, they cannot be identical. So, what gives here?

BG: Yes. That's a bit of a pickle for perdurantists. Two principles that perdurantists regard as constitutive of identity (the mereological principle and Leibniz's Law) appear to yield incompatible verdicts in the Lumpl/Goliath case.

But one well known perdurantist, David Lewis, claims that appearances are deceptive. According to Lewis, we can hold that Lumpl is identical to Goliath compatibly with Leibniz's Law (Lewis, 1971).

JJ: Intriguing. How can this be done?

BG: Lewis thinks that the verdict that Lumpl isn't Goliath stems from the following kind of argument:

1. Goliath is essentially statue-shaped.
2. Lumpl is not essentially statue-shaped.
3. So, Lumpl isn't Goliath.

But, according to Lewis, this argument is invalid.

JJ: Hmm. Isn't this just an instance of Leibniz's Law (or, rather, its contrapositive)?

BG: No, not according to Lewis. Lewis rejects transworld identity in favour of similarity relations between world-bound individuals. According to his so-called counterpart theory, an object A is essentially F just in case all A's counterparts (entities in other worlds similar to A in relevant respects) are F. But there are a range of counterpart relations, and which relation a modal predicate picks out depends on how the object in question is named or described. An object may have one set of counterparts when named or described in one way and a different set when named or described in another way.

JJ: With you so far. But how does this help with the Goliath and Lumpl case?

BG: Well, since 'Goliath' is the name of a statue, the first premise of the above argument attributes to Goliath the property of being such that all of its statue counterparts are statue-shaped. Since 'Lumpl' names a piece of clay, the property that the second premise denies of Lumpl is that of being such that all of its piece-of-clay counterparts are statue-shaped. These are different properties: the property attributed to Goliath is not the property denied to Lumpl. Thus, we can hold that the premises of our argument are true but its conclusion false, consistently with Leibniz's Law.

JJ: Hmm. Doesn't this conflict with the necessity of identity?

BG: I take it you're referring to Saul Kripke's thesis that if A = B, necessarily A = B (where 'A' and 'B' are, e.g., proper names). Yes, Lewis rejects this thesis. For him, "Lumpl is Goliath" is true (in our imaginary world) but not necessarily true. In possible worlds that start out like Gibbard's world, but in which Lumpl is squeezed into a ball, Lumpl is not identical to Goliath. Lewis takes this to be an acceptable consequence of his theory, not a counterexample to it.

JJ: Where does this leave us? Which theory of persistence better accounts for the puzzles? The endurantist's or the perdurantist's?

BG: I think neither account is without its problems. Endurantists and perdurantists agree that David isn't Lump but disagree over the truth of the mereological principle (endurantists reject it, perdurantists accept it). Endurantists hold that Lumpl isn't Goliath, even though spatially coincident at all times at which they exist. This offends against the intuition that if two objects are numerically distinct, they differ in their life-histories. On the other hand, perdurantists maintain that Lumpl is Goliath but have to resort to counterpart theory in order to render their view consistent with Leibniz's Law, and counterpart theory is controversial. Overall, it isn't clear which theory is the best.

References

Garrett, B. (2017). *What is this thing called metaphysics?* 3rd edn. London: Routledge.

Gibbard, A. (1975). Contingent identity. *Journal of Philosophical Logic, 4*(2), 187–221.

Lewis, D. (1971). Counterparts of persons and their bodies. *The Journal of Philosophy, 68*(7), 203–11.

Locke, J. (1694/1975). Of identity and diversity. In P. Nidditch (Ed.), *An essay concerning human understanding*, 2nd edn. Oxford: Oxford University Press.

Chapter 28
On Personal Identity

Abstract In this discussion, we focus on central metaphysical questions about persons and the theories that try to answer them.

JEREMIAH JOVEN JOAQUIN: Perhaps, the best way to start our discussion on this topic is by looking at the three philosophical questions that you outlined in your 1998 book, *Personal Identity and Self-Consciousness* (Garrett, 1998).

BRIAN GARRETT: OK. But you have to remind me what those questions are.

JJ: There's the question about our nature. What are we? Are we persons (i.e., rational, self-conscious beings, in accord with John Locke's famous definition of 'person')? (Locke, 1975). Are we material or immaterial? There's also the question about our persistence over time. What, if anything, constitutes our identity over time? Is it psychology continuity or continuity of the body? Finally, there's a question about the importance of personal identity itself. Does being the same person over time matter in decisions about prudential concern (i.e., decisions we make about our own future welfare)? We can label these questions as the nature question, the identity question, and the "what matters" question, respectively.

BG: Ah, yes, I do remember these questions.

JJ: Shall we begin with the answers to the nature question then?

BG: I think that it would be better to first discuss what these questions amount to and how they are related to one another.

JJ: Alright. So, how do you wish to proceed?

BG: First, in asking the nature question, we are asking a question in ontology – a question about the kind (if any) that we essentially belong to.

Second, some philosophers – most notably, Locke – think that we are essentially persons. That is, they think that we are essentially rational, self-conscious beings. But this view doesn't really answer the nature question

B. Garrett, *Time, Identity and the Self: Essays on Metaphysics*, Synthese Library 442, https://doi.org/10.1007/978-3-030-85517-8_28

(as we've characterised it) since it doesn't tell us which kind we belong to. (Locke himself does not presuppose any particular view about the kind of thing persons are.)

Third, the identity question (as you've characterised it) is about the necessary and sufficient conditions for our identity over time. Our answer to this question is closely connected to our answer to the nature question. After all, if we are fundamentally Fs, then our identity or survival conditions are those appropriate to Fs. So, the answers to the identity and nature questions need to harmonise.

JJ: Alright. But what of the third – "what matters" – question?

BG: The topic of personal identity lies at the intersection of metaphysics and morals. For many philosophers, therein lies its real importance. Any answer to the nature and identity questions will influence how we answer the question about what matters.

Some philosophers – in particular, Derek Parfit – have tried to forge an interesting connection between theories of persons and value theory (ethics and rationality) (Parfit, 1984). Parfit has argued that, on the best theory of personal identity (which, for Parfit, is psychological reductionism), identity is not what matters. What matters is the preservation of psychological relations such as 'apparent' memory, belief, desire and character, etc. Unlike identity, these relations can hold between one person and two or more later persons. They can also hold to varying degrees (for example, I can acquire a more or less different character over a period of years, or more quickly).

I have already said my piece on the "what matters" question in one form or other.[1] And I know that you have so as well.[2] So, we could pursue this topic if it comes up in our discussion.

JJ: Alright. Let's just focus for now on the nature and identity questions.

BG: Jolly good.

JJ: In your 1998 book, you distinguished between materialist and immaterialist answers to the nature question. Immaterialists, such as the seventeenth century French philosopher, Rene Descartes, thought that we are non-physical (yet embodied) beings. On this view, we continue to exist so long as our immaterial souls exist. Materialists, on the other hand, deny this. They think that we are fundamentally a physical entity of some sort. One materialist view, the animalist theory, identifies us with the human animal in our shoes. Another view, the body theory, identifies us with a human

[1] See Chapter 24 of this volume and (Garrett, 1998, chap. 6).

[2] See Joaquin (2017).

body. (But is the animal distinct from the body?) A third view, the brain theory, identifies us with the physical seat of our mental lives, which we have discovered to be the brain and central nervous system. Each materialist view, of course, implies a corresponding view about the conditions of our identity over time (i.e., what changes we can survive; what changes kills us).

BG: That's one way of surveying the field. In a later work I discussed four main theories of persons: dualism, animalism, constitutionalism, and the view of Hume-cum-Parfit (Garrett, 2017, chap. 2). I argued that all theories face serious problems.

JJ: Alright. Let's focus on these four theories, starting with dualism.

BG: Perhaps the most famous dualist was Descartes. In this Sixth Meditation, he wrote:

> I have a clear and distinct idea of myself, in so far as I am a thinking, non-extended thing; and [...] I have a clear and distinct idea of body, in so far as this is simply an extended, non-thinking thing [...] [A]ccordingly it is certain that I am really distinct from my body, and can exist without it (Descartes, 1996, 54).

For Descartes, soul and body are distinct substances – the soul essentially a non-extended thinking substance, the body essentially an extended non-thinking substance – and the soul can survive the death of the body. Accordingly, the soul is a simple or indivisible mental substance, whose identity over time is primitive and unanalysable.

JJ: So, for Descartes, does our identity over time consists in the continuing existence of our soul – the seat of our mental lives?

BG: Yes. According to Descartes, it is precisely because we can "clearly and distinctly" conceive ourselves surviving without a body, that we are entitled to conclude that we are immaterial.

JJ: Of course, Cartesian dualism faces many problems. But let's focus on the causal interaction problem. Could you tell us something about it?

BG: Yes. Let's note that Descartes was an interactionist dualist. That is, he acknowledged that the mental and the physical causally interact. Such interaction seems undeniable. When I stick a pin in your leg, you feel pain; when you desire a coffee, and believe the coffee shop is over there, you start walking in that direction. But if the mental and physical are so different, as Descartes believed, how can there be such interaction?

JJ: But why is this a problem for Descartes? As you said, the interaction between the mental and the physical is undeniable. Couldn't he just take the causal interaction as a given and leave it at that?

BG: Well, we have good reason to think that the physical world is causally closed; i.e. that physical effects have physical causes, sufficient to explain those effects. The success of science makes it reasonable to believe that the physical world (including all bodily movement) is causally closed. This is a problem for Cartersian dualists since they hold that some physical events (for example, my hand rising) have non-physical causes (for example, my desire to acknowledge a friend).

JJ: So, does this mean that Descartes's dualism is incompatible with the causal closure of the physical world?

BG: Not immediately. Cartesian dualists can secure the compatibility but at the cost of commitment to an implausible over-determination thesis, where human actions always have two separate causes (or sets of causes), one physical and the other non-physical, each sufficient to bring about their effect. Now events are sometimes over-determined (think of the condemned man being shot simultaneously by multiple shooters). But it is hard to believe that every human action involves such over-determination.

JJ: So, a Cartesian dualist will have a dilemma: either deny causal closure or accept the over-determination of human action.

BG: Yes. However, a dualist who accepts causal closure could avoid the problem of over-determination by becoming an epiphenomenalist (hence non-Cartesian) dualist. Such a dualist thinks that mental events are caused by physical events, but that mental events (such as beliefs and desires) don't cause anything. However, this is hardly a congenial position either. Perhaps the best strategy for the dualist is to reject the first horn of the dilemma and deny the causal closure of the physical, claiming, not unreasonably, that mental/physical interaction is a special case, and hence an exception to causal closure.

JJ: But wouldn't this go against the physicalist tide of twentieth/twentyfirst century philosophy?

BG: Maybe, but contemporary popularity is no guarantee of truth and, despite its problems, dualism deserves to be taken seriously.

JJ: Alright. Let's now turn to another theory of persons. Tell us something about animalism. I know that you've been critical of this view.[3]

BG: Yes. I've been one of its most ardent critics. As I understand it, animalists (notably Paul Snowdon and Eric Olson) think that we terrestrials are fundamentally human beings. In other words, each of us is numerically identical to the human animal in our shoes.

---

[3] See Chaps. 16 and 17 of this volume.

JJ: So, I am just an animal that belongs to the species *homo sapiens*?

BG: Yes. You, me, and the rest of humanity are human animals. This is not to say, however, that most of us aren't persons (i.e. beings that have a self-conscious mental life). Of course we are persons except when we are fetuses or senile. But we are not fundamentally or essentially persons; the concept *person* is not a fundamental concept. In robot worlds, robot persons are fundamentally robots; in soul worlds, soul persons are fundamentally souls. But we (human persons) are identical to human beings.

JJ: Are there arguments in favour of animalism?

BG: Yes. One compelling argument runs as follows. Suppose that 'A' names the human being in my shoes. Since A has my brain and body, he presumably has all my mental characteristics, too. But this means that A is a self-conscious being like myself. But if A is self-conscious, and we want to avoid the absurd conclusion that there are two self-conscious beings in my shoes, we should identify myself with A and so conclude that I = A. And that is precisely the thesis of animalism.

JJ: Do you think this argument is any good?

BG: Despite the plausibility of this reasoning, animalism cannot be right.

JJ: How so?

BG: According to the animalist, we are each identical to the human being in our shoes. So if 'A' names the human being in my shoes, I = A. Now, if X = Y, then, by Leibniz's Law, every property of X is a property of Y, and vice versa. This means that if I = A, then every possibility for me must be a possibility for A, and vice versa. But there seem to be a range of possible scenarios in which either A survives but I do not or in which I survive but A does not. In which case, I cannot be A.

JJ: I reckon that the familiar thought experiments in the personal identity literature could be given as objections here.

BG: Yes, they could. But let's focus on the famous Brown/Brownson thought-experiment first introduced into the literature by the contemporary American philosopher Sydney Shoemaker.

> It is now possible to transplant certain organs ... It is at least conceivable that a human body could continue to function normally if its brain were replaced by one taken from another human body. Two men, a Mr Brown and a Mr Robinson, had been operated on for brain tumours, and brain extractions had been performed on both of them. At the end of the operations, however, the assistant inadvertently put Brown's brain in Robinson's head, and Robinson's brain in Brown's head. One of these men immediately dies, but the other, the one with Robinson's head and Brown's brain, eventually regains consciousness. Let us call the latter 'Brownson'. When asked his name he automatically replies 'Brown'. He recognizes Brown's wife and family. And is able to describe in detail events in Brown's life. Of Robinson's life he evidences no knowledge at all. (Shoemaker, 1963, 23–24)

Almost everyone agrees that the best description of this case is that Brown is Brownson. Few philosophers think that Brown dies and Robinson acquires a new brain and psychology. So, if I underwent such an operation, I would survive in a new body, but A (the human being) would cease to exist. It's true that part of A (his brain) would continue to exist, but A himself would no longer exist. This result contradicts animalism. (To bring out the intuition in a stronger way, imagine that my old brainless body is kept alive, while I occupy Robinson's body. Then A still exists, but I exist elsewhere, so obviously we cannot be identical.)

JJ: But doesn't this thought-experiment already presuppose that our mental life is fundamental to our nature?

BG: Not really. The dialectic so far proceeded this way. Animalists think that each of us is fundamentally a human being. But the Brown/Brownson case presents a scenario where a particular person, Brown, survives but is no longer identical to the human animal he originally 'cohabited' with.

JJ: But isn't this just a matter of how we respond to the thought-experiment? That is, the conclusion that Brown survives but now inhabits Robinson's body is just the intuition that most philosophers get. But intuitions could be false, right?

BG: Yes, it's true that the use of thought-experiments in philosophy has been subject to a number of criticisms. It has been claimed that we shouldn't take our intuitions about thought-experiments as guides to philosophical truth, since such intuitions may be prejudiced and unreliable. This criticism is, I think, over-stated. For one thing, it ignores the frequent and legitimate use of thought-experiments in virtually all traditional areas of philosophy (most notably, for example, in epistemology and in ethics).

Second, and more important, a thought-experiment can be useful in understanding the structure of a concept and the relative importance of its different strands, provided that there is general agreement about the best description of the thought-experiment. It's true that some philosophers have tried to gain mileage from thought-experiments in the absence of such general agreement. But it would be unwarranted to infer from the existence of such abuses that thought-experiments can never perform any useful function in philosophy.

JJ: Let's leave the question about philosophical thought-experiments and intuitions aside for now. Let's focus on constitutionalism, which is another theory of persons you're critical of.[4]

[4] See Chap. 18 of this volume.

BG: This view occupies a kind of halfway house between dualism and animalism. According to (Lynne Rudder Baker's version of) constitutionalism, we are not immaterial souls, but nor are we numerically identical to any material or biological substance (such as a brain, body or human being). We are, however, constituted by such a substance (Rudder Baker, 2000).

JJ: So, for constitutionalists, constitution is not identity?

BG: Yes. We can define the relation of constitution as follows: X constitutes Y just if (i) X is not identical to Y; (ii) X and Y are composed of the very same atoms and molecules; (iii) X is the ontological ground of Y, but not vice versa.

JJ: This is true of the statue/lump example we discussed previously.[5]

BG: Yes. The ontological ground of the statue is the lump of clay, but not vice versa. That is, the statue owes its existence and properties to the existence and properties of the lump of clay, not vice versa.

Similarly, according to constitutionalists, I am numerically distinct from the human being in my shoes, yet we are composed of the same atoms and molecules. Further, I owe my existence and properties to the existence and properties of the human being that constitutes me, not vice versa.

JJ: Does constitutionalism imply that I cannot exist without this human body I now inhabit?

BG: Well, no. On one version, you could come to be constituted by a different substance (for example, a bionic one), provided that substance preserved your psychological life. Nonetheless, whatever substance constitutes you at any given time, you owe your existence and properties at that time to the existence and properties of that underlying substance.

JJ: So, according to constitutionalists, I could be constituted by one underlying substance at one time and be constituted by a different substance at another time. Isn't this just what dualists say?

BG: Not really. Dualists claim that we could exist apart from any material substance. This isn't what constitutionalists claim. While we do have psychological lives, we are still constituted by some underlying material substance.

The motivation for constitutionalism is based on two quite plausible views: (i) an unwillingness to embrace dualism; and (ii) the belief that some possibilities for me are not possibilities for the human being that constitutes me, and vice versa, and hence that I cannot be numerically identical to (one and the same thing as) a human being.

[5] See Chap. 27.

JJ: Alright. So, constitutionalists hold that I am not identical to the human animal in my shoes, but nor am I identical to anything immaterial (since I am fully constituted by the flesh and blood of this human animal).

BG: Yes. And this leads to a problem for constitutionalists.

JJ: How so?

BG: We have to agree that each of us is a self-conscious subject of experience, a person. You, me, and the rest of our kin are self-conscious.

JJ: That's right.

BG: But what about the human being – the human animal – in our shoes? Is that human animal self-conscious? Suppose the constitutionalist says: "No; the human animal is just an animal and so has no mental states, only physical ones". The trouble with this answer is that the human animal in my shoes has all my physical attributes, including my brain and brain states. It is now generally accepted, and accepted by the constitutionalist, that mental states are causally dependent on, and generated by, brain states. (Remember the constitutionalist doesn't think we are immaterial entities). If I'm material and have mental states, then why deny the full range of mental states to the human animal in my shoes? Thus, 'No' cannot be the right answer.

JJ: So, 'Yes' is the right answer here? That is, "Yes, the human animal in my shoes is self-conscious".

BG: Well, let's see. Suppose the constitutionalist says: "Yes, the human being has all my mental states and is self-conscious". Remember that the question we are answering arose on the constitutionalist's assumption that each one of us is not identical to the human animal in our shoes. So, if I'm self-conscious, and it is conceded that the human animal in my shoes is also self-conscious, it follows that there are two people in my shoes! Generalising from my case, it follows that the population of the planet is twice what we thought it was. But this is absurd. 'Yes' cannot be the right answer either.

JJ: So, constitutionalists face a dilemma: Either the human animal in my shoes is self-conscious or not. If it is, constitutionalists would have to say that there are two people in my shoes right now. If it isn't, the constitutionalists would have to deny that our psychological life is dependent on, and generated by, the physical goings-on in our brain.

BG: Yes. This dilemma is fatal for constitutionalists.

JJ: Let's now turn to the final theory of persons, which is the Hume/Parfit view. I reckon that you're not a big supporter of this view either.[6]

[6] See Chaps. 19, 20, and 24 of this volume.

BG: Well, I've been critical of the reductionist aspect of this view, and the conclusion Parfit wants to draw from the fission case.

JJ: Before getting into your objections to the view, let's try to understand what it is first.

BG: I think we better start with some ideas from the eighteenth century Scottish philosopher, David Hume. According to Hume, we are not substances. A standard example of a substance in this sense would be a particular horse or tree, for example. An example of a non-substance would be, e.g., a constellation such as Orion's Belt. Instead of being substances we are but bundles of experiences, with no unifying core. If experiences e1 and e2 belong to a single person, that is not because they are had by the same substance (whether biological or psychic). Rather, it is because of the relations between e1 and e2 (or perhaps because those experiences causally depend on the same brain). In elucidation of his bundle view, Hume compared:

> the soul ... to a republic or commonwealth, in which the several members are united by the reciprocal ties of government and subordination, and give rise to other persons, who propagate the same republic in the incessant changes of its parts. (Hume, 1978, Book 1, Part IV, Section VI, paragraph 19)

Parfit, a modern Humean, has made much of this analogy. Just as the constituents of a republic (its inhabitants and land) can be understood without reference to the concept of a republic, so the constituents of the self (thoughts, experiences, brain, body, etc.) can be understood without reference to the concept of a person. Hume's analogy provides the model for Parfit's reductionism about persons, encapsulated by his so-called "Impersonality Thesis".

JJ: Could you spell out this thesis a bit more?

BG: Sure. According to Parfit's Impersonality Thesis:

1. The fact of a person's identity over time just consists in the holding of certain more particular facts.
2. These facts can be described without either presupposing the identity of this person, or explicitly claiming that the experiences in this person's life are had by this person, or even explicitly claiming that this person exists. These facts can be described in an impersonal way.
3. Though persons exist, we could give a complete description of reality without claiming that persons exist. (Parfit, 1984, 210–212)

Parfit's idea is that a description of reality can be complete, i.e. contain all truths, and impersonal, i.e. make no reference (explicit or implicit) to persons or subjects of experience. In particular, the mental features that make up our psychological lives (pains, tickles, beliefs, desires, intentions, memories, etc.) can be completely described without reference to a subject who has or owns such mental characteristics.

JJ: So, like Hume, Parfit thinks that we are just a collection of mental states. I can now see why you're critical of this view: you're not a reductionist!

BG: Well, I wouldn't be so definitive, but I can certainly see a couple of problems for Parfit's reductionism. First, it's hard to make sense of simple mental states, such as pains and tickles, other than as had by a subject. We can make little sense of an unowned or free-floating tickle. Second, a special problem is posed by more sophisticated mental states such as memory and intention. These states seem to have reference to persons built into their content. My memory of tasting coffee yesterday not only requires a current bearer but appears to implicate me in its content: I remember that I tasted coffee yesterday. How, then, can memory, a crucial feature of our psychological lives, be described impersonally?

JJ: Surely, Parfit has replies to these points.

BG: Yes, he does. With regard to the first problem, Parfit concedes that we don't talk of unowned pains, but urges that this is merely a feature of our subject-predicate language and that we shouldn't read any metaphysical thesis into it. The trouble with this sort of reply is that it's very hard to evaluate. Parfit might be right; but then again he might not.

With regard to the second problem, Parfit insists that memory is a composite concept built out of identity and quasi-memory (q-memory). The latter concept is stipulated to be like memory in all phenomenological and causal respects, yet does not presuppose identity. Thus, as a result of a donor brain graft, for example, I can have q-memories of someone else's experiences. What we call memories are just q-memories of our own experiences. Q-memories can thus yield knowledge of one's own or another's past.

JJ: You don't find this q-memory reply compelling?

BG: Well, no. I think that it's still an unresolved question whether memory is a composite concept along the lines Parfit has in mind or whether it's a unitary concept irreducible to more basic conceptual atoms. If it's the latter, Parfit's reply won't work.

JJ: You mentioned about your qualms about the fission case. Could you elucidate on this?

BG: Well, this thought-experiment has featured heavily in discussions of personal identity. I believe that it was first introduced into the literature by David Wiggins and is prominent in the work of Derek Parfit. It goes something like this:

> Suppose that the two hemispheres of my brain are functionally identical, and that surgeons transplant each hemisphere into its own (brainless) body. After the operation, two people wake up – call them Lefty and Righty – each of whom is psychologically continuous with me (each has my beliefs and character, and both seem to remember my past life). They are psychologically exactly similar to each other upon waking but begin to differ thereafter.

How should this case be described? Since Lefty is not the same person as Righty, it seems there are only three options: (1) I am Lefty; (2) I am Righty; (3) I am neither Lefty nor Righty. For any non-dualist, including Parfit, there is no reason why (1) would be true and (2) false or vice versa. They cannot both be true, so neither is true. Hence, says Parfit, (3) is the best description.

Yet, thinks Parfit, my relation to Lefty and to Righty contains what matters. (After all, I much prefer division to death.) Since I'm not identical to Lefty or Righty, it follows that identity (continuing to exist) cannot be what matters. What matters instead is the relation I stand in to Lefty and to Righty, viz. the relation of psychological continuity and/or connectedness (what Parfit calls "relation R"). Hence, identity is not what matters; what matters is relation R.

JJ: But is this a good argument?

BG: Well, here's a reason to think not. Suppose that you will divide tomorrow, and you know that Righty will suffer toothache. Parfit thinks that, in virtue of Righty's R-relatedness to you now, you ought to have the very same concern for Righty as you would have if you were going to suffer toothache tomorrow. In this way, then, identity does not matter.

But what is the concern that you have for both Righty and yourself? You have self-concern for your own future, but you cannot have self-concern for Righty's future, since he is not you. So, it seems that you cannot have the same kind of concern for both yourself and Righty.

JJ: Parfit must have a reply to this.

BG: Yes, he does. He agrees that you can't call your concern for Righty "self-concern", but he regards that as a trivial verbal point. Parfit thinks that there is a relation of q-concern that stands to self-concern as q-memory stands to memory. So, self-concern is just q-concern for yourself.

JJ: OK, how does this help Parfit?

BG: Well, Parfit can now claim that you can have essentially the same concern for Righty as you have towards yourself: q-concern. Q-concern can be directed towards yourself or towards Righty, it's just that in the latter case we can't call it "self-concern". But that is a merely verbal point.

JJ: I'm seeing similarities with the discussion of memory above.

BG: Indeed. The same question arises: whether a given concept – memory or self-concern, as it may be – is or isn't a composite concept. Parfit wants to answer 'composite!' in both cases, but the jury is still out.

JJ: Well, we've gone through four main theories of personal identity: dualism, animalism, constitutionalism, and Humeanism. We found serious objections against all these views. So, I ask you now: What is your view? What are we fundamentally?

BG: Well, that is the big question, isn't it?

References

Descartes, R. (1641/1996). *Meditations on first philosophy*. Cambridge: Cambridge University Press.

Garrett, B. (1998). *Personal identity and self-consciousness*. London: Routledge.

Garrett, B. (2017). *What is this thing called metaphysics?* 3rd edn. London: Routledge.

Hume, D. (1739/1978). *A treatise of human nature*. Oxford: Oxford University Press.

Joaquin, J. J. (2017). Personal identity and what matters. *Organon F, 24*(2), 196–213.

Locke, J. (1694/1975). Of identity and diversity. In P. Nidditch (Ed.), *An essay concerning human understanding*, 2nd edn. Oxford: Oxford University Press.

Parfit, D. (1984). *Reasons and persons*. Oxford: Oxford University Press.

Rudder Baker, L. (2000). *Persons and bodies: A constitution view*. Cambridge: Cambridge University Press.

Shoemaker, S. (1963). *Self-knowledge and self-identity*. Ithaca: Cornell University Press.

Name Index

B. Garrett, *Time, Identity and the Self: Essays on Metaphysics*, Synthese Library 442, https://doi.org/10.1007/978-3-030-85517-8

Subject Index

B. Garrett, *Time, Identity and the Self: Essays on Metaphysics*, Synthese Library 442, https://doi.org/10.1007/978-3-030-85517-8

CPSIA information can be obtained
at www.ICGtesting.com
Printed in the USA
BVHW052011270223
659328BV00007B/98

9 783030 855192